Robert M. Randolph (MBA, Northwestern University) is
President of the Professional Management Institute and
President of the education and consulting firm, Planagement,
Inc. Bob has been developing the Planagement® System for
thirty years, and has taught its principles to thousands of
individuals in leading organizations. He is a popular speaker
and workshop leader in addition to having published over
100 articles, as well as numerous manuals, workbooks,
cassettes, and professional management skill building kits.
He is also the author of the highly successful book,
Planagement® : Moving Concept into Reality.

"Thank God It's Monday!"

ROBERT M. RANDOLPH

Institute for Business Planning, Inc.
IBP Plaza
Englewood Cliffs, New Jersey 07632
A Prentice-Hall Company

©1982 by Institute for Business Planning, Inc.
IBP Plaza
Englewood Cliffs, New Jersey 07632

Library of Congress Cataloging in Publication Data

Randolph, Robert M., 1934-
    Thank God it's Monday!

    Includes index.
    1. Management. 2. Success. I. Title.
HD31.R28 1982   658.4'09   82-11926
ISBN 0-87624-623-4

Printed in United States of America

Current printing:
10 9 8 7 6 5 4 3 2 1

CONTENTS

Preface iv

1
Learning to Lead: Know Thyself First 1

The Whole Person 2
Putting Your Act Together 3
The Planagement Approach: Maximizing Performance
  and Work Satisfaction 4
Success is in the Eye of the Beholder 5
Understanding the Learning/Thinking Process. The "Thinking Gap" ... 6
Roadblocks to Thinking 8
How Our Minds Work: Overcoming Roadblocks 9
Taking the Steps to Working Smarter 10
  Step 1: Decide to Learn and Grow 11 / Step 2: Develop Learning
  Skills 11 / Step 3: Develop Learning Targets 13
Filing a Flight Plan For Your Life 13
The Keys to High Performance 14
  Accentuating the Positive 14 / Learning to Lead 16

Creativity 18

    Brainstorming 19 / Thinking Techniques 19 / Tensions and
    Opposites 21

Option-Loaded Decisions—Or, Making Things Happen 22

The Philosophy of Excellence 27

2

Planning Your Position in Life 29

Looking Toward Your Future 30
    Taking One Day At a Time 31

Can You Get There from Here? 35

Before Making Your Decision 36

    A Positive Perception of Human Nature 36 / The Importance of a Sound
    Management Philosophy 37 / The Importance of Accepting Certain
    Responsibilities 38 / Compare. . . Cooperate 40

The Choice is Yours 41

    Choice No. 1: To Manage Life Like an Amateur 41 / Choice No. 2:
    To Manage Life in an Inconsistent Manner 41 / Choice No. 3: To Manage
    and To Plan Life Professionally 41

3

Climate: People Are the Organization 42

Taking Steps 43

Setting Up the Right Job 45

The Planagement® System: Placing the "Right" People in the
"Right" Jobs 49

    Step 1: Develop Position Descriptions 51 / Step 2: Give Out Selection
    Kits 51 / Step 3: Get Back Selection Kits 52 / Step 4: Rank-Order the
    Candidates 52 / Step 5: (Optional): Narrow Recommendations Further 52

A Practical Approach to Management Development 53
    A Good Fit 53

Measuring and Rewarding Performance 55

    Premise 1: Jobs Have Measurable Standards 56 / Premise 2: Measure by
    Results Achieved 56 / Premise 3: Challenge to Beat Standards 56 /
    Premise 4: Compensate According to Achievements 57 /
    Premise 5: Expect Change 57 / Linking Compensation to
    Performance 58 / Step 1: Establish a Policy 58 / Step 2: Describe Each
    Position 58 / Step 3: Specify Standard Objectives 58 / Step 4: Spell Out
    the Gain 59 / Step 5: Establish a Compensation Plan 59

4

Motivation: Releasing the Angel from Within 61

A Six-Step Formula of Motivation for Increased Performance 62

Step 1: Be a Participative Manager 62 / Step 2: Establish Clear-Cut
Organizational Direction 63 / Step 3: Balance Freedom with
Discipline 63 / Step 4: Plan for Human Resource Development 63 /
Step 5: Understand Human Needs 64 / Step 6: Get Feedback to
Measure Motivation 65

This Power from Within 65

Motivation Through Education 69

Taking Steps to Teach 72

Step 1: Decide What Can Be Taught by Practice 72 / Step 2: Teach at the
Students' Level 73 / Step 3: Encourage Feedback of Results 73 /
Step 4: Use Varied Teaching Techniques 73 / Step 5: If You Just Can't
Teach . . . 74

5

Keeping the Monkey Off Your Back 75

Getting Started 76

Self-Discipline 76 / Direction 77

How to Sell More in Less Time 79

Step 1: Know and Compare Your Product 79 / Step 2: Diagnose
Customer Needs 80 / Step 3: Concentrate on Key Accounts 80 /
Step 4: Develop a Sales Plan 81 / Step 5: Continue to Learn Your
Trade 81 / Step 6: Establish a Career Plan 82 / Step 7: Provide for
Feedback 82

Delegation 83

Decide to Delegate 84

Step 1: Decide What to Delegate 84 / Step 2: Assign Some Tasks to
Others 85 / Step 3: Extend Delegation Further 85

Delegation and Development 85

Step 1: Describe Your Position 86 / Step 2: List Details 86 /
Step 3: Assess Time 86 / Step 4: Categorize Tasks 87 / Step 5: Select
Appropriate People 87 / Step 6: Note Time Saved 87 / Step 7: List
Future Tasks 87 / Step 8: Prioritize Tasks 88 / Step 9: Estimate
Time 88 / Step 10: Make Up Your New List 88 / Step 11: Plan the
Delegation Timetable 88 / Step 12: Do It! Redo It! 88

Planning 89

Strategy 93

Example 1: Military 93 / Example 2: Large Retail Business 94 /
Example 3: Automotive Industry 94 / Develop Strategy 95

Strategic Sequencing 95

Bridging the Communication and Knowledge Gap 97

6

Management by Cause and Effect 100

One Most Important Skill 101
Diagnosis 103
    What is Diagnosis? 103 / How Does the Diagnostic Skill Work? 104 /
    Can the Diagnostic Skill be Taught? 104 / An Early Warning System 104
Discipline 106
    The Discipline Checklist 106 / Types of Discipline 109 / Is Discipline
    Tough, Demanding, and Work-oriented? 110 / The Discipline Habit 110
Implementing the Cause-and-Effect Approach 112
    The Price of Professionalism 115
The 80/20 Rule and Your Diagnostic Skill 117
    A Guideline to Effective Control 117

7

The Professional Manager's Approach 121

Traditional Versus Professional Management 121
Theory X and Theory Y 124
Profile of a Professional Manager 125
    Philosophy of a Professional 128
The Traditional Versus Professional Manager 130
Inverting the Top-Down Organizational Theory 142
Taking Steps Toward a Positive Climate 143

8

Turning Potential Into Results 146

The Three-Level Forecast: Simple but Productive 147
    Step 1: Guesstimate the Best 147 / Step 2: Guesstimate the
    Worst 147 / Step 3: Make a Practical Forecast 148 / Benefits 148 /
    Example 149 / The Living-Rolling Forecast 150
A Formula for Managing Your Future Into Reality 150
    Step 1: Define Growth Expectations 151 / Step 2: Identify
    Opportunities 151 / Step 3: Compare Present and Future 153 /
    Step 4: Chart the Potentials 153 / Step 5: Write a Plan 153 /
    Step 6: Develop the Plan 153
The Crescent Company Example 153
From Potential to Results 158

9

How to Build a Successful Business 159

Taking Steps to Build a Successful Enterprise 160

Step 1: Be Sure You're Committed 160 / Step 2: Become a Qualified
Manager 160 / Step 3: Manage Each Phase 164 / Step 4: Establish
a Resource Base 165 / Step 5: Adopt a Balanced Philosophy 167

Eagles Beware: Ten Reasons Why Companies Fail 167

1. Poor Management 167 / 2. Inadequate Capital 168 / 3. Inadequate
Backup 168 / 4. Lack of Delegation 169 / 5. Lack of Sound Business
Administration 169 / 6. Lack of Marketing Orientation 170 / 7. Lack
of Innovation 170 / 8. Poor Time Management 170 / 9. Inadequate
Interpersonal Skills 170 / 10. Lack of Discipline 171

Making the Going Business Go 172

Changing Over to Participative Management 172

Step 1: Select Individuals 174 / Step 2: Write a Company Guideline
174 / Step 3: Develop Individual Supporting
Plans 175 / Step 4: Consolidate and Integrate 175

Productive Meetings 175

Step 1: Establish a Team Charter 176 / Step 2: Select Team
Members 176 / Step 3: Establish Agenda 177 / Step 4: Select
Chairperson 177 / Step 5: Document the Meetings 177

The Management Game of Synergistics 179

Example 1: A Small Business 180 / Example 2: A Large
Conglomerate 182 / How it Works 182 / The "Payoff" is High! 186

10

Profitability 187

Managerial Productivity 188

Orient Yourself to Growth 189

Create Your Own Position Description 189

Adopt an Asset-Management Approach 190

Generate Position Descriptions and Compensation Programs for
Others 190 / Get the Right Person in the Right Job 191 / Take
Control and Get Feedback 191 / Adopt a Participative Style 192 /
Don't Let Opportunity Run Out 192

Lead the Way 192

Think Planning 192 / Formulate a Sound Strategy 193 / Organize
For Simplicity 193 / Use Project Management 194 / Keep Your MIS
Simple Too 194 / Encourage the Company Over Empires 194

Practice Professional Management 194

Step 1: Enhance Your Understanding 195 / Step 2: Relate to the Five
Business Needs 195 / Step 3: Identify Gaps 196 / Step 4: Tailor a
Sound Management System 196 / Step 5: Develop an Action Plan
196 / Step 6: Measure Cost-Effectiveness 196

11

The Paradox of Power 203

One Approach to Power 203
...And Another 205
The Paradox of Power 206

12

Knowing When You Reach the Top 208

Mastering a Creative Skill for Fun and Profit 210
Deciding to be Creative 212

13

America: What We Were, What We Are, What We Can Be 216

Life Cycle of a Civilization 216
  1. Bondage 216 / 2. Spiritual Faith 217 / 3. Courage 217 /
  4. Liberty 217 / 5. Abundance 217 / 6. Selfishness 217 /
  7. Complacency 218 / 8. Apathy 218 / 9. Dependence 218 /
  10. Bondage! 219
Resurgence 219
  Drive 220 / Direction 220 / Discipline 221 / Development 221
Momentum Versus Renewal 222
  Maintenance 223 / Improvement 224 / Agressiveness 224 /
  Expansion 224
Last Word: A Beginning, Not an End 227

Appendix: Apply the Seven-Step Process 228

Glossary 233

Bibliography 240

Index 242

Preface

How can anyone possibly say, "Thank God It's Monday"? This book shows you how a thank-god-it's-monday frame of mind helps both you and your company achieve success—and helps you get what you want out of your job at the same time. Whether you are an up-and-coming young professional or a company president who has put in many years "on the job," you will find that, by strategies and techniques, you will master the skill of management. The rewards are many: You will see how you can become a master of your job or business—and not a slave to it. The economic rewards include increased compensation and perhaps financial independence whereby you have the freedom to spend time as you want to—not as you have to. How, specifically, can you do all this?

First, you must make a commitment to plan and manage yourself, your career, your organization, and your future. Obviously, this commitment involves a continuous program of self-improvement. Yet is is a small price to pay in light of the tremendous payoff.

If you follow the clearly defined "flight-plan" that this book provides, the trip to success is far less difficult and more orderly. For those of you who are already managing your career to full potential and who would like to pass on the feeling of TGIM to others, this book shows you how.

Too many people who become unhappy in their work begin to feel trapped. Yet somehow they do not get out of the trap. Their plight is due in part to a desire for security and to a fear of change. More predominantly, however, their reason for staying in a job is a lack of direction. Also, people generally cannot perform well on a job they do not like. So if you manage others and want them to produce for you or your company, you must be able to teach as well as to learn. This book contains specific guidance on counseling and on helping your subordinates to love their jobs as much as you love yours.

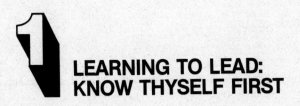

LEARNING TO LEAD:
KNOW THYSELF FIRST

> Man is obviously made to think. It is his whole dignity and his whole merit, and his whole duty is to think as he ought.
>
> —Blaise Pascal

Managing another person is an enormous responsibility. In many ways, such an assignment places a tremendous obligation on managers, because they are charged with the difficult challenge of seeing the best in others, at the same time giving the best they have. The task requires a great deal of personal understanding, direction, and consistent discipline. Little wonder that a truly effective manager is a very rare and sought-after person.

To become such a manager, you must first learn how to *manage yourself.* Unless you do so, you will not be able to manage anyone. All you will do is exert an influence that is created by mutually accepted principles, policies, and procedures. In turn, to manage yourself, you must be able to understand yourself and others as whole persons.

Another fundamental requirement—and part of knowing yourself—is the continuous application of the *learning/thinking*

1

process. This natural phenomenon, although common to us all, is rarely exploited. Those who choose to make the best use of it then have the commitment to take the necessary steps to become much more effective leaders and managers.

Let's begin with a look at the whole person.

The Whole Person
What is the human resource? What is a human being? A human being is a whole person with a hierarchy of needs and is constituted of four primary parts. Each of these parts, although synergistically interrelated with the others, can be viewed as a separate element, as follows:

1. The *mental*—the brain with its enormous, untapped potential;
2. The *spiritual*—the philosophy, including the individual's beliefs;
3. The *social*—the normally inherent desire to interact with others; and
4. The *physical*—the protection and enhancement of the body.

In the past, managers felt that there was a working person apart from the whole person, but such is not the case. The whole person comes to work everyday. So the manager must deal with whole persons, as well as with priorities that they place on the four individual parts. For example:

- Individuals who place a high priority on the development of their *mental* faculties will, in all probability, be incompatible with a stable or declining company. They would likely resent routine jobs that do not provide challenges.
- On the other hand, persons who strongly emphasize *physical* things may be very happy to dig a ditch or to manhandle boxes.
- Individuals whose *spiritual* bent tends to be puritanical might not be at all compatible with a libertine manager whose philosophy is to win at all costs.
- For those who place great emphasis on their *social* activities, the organization that sponsors company picnics and Friday

night get-togethers might be more appealing than the company that requires a lot of solo travel or working alone.

What type of whole person are you? The answer to that question dominates your management style and results. If you are not a sound person, you probably will not be a very effective manager. If you understand and respect yourself, the chances are good that you will be a manager who can make a great contribution. This primary requirement holds for any organization, whether business- or family-oriented. The most awesome management responsibility of all is the one you take on when you give life to a child, not to mention the marriage that customarily goes along with having children. Usually, if you mishandle these, your performance as a manager on the job will be adversely affected.

Understanding and managing yourself are not easy tasks. Yet they are musts, if you are to manage by example and operate on the authority of earned prestige. Self-knowledge and self-management are rapidly becoming needed management skills to meet today's management requirements, as well as tomorrow's.

Putting Your Act Together

Gaining an objective and accurate insight into just what kind of person you are now is one of the most difficult parts of managing yourself. Very few people can analyze themselves. Because our world is changing faster and becoming more complex, more and more people are becoming less and less able to cope, and they need the right kind of skilled help to "put their act together." Yet, because they know analysis is needed from time to time, the intelligent ones go to professional counselors, just as they would go to an attorney for an important legal matter or to a CPA for a complex tax situation.

Another problem is that people have their own unique and very personal acts, which sometimes become incompatible, for example, between a husband and wife, a parent and child, a manager and subordinate, or an individual and the job or company. When such incompatibility occurs, the individual really has three fundamental choices:

1. Try to be compatible with the situation and its inherent responsibilities and obligations.
2. Attempt to change the situation so that it becomes compatible.

3. Give up the situation and attempt to find a new one that is more compatible and supportive.

One thing is for sure: Until you put your own act together, you should not accept or request a management role over other persons who are looking to you for leadership and help in putting their own acts together.

The Planagement® Approach: Maximizing Performance and Work Satisfaction

To match the person with the "right" job, you once again have to make an objective and accurate appraisal, this time of both the person and the job. Certain tools and skills are available not only to assist individuals and organizations in making such analyses, but also in identifying gaps between the person and the job and in establishing an appropriate supporting program. Such a program either minimizes the gaps between person and job or, if they cannot be bridged, assists the individual in accepting the gaps as a part of life. Or perhaps the employee needs to focus sharply on a sound new career path that fits the person. (See Figure 1-1.) Part of the Planagement® System is designed to establish the right person in the right job. It works this way:

The person—with or without a counselor—honestly answers in *writing* a series of questions designed to establish profiles of the person and of the job as it exists. Some of these questions follow:

FIGURE 1-1. The right person in the right job system.

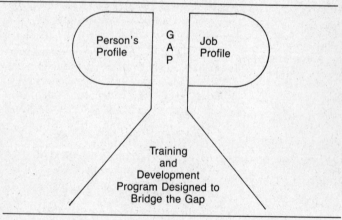

4

1. How do you define yourself as a person?
2. How do you describe the job which you can do best?
3. What are your personal missions in their order of importance? What are the most important results you wish to achieve for yourself and on the job?
4. What are the missions and results of your job in their order of importance?
5. What gaps exist between the reason and the job?
6. How can the gaps be bridged and by when?

Success Is in the Eye of the Beholder

Frequently, and sadly, even after analyses of both the persons and the job, many individuals with managerial responsibility blame the job and their situation rather than themselves for less-than-satisfactory or -happy results. The Planagement® System has, over the years, led to the remarkable insight that the person, not the situation, is almost always to blame. Another way of looking at this finding is reflected by the old Dutch proverb: "If everyone would sweep his own front porch, the whole city would be clean." Perhaps a favorite story of mine best makes the point.

A tourist walked over to an old man sitting under a shade tree and asked, "Old man, what kind of people live in this town?"

The old man responded by asking the tourist, "What kind of people live in your town?"

The tourist answered, "The people from my own town are losers. They lack consideration for others. They're selfish and self-centered, and it's difficult to have any respect for them or to want to be with them."

The old man then responded, "The very same kind of people live in this town—so you should feel very much at home."

Shortly after this brief visit, another tourist came up to the old man and asked the same question,

"Old man, what kind of people live in this town?"

The old man again asked, "What kind of people live in your town?"

The tourist replied, "The people from my town are wonderful people who go out of their way to help others and who always do the very best they can." He further stated that the people from his town were "ambitious," because they worked hard at improving themselves and were constantly able to make greater contributions to themselves, to their families, to their work, and to their community. As a result, the town was a prospering place to live, fun, exciting, challenging—an environment that contributed to everyone's happiness and peace of mind.

The old man smiled and said to the tourist, "You are a most fortunate person, because that is exactly the type of people who live here. That is just the kind of town we have. You should feel very much at home and have a wonderful time."

How do you regard your "town"—or company? Is it filled with self-centered and selfish people? Or are the people there ambitious and giving? Do they work together in good spirit? Are you having a wonderful time as a manager? Do you meet responsibilities? Do you love your work? Are you happy in your present situation?

Do you look forward to Monday mornings?

If your managerial style is characterized by discontent, by restlessness, or by continuous frustration, then perhaps you need to assess both yourself and your situation. Decide whether to accept the situation as is, attempt to change it, or find another more compatible situation. To make such a decision, however, you need first to know yourself.

Understanding the Learning/ Thinking Process: The "Thinking Gap"

Before you can look forward to the challenge of Mondays, before you can elect to manage your life professionally, and before you can hope to manage others, you have to understand the "Thinking Gap." This gap is the wide discrepancy between what our minds are capable of doing and what they actually do. In almost all cases, we fall far short of our potential; that difference is called the Thinking Gap.

How much of a Thinking Gap do you have? How much of your potential for profit and growth are you actually achieving? Most owners and managers feel it is not nearly as it should be. When several hundred managers were asked this question, most felt that they were getting less than 50 percent of the profits and growth that they should be getting from their businesses.

The next question is "Where does this potential exist in a company?" The standard answer comes back that the greatest potential for improvement rests with the people's ability to work smarter, not just harder. The general feeling seems to be that the amount of work or the activity of the people frequently does not generate the anticipated or possible results.

A published study indicated that inefficiency is costing United States business $482 million every single day. This loss represents a tremendous potential for increasing profits, which, in turn, could be allocated, at least in part, for stimulating growth. Actually, the loss is probably much more like $2 billion each day because we are not only inefficient, but we are often ineffective as well. Sometimes we don't do things right (efficiency), but at times we may not even be doing the right things in the first place (effectiveness). This greatly multiplies the loss due to inefficiency alone.

Why does this situation exist? And what can be done about it? how can we clearly identify where the potential exists? And how do we establish a process for reclaiming the loss?

First of all, we need to find out where the potential for improvement exists in people. Past research has provided valuable direction in this regard. Apparently, we do not use our "thinking machines" very well. Psychologists tell us that the average human being uses only 5 percent of the mind's true capacity. They tell us that the skills and disciplines we must employ as managers require between 10 and 13 percent of our mind's capabilities. According to the scientists, Einstein, who was one of our greatest thinkers, used only 22 percent of his mind's potential.

When I first heard these percentages, I asked how they were established. It seems that our brains have the capacity to store 2,000,000,000,000,000 (2 quintillion) bits of information. Put in other terms, we have the mental capacity to store more than 20,000 times the information contained in the entire *Encyclopedia Britannica*. How do we know? Apparently some scientists have determined that the cells in our brain are a different color depending on whether they are used. So the 5-, 10-, 13-, and 22-percent figures come from dividing the total number of cells into the different colored cells that we "turn on" by using them. With present technology, it would take a computer larger than the earth itself to duplicate the capability and capacity of the 3¼-pound computer that we carry around in our heads.

Such is the theory, and, frankly, some people strongly disagree with the conclusions. Nevertheless, almost everyone feels that we are not living up to our true potential, because, as human beings, we have some rather serious roadblocks to working smarter.

Roadblocks to Thinking

What are these roadblocks? Here are some of them:

1. Human beings do not like to do three things: to think; to use orderly procedures; to do paperwork.
   Yet these disciplines are the keys to exercising our minds and to turning on more of our cells to do more in less time with better results. While psychologists tell us we don't like to think, it has been shown that *people do like to think when they know how.* But most people have not learned the simple and productive process for thinking.

2. We are prone to establishing habits. Enraptured with the routine, we content ourselves with managing momentum rather than with doing the thinking required to manage the potential. This common, human approach does not challenge and exercise our minds.

3. Although we tend to fear and resist change, we live in a world where change is the only constant. As a result, most individuals and organizations allow change to determine their future, rather than apply some good hard thinking to frame the future.

4. Our language creates additional roadblocks to understanding what is on people's minds, including our own! The 500 most commonly used words in the English language have over 14,000 definitions. Managers frequently use words that do not have a commonly understood definition: planning, growth, thinking, strategy, and the like. Different backgrounds and experiences, along with the concomitant different frames of reference, also add to the complexity of this communication problem.

5. People often procrastinate. Putting things off—how can we make our ideas happen when we can't even get started?

6. Unfortunately, some people regard a question as a sign of stupidity or lack of experience. Ironically, the questions we ask others, as well as those we ask ourselves, are stimulators of thought. They represent a healthy, inquiring, open, and growing mind. On the other hand, reaching a final or perfect answer turns the "thinking machine" off, not on, and results in stability and stagnation of the mind. A great many people, referred to as "dropouts," have just stopped growing. Many of these "dropout" or "obsolete" managers are only anxious talkers with a lot of answers, rather than skilled listeners with the right questions in a logical sequence.

7. There exists an unstructured balance between logic and emotion. Rationality and feelings are frequently viewed on an either/or basis, rather than as a natural combination. Although both are usually present, they are typically not communicated, but rather left to the interpretation and empathic capacity of others. Other times, we let our "feel" for a situation dictate what we do, without thinking out why we feel as we do. Individuals are startled when someone asks them, "Do you know this to be true, and if so, why?" Or, "If you are guessing, what is the basis of your guess?" Yet this kind of question is the beginning of conscious and communicated thought, as well as of improved understanding.

How Our Minds Work: Overcoming Roadblocks

How do we overcome some of these roadblocks? We apparently must have a better understanding of how our minds work. We would then have the opportunity to work our minds better. A systematic approach to thinking should assist us in doing more in less time and with better results, because we would have a more rapid way to identify, gather, organize, present, or consider the minimum amount of information we require to make the right decisions faster.

Suppose we could stop our rapidly spinning minds. Suppose we could look at the mind's step-by-step logic process. What would we see? We would see it function essentially as shown in Figure 1–2.

FIGURE 2–2. The mind's process

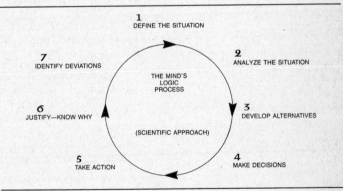

The unconscious application of this process is often called "by the seat of the pants"—an interesting idiom. Conversely, its conscious, documented application is frequently referred to as "planning" or "scientific management." Whatever you call it, the logic process is nothing more than the basic process of planning and managing a situation. This planning/management process helps overcome roadblocks through a better understanding of how the mind works, with a simple approach that helps anyone work smarter.

A depiction of the planning/management process that combines scientific management (facts) with the behavioral sciences (gut feel, judgment, emotions) might look as shown in Figure 1-3. This sound checklist for decison making helps us develop and document plans as individuals for our particular jobs and collectively for our companies, regardless of size. The conscious and consistent application of this powerful discipline contributes directly and measurably to increasing profits and accelerating sound growth. Most people would agree that the growth and development of an organization is directly dependent on the growth and development of its people—who *are* the organization.

FIGURE 1-3. Professional management process.*

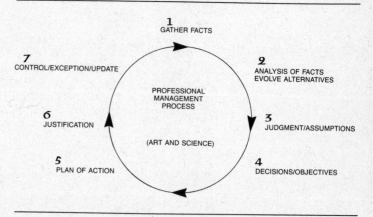

*For a brief example of this seven-step process applied, see the appendix.

With this newfound awareness, your next step requires application and self-discipline. You must learn to overlay the process onto just about every situation you come across, since every situation contains something of value. Learn whatever you can whenever you can, and store it away for use at an appropriate time in the future.

But where do you start? Part of the Planagement® program includes a series of steps that increases learning, improves performance, and enhances personal job satisfaction. Here is how it works.

STEP 1: DECIDE TO LEARN AND GROW

Make the basic decision that you want always to *learn and grow.* Unless you have the *drive* for improvement, you won't be able to make the needed effort to overcome the inertia of a mind at rest. Henry Ford said, "Thinking is the hardest work of all—that is why so few people do it." No question about it. Learning takes effort, just like any exercise. The more consistently you apply the effort, the easier it gets. Eventually, the bad habits of not learning and not thinking are replaced with the good habit of constant learning—with all its priceless rewards and abundance. You must accept the fact that the learning process is never-ending.

STEP 2: DEVELOP LEARNING SKILLS

Develop *learning skills,* some of which follow:

- *Use active listening:* Recognize the lesson of our two ears and one mouth. Discipline your mind to focus and concentrate on the outside input with the objective to do twice as much listening (input to the mind) as talking (output).
- *Ask questions:* Develop the *diagnostic* skill. Some people define the education process as a series of questions and answers; the first such series causes confusion and frustration, resulting in the formulation of a new series of questions at a higher level on more important things. In this never-ending process, we must always learn to tolerate—and even enjoy—the inherent frustration of acquiring and understanding new knowledge. The professional manager's most important skill is the ability to ask the right questions in the right sequence at the right time to the right person.
- Consciously *apply several senses* to a learning experience: *Multisensory* learning allows you to capture a much higher percentage of whatever there is to be learned. If you only

hear something, the chances are great that you will retain less than 10 percent of what you hear. If you hear it and see it, the percentage goes up. And if you write it ("touch" it), then the percentage for retaining the learning experience is significantly increased.

The guideline for learning is then: To hear it is to forget it, to write it is to remember it, and to live it (or apply it) is to understand it. Once you understand something, it remains with you all your life until a better or different understanding takes its place or builds upon it. The learning is in the doing. The education is the application.

- Use *repetition* to force new knowledge past the human filters that block out so many experiences and insights. Research has shown that, if something is repeated six times or more, it becomes part of our brains and an available resource forever.

- Be *selective*. With *selection* skills, you continuously seek the minimum amount of information needed to understand, to make the required decision, and to implement the best action program for carrying out the decision with the maximum cost/benefit. Utilizing techniques in a systematic approach, you identify the 20 percent that impacts on the 80 percent. Hence you are able to do more in less time with better results.

- Consciously apply the *learning/thinking* skills through a closed-loop activity that works as shown in Figure 1–4. This process provides an invaluable checklist for learning, and it should be used as frequently as possible.

- Establish the skill of *visualization*. Since the mind thinks in pictures, make every attempt to convert an important concept, experience, or direction into a picture form. Such a picture almost always communicates more understanding than a thousand words.

- *Discipline* your mind to develop a balance between the conceptual and executor sides of your brain. Studies have shown that one part of the brain emphasizes planning, while the other side emphasizes managing or doing. Because one side usually develops much more than the other in most people, you observe two kinds of people: those who have a tendency to think, and those who have a tendency to act. Balancing these important skills makes you more productive as a person. You tend to be Creactive©, that is, you develop the ability to move concepts into reality. The person who has not

FIGURE 1–4. The closed-loop learning thinking process

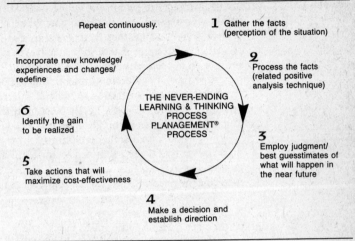

©Copyright, 1978, Planagement, Inc.

only developed good ideas, but who also has the necessary *discipline* to make those good ideas happen, is much more effective.

STEP 3: DEVELOP LEARNING TARGETS

Develop *learning targets* that enable you to move foward in your established present and future direction. You must always be comparing where you are now to where you want to be in the future. The gaps that you identify provide you with the guidance—the targets—for additional learning and the action needed to move ahead. Ideally, this learning development process never ends. Instead, it results in an uncommon, productive, and rewarding life through the constant application of your learning process.

Filing a Flight Plan for Your Life Let's say that you make yourself more conscious of the learning/thinking process. Or, if you were already aware of it, let's say you put it to greater use now. What good does this process do for you? You become someone who makes the greatest possible use of a capability that everyone has. You distinguish yourself from the great

13

majority of people who fail to make the most of their minds. For example, because of people's generally undisciplined, underutilized, and inconsistent minds, pilots are required to follow a flight plan and a check-list every time they fly—regardless of their experience, track record, expertise, or established habits. They need the enforced orderliness of the flight plan and checklist to get where they're going.

Yet most people fly through life without a plan, without checklists, without orderliness. These same people, however, would not think of trying to put a jigsaw puzzle together without a picture as a guide. To get an idea of how hard you make things for yourself when you don't take an orderly approach, try flipping the jigsaw pieces over so that the backsides are face up. There's no picture to guide you. All the pieces are one color. How much faster could you assemble the puzzle if you had the colored sides and the finished picture as a guide? If each of those pieces were a piece of the irreplaceable time in your life, wouldn't you be interested in "getting it all together" with as little waste as possible?

In this age of change and challenge, the ability to think is more than a key to unlocking your potential. It is the key to your survival! If persons can become what they think about, you cannot hope to become much if you don't think at all. Following the mind's process enables you to "think big."

The Keys to High Performance

ACCENTUATING THE POSITIVE

For optimum high performance, take the lid off your capacity for learning and growth. Have you ever met a person who is proud of having had twenty years of experience? Have you then discovered, once you became more familiar with the person's knowledge, that the person has had only one year of experience twenty times over? On the other hand, you have probably observed another type of person who seems to catch on faster than most to new experiences and knowledge. What makes the difference between these two types of individuals, who have the same amount of time, and, in some cases, similar backgrounds, training, and experience?

The difference is how each person applies his or her inherent capacity to learn, which, in turn, is determined by how well each applies the learning process. God grants us time, but it is up to us to determine its value. Individuals who are not aware of the learning process—the 5-percenters who use only a fraction of their brain power—meander through life managing their own mediocre mo-

14

mentum. On rare occasions, they think hard enough to wonder why life has passed them by and decreed that they should be "just average." By learning how to apply the process, you greatly enhance your capacity for development, thus setting yourself off from most others.

Many of us find such a reorientation difficult, because tragically our educational system does not focus on the learning (or thinking) process. We have received an "education," but we have not necessarily learned how to learn. Although many teachers will tell you that they are attempting to teach their students how to think, they are unable to communicate that very process. Hence, the very essence of the teacher/pupil relationship remains obscure and fragmented to both, with the unfortunate result that over nine out of ten people never learn how to learn. In other words, most "educated" people never learn how to consciously apply their capacity to think.

In addition, the normal approach to education—whether in the classroom or in organizational training—seems to focus on the negative. For example, asking questions is frequently interpreted as a sign of ignorance, instead of an inquiring, growing mind. Yet questions are often answered with a response like, "Why are you asking that question? Haven't you done your homework?"

This negative emphasis extends even into the areas of problem solving and testing. For instance, a well-known trainer recently said to a group of managers, "Managers can only learn in the context of a perceived problem." Further, he stated, "No learning experience can take place unless the individual has a problem." Yet why does the learning experience have to be stimulated by a negative (a problem) instead of by a positive (an opportunity)? Why do we always get thirty *wrong* out of a hundred instead of *seventy right?*

Perhaps this negative orientation persists because managers think they do better with it! A not uncommon perception of managers about managers is that they are paid to solve problems. So the more problems they have to solve, the more they are needed and the more job security they have. As a result, managers are prone to look for problems and even to magnify them. They have limited, if any, opportunity to learn new and better ways—only time to move from one crisis and problem to another crisis and problem. Activity becomes their preoccupation, because they are being paid to be busy and indispensable. They react to and solve problems. No wonder managers have "no time" to seek out and to exploit operational improvements. No wonder they are reluctant to take time to think and to develop the anticipative skills of becoming problem-preventers. Should they learn how to prevent rather than react to problems, they may appear to have little to do and to be unneeded.

The result? Individuals are reluctant to ask questions or to take the time to think before taking action. "The busier the better" becomes the motto and the prevailing modus operandi. This orientation forms the basis of the accepted norm, which is to manage momentum, to solve problems, and generally to act like everybody else.

Becoming conscious of the learning/thinking process is only the first step toward rejecting this common way of life. This one basic phenomenon underlies all the related activities not only of learning and thinking, but also of planning, management, decision making, control, creating, communicating, mental development, and problem preventing and solving. It is little more than applied common sense—that is, how the mind works naturally. Yet if we are not practiced in this vitally important process—if we do not exercise our minds—then mentally we become lazy, inconsistent, and eventually dormant.

LEARNING TO LEAD

For managers, the most beneficial effort of living out the learning/thinking process is that they become better leaders. Shelves of books have been written on leaders and leadership. Seminars and workshops attempt to develop leaders. Numberless individuals strive to become leaders, for the recognition and reward, but few have the capacity. Sadly, all this effort has produced precious few urgently needed leaders. In fact, a growing majority today believe that our nation's biggest problem is a lack of leaders, not only in government, but in business and education as well.

How, then, does effective leadership arise from self-knowledge and a rational approach to life? Leaders who have taken the trouble to understand their own needs and desires are able to appreciate the needs of others. By reason of their thoughtfulness and rationality, they can also lend direction, purposefulness, and confidence to others, necessary to achieve a common objective. So, although some leaders may be born, other apparently "born" leaders can be "made."

Let's look at some of the more important and common attributes of a successful leader to see how they derive from all we've discussed:

16

1. *A positive self-image:* Leaders must have an internal insight and a respect for themselves that feeds a powerful self-confidence and a drive to lead. Without this drive to lead, no individual is very likely to become an outstanding leader.

2. *A clear philosophy:* A leader has an established philosophy that translates into a communicated direction. The intensity of that philosophy, along with the resulting clarity of direction, attracts followers of a similar philosophy, as well as those who need a direction set for them.

3. *Strong communication skills:* The ability to communicate is one of the most important assets of a leader. "Charisma" is a form of nonverbal communication that has considerable impact on others who are attracted to the leader. They get a feeling of confidence in the leader, and they understand the leader's purpose.

4. *A sensitivity to needs and goals:* An important strength of leaders is their ability to combine their own direction with the needs and goals of their followers. By so doing, leaders evoke a closeness and dedication that is of vital importance to a continuity of programs.

5. *Setting an appropriate example:* To maintain the continued support of others, leaders must maintain confidence by setting a continuous example that is appreciated and that may even be inspirational to the followers. This example needs to be tailored so that it fits both the philosophy of the leader and the needs of the followers. The fact that both Hitler and Churchill were considered leaders by their respective followers provides a vivid example of how different philosophies may be found in those with the capacity to lead.

6. *Courage, determination, and persistence:* One of the most common characteristics of successful leaders is their ability to overcome adversity and failure. This consistent ability to learn from mistakes and to bounce back from disappointments is of critical importance to those who choose to lead. Courage, determination, and persistence provide the continuity for increasing the confidence and support of followers.

7. *The ability to demand:* Strong leaders see the best in others while giving the best they have. They demand the best ef-

fort from their followers, because they know that to expect and require the best brings out the best in people. This attitude becomes a building and strengthening process, which is good for the followers and which increases the results achieved.

8. *Personal integrity:* Leaders may be wrong, but they are always honest and consistent with their philosophy. This trait provides a consistency on which others learn to trust, respect, and have confidence.

9. *Superior management ability:* Leadership requires a consistent ability to manage inconsistent situations in a way that produces constant gain. The ability to plan successfully, organize, delegate, and control is a fundamental requirement of leadership. Time management skills, which result in your being able to do more in less time with better results, are also major contributors to successful leadership. Being able to discern and to concentrate on the 20 percent of the factors that control 80 percent of the results is of great importance. Combining effectiveness (doing the *right things*) with efficiency (doing *things right*) is also a key ability.

10. *Discipline:* To lead well, persons must have not only drive and direction, but also discipline. Discipline, which is basic to leadership, may be expressed in a number of ways. For example, leaders may apply the self-discipline required to progress continually and to develop in support of the established direction. Or they may exert discipline by making timely, sound decisions, by project management, by setting priorities, and by doing the required follow-up.

These characteristics can be acquired through study and practice. You can *learn* leadership, but only through the consistent application of sound leadership concepts. Becoming a competent leader is not easy, but you can become one if you have the need, the drive, the determination, and the discipline.

Creativity Although creativity is a trait normally associated with flamboyant Picassos and temperamental divas, it is actually only an extension of every person's thought process. While some individuals seem to be born with more creative capability than others, all persons may increase their creativity. They may do so by emulating the personal characteristics of creative people and by continuously applying certain disciplines, tools, and techniques that have been researched and designed to increase creativity.

These tools and techniques have been used to increase creativity not only in individuals, but also collectively in companies. Frequently the results have been good. Where less than satisfactory results have been experienced, they were often due not to the concepts' lack of soundness, but rather to a poor understanding of them, usually combined with an inept implementation program.

BRAINSTORMING

The purpose of brainstorming is to generate as many ideas as possible. Although this technique is frequently used for creative problem solving, it works just as well for creative opportunity identification. The steps of this method might be summarized as shown in Figure 1–5. The completion of these seven steps develops a creative solution that frequently was not apparent at the outset. It also offers significant advantages over no solution at all, of course, or even over the first idea that comes to mind. Probably one of the reasons that brainstorming has proven to be so valuable is that usually one good idea sparks another, and then the two combine to be of more value together than either could be individually.

THINKING TECHNIQUES

Another way to stimulate creativity is to apply your pattern of thinking in new ways about what has existed in the past or what exists now. In other words, you should try to see things as they might be rather than how they really are. Correlative suggestions include:

1. *Think association*—relate various elements, using a key word technique.
2. *Think combination*—combine various elements in new or different ways.
3. *Think adaptation*—for example, records and cassettes originally developed for entertainment were adapted for instruction and education.

FIGURE 1–5. The brainstorming technique

1. Clearly define the entire opportunity or problem in writing.
2. List all the known facts about the opportunity or problem.
3. List and use all important sources of information that would relate to the opportunity or problem in order to gather additional facts, judgments, experiences, and ideas about the opportunity or problem.
4. Write down all the information gathered from the sources listed in step 3.
5. Generate as many ideas as you can—individually and/or in a group—and do this brainstorming (thinking) with the "judgment brakes" off. Do not try to decide at this point whether the idea is good or bad: You are after only as many ideas as you can generate. There are four basic rules in brainstorming:
    1. No negative thinking.
    2. The wilder the idea, the better.
    3. A large number of ideas is essential.
    4. Combination and improvement of ideas is a primary goal.
6. After generating all the ideas you can, rank-order them based on their feasibility, ease, value, practicality, effectiveness, or suitability. These, and perhaps other, important factors sequence your ideas according to which is best, next best, and so on.
7. Develop action plans for the best ideas. These action plans should include:
    a. estimated time,
    b. cost,
    c. materials,
    d. other required resources,
    e. who has to do what,
    f. when it needs to be done, and
    g. the sequence of actions, with due dates.

4. *Think substitution*—what different material or source of energy could you use in your business?

5. *Think magnification*—think big: how to make things larger and the benefits of size.

6. *Think minification*—consider the shift from table radio tubes to the pocket transistor, as an example.

7. *Think rearrangement*—turn things around, for instance the new fur coats with the fur on the inside.

All these alternatives exercise your mind and contribute to increase your creative capability and possibly generate that "unbelievably great idea."

TENSIONS AND OPPOSITES

The use of tension and intentional opposites also stimulates creativity. Of the many well-known examples of this technique, some are expressed in the following statements:

1. The Two Horns of the Dilemma.

2. Necessity is the Mother of Invention.

3. The creative speed of "the dog running after its dinner" as compared to "the rabbit running for its life."

4. Michelangelo's Agony and the Ecstasy.

5. Balancing freedom of the mind with discipline of supporting actions.

6. The ability to know what time it is and also to know how to build the watch.

7. The feeling of many creative persons that:

> I burn the candle at both ends;
> It won't last through the night.
> But oh what a joy to watch it burn,
> Because it burns so bright.

In other words, although a significant creative synergism results from combining opposites, if it is carried to extremes, it can burn itself out and "not last through the night."

If in this tension-and-opposites theory, there is a key word, it would probably be "balance." And perhaps one of the best examples is found in the roots and growth of the United States. Among the most basic principles of the United States is the challenging combination of individual rights and the rule of the majority. These seemingly contradictory concepts have been balanced in such a manner as to create the most creative and abundant society that the world has ever known.

To remain a leader—either as a nation, or as a business, or as a person—our creative capacity cannot be left to chance. Being creative is hard work, and it requires a great deal of self-discipline in continuously thinking, planning, and taking action. This is a never-ending process, because, if we stop being creative and become complacent, we will stop growing and quickly become obsolete.

Option-Loaded Decisions— Or, Making Things Happen

Most people pass through periods when they devote a considerable effort to developing plans for self-improvement—in other words, when they are not happy with themselves or with what they have accomplished. Perhaps the reason for so many people's feeling this way so often is that they are subconsciously recognizing the fantastic potential within everyone. Most people have a tremendous number of good thoughts. Stop and think how many good ideas you have had in the past few days that you did not, or have not, implemented. Some of them you can still do, and some of them you can never do, because the situation has passed. Some of them you should have discarded, since they were not worthy of implementation. While we are often encouraged by others to create and to act on our good ideas, we owe it to ourselves to bring more of our ideas to fruition on our own. We need to think of alternative options—then choose one to start acting upon.

Remember: action, not thought, brings results. How do we do this? Of the many excellent ways, concentrate on one word, "action." More thoughts won't automatically produce more results. As a matter of fact, they could produce fewer. You may have one, several, or a hundred thoughts, but you will achieve results only to the degree that you take action. In other words, action has a direct correlation to results. More thoughts can *help* to produce better and more results, but *only* in connection with more action.

One of the ways to accomplish more is to develop the *habit of action*. "Get it done," "Do it now," and other stimulative phrases could help to remind us of the importance of action.

Let's take a closer look at another such phrase: "Make things happen." Making things happen implies action. *You* are the doer or maker, and the "things" can be physical items, thoughts, ideas, or whatever. "Happen" implies change or results. In effect, you take action on something to produce results.

Make things happen = More results
You take action with things to produce change = More results

Your thoughts are directed toward results and action, not just toward producing more thoughts or doing evaluations of your ideas. Doing something and making mistakes is usually better than doing nothing. You accomplish something, you gain experience, and you will probably do it better next time.

So how does it work? Basically, you consistently remind yourself that you are a doer and that, if you want results, you must make things happen. The time to make the tool work is when you have a good idea, when you are excited about it, when you want to produce a certain result. At that point, think immediately, "Make things happen." Immediately take some kind of action that helps to produce the result. If the result cannot be accomplished right then, do something that does enhance it.

The best way to produce results is to develop many alternatives or options. As you develop more and more alternatives, many things happen:

— your chances of effecting the result get better;

— you give more evaluation to your idea;

— you practice the discipline of thinking; and

— you are likely to achieve better and better results.

Let's look at an example.

Idea	Normal Reaction	Result
Want to purchase a new home	1. Can't afford it. 2. Will do it later. 3. Too busy to look. 4. Call real estate agency. 5. Look at ads in paper.	May or may not get results

Idea	Make Things Happen Develop Alternatives/Options
Want to purchase a new home	1. Can't afford it: a. Do new financial statement. b. Check latest loan requirements. c. Let real estate agency submit a loan application. d. Evaluate alternate cash assets: (1) Stocks (2) Insurance policy cash values (3) Garage sale (4) Part-time work (5) Appraisal of present home (6) Equity in other items. e. Talk to contractor about doing some of the work to cover the down payment. f. Maybe present owner will take small second mortgage. g. Look for house for sale where owner will finance. h. Check special government loans. i. Have smaller new home built and plan to add to it later. j. Borrow long term from the family. 2. Read advertisements in paper. 3. Call two real estate firms and let them know with specifications what you want. 4. Drive around the area where you want to live and look. 5. Tell friends you are looking. 6. Visit a contractor and tell him/her your specifications. 7. Place an ad in the paper—Home Wanted—with specifications. 8. Visit a builder of modular housing. 9. Rent a house with option to buy.

The chances of winding up with a home are much better with this skill and discipline. Figure 1–6 pictures the process for making things happen.

"Immediate action" alternatives are especially important if you have included some procrastination options. "Will do it later" or "Too busy to look" are only two of many alternatives, if you're attempting to make things happen. Although such options can be stoppers, they can be overcome with this technique. For example:

FIGURE 1-6. Make things happen

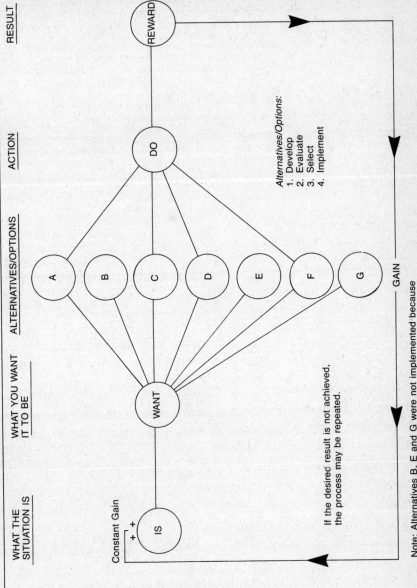

WHAT THE
SITUATION IS

WHAT YOU WANT
IT TO BE

ALTERNATIVES/OPTIONS

ACTION

RESULT

Constant Gain

IS

WANT

A
B
C
D
E
F
G

DO

REWARD

GAIN

Alternatives/Options:
1. Develop
2. Evaluate
3. Select
4. Implement

If the desired result is not achieved,
the process may be repeated.

Note: Alternatives B, E and G were not implemented because
they were eliminated by the evaluation.

Idea	Normal Reaction	Result
Want to sell a key customer (male) a special product	Present the product to him on the next visit.	May or may not buy

But, if you really want to make it happen:

Idea	Develop Alternatives or Options
Want to sell a key customer a special product	1. Write him ahead of the presentation and tell him you have something very special to show him. 2. Review your presentation and try to improve it. 3. Present the product to a friend or fellow salesman and ask him to offer suggestions on presentation. 4. Call some customers who are using the product and ask them what they like best about it. 5. If any of your customers using the product know your key account, ask for letter of recommendation. 6. Prepare a proposal and outline of key features to leave with customer. 7. Follow up with a proposal showing where the product meets his expressed needs. 8. Send copies of letters from satisfied users. 9. Make sure you know who will make the decision and that the information is getting to him. 10. Make sure you know when the decision will be made and plan your follow-up activities accordingly. 11. Develop special closing stimulators, such as pricing approvals, credit terms, delivery, service. 12. Make arrangements to take him to a customer who is using the product. 13. Would he try just a few on a "no risk" basis—if possible, depending upon the product? 14. Ask a lot of questions and listen when you meet with him. 15. Consider having another salesman or consultant go along and make the presentation and help observe reaction.

Idea	Normal Reaction	Result

16. Make a logical, simple presentation supported by visuals.
17. Follow up with a letter of appreciation.
18. How can you get him personally?
    a. What are his hobbies, interests, personal concerns?
       (1) Football fan—send him two tickets to the big game.
       (2) Like to play tennis—send him interesting article or new book on tennis.
       (3) Take him to lunch at his favorite restaurant.
19. If he doesn't purchase, make sure you know why:
    a. Will they buy later; when?

Let's go over this discipline once again:

1. You have a lot of good thoughts.
2. You can make things happen.
3. You can get more results by developing the discipline to make things happen.
4. When you have a good thought, respond immediately with "make things happen" and begin the process of developing options.
5. Selecting one, move *now*. Do it. Do it *now*. Do it *right now*.

To avoid a very deep discussion about what contribution this approach makes to your attitude, confidence, rhythm of success, and the like, suffice it to say that:

More Results = More Satisfaction = A Happier You

Isn't that what life's really all about?

The Philosophy of Excellence

Napoleon used to instruct his intelligence force to forget about the size of the enemy army, and rather to identify the opposing generals. If Napoleon knew the other generals, he would study their philosophy, gain an insight into their strategy, and thus correctly anticipate their tactics. Napoleon's numerous wins in the field supported his reasoning.

Fundamentally, what separates the winners from the losers is the quality and type of their attitude, which might be defined as the

27

thought behind what is done. Napoleon understood this point. He knew that behind the enemy leader's thought was an attitude, which derived from a personal philosophy, the leading edge of a person's thinking. Hence the soundness of the philosophy is crucial to the soundness of the person. Bad philosophy generates a bad attitude, which in turn, generates bad thinking, bad actions, and bad results. Hence, some are bound to win and some are bound to lose.

Many statements show the interrelations among philosophy, attitude, thinking, action, and results.

"As you think, so you produce."
"What you are speaks much more loudly than what you say."

This latter statement is confirmed through research, which indicates that effective communications are dependent:

9% on the words we use;
38% on how we say the words;
53% on body language.

Assuming this research is correct, we can say that 91 percent of our communications is directly related to our attitude, as attitude will have a dominating impact on how we say things and our body language will be predominatly controlled by our thinking and emotional state, which in turn, are largely determined by our philosophy.

To pursue excellence, you must continually commit to the disciplines of professional management: developing yourself and then contributing to the development of others. By making this basic commitment, you will often find yourself the sole spectator of your effort. The only satisfaction you can count on absolutely is knowing you have done your best, are doing your best, and will always do your best. However, you will be a winner regardless of your chosen field and level of attainment, because, in doing your best, you will have discovered what truly constitutes life's success.

PLANNING YOUR POSITION IN LIFE

Nothing is really work unless you would rather be doing something else.

—James M. Barre

If, as a professional manager, your responsibility is to create balance, establish purpose, and provide for a learning climate in the life of your organization, then you must do the same for your own life. Hence, career planning becomes extremely important to both you and your firm. Your role as a professional manager obliges you to plan your own career carefully and purposefully, as well as to provide the example and resources for your subordinates to plan their careers also.

The critically important question is do you enjoy your work, or is it drudgery? Your answer determines whether you are working in a job or pursuing a career. The difference between the two is bigger than you might think. A *job* is something you have to do. A *career* is your progress in your chosen field. If you are not happy in your work, your chances for being happy in your life are diminished. So the key to being happy in your work and probably in your life is to develop a career plan that fits *you*. You must then continually implement your career plan while making the needed changes as you change.

So important is career planning that an increasing number of educational institutions, as well as business organizations, are establishing career programs and services. Independent career counselors and services are also becoming more numerous, as are products and books on the subject.

Yet, even though the vast majority of individuals and organizations recognize career planning as very important, they do not apply career planning, either because they do not know how or because they do not want to be bothered. Organizations in particular often do not want to offer or to encourage career planning, because they fear that their employees might become dissatisfied with their present jobs and leave the company. Individuals resist career planning, because it requires great effort: thinking, applying self-discipline, establishing direction, and then taking developmental actions to correct the identified gaps. Such resistance is hard to understand when you stop to think of the benefits of having such a plan. The 2 percent of the population who are independently working out formal plans are usually the leaders in their chosen fields. In addition, these same individuals are not only living happy lives, but typically they are also secure, both psychologically and financially.

This chapter, therefore, takes three steps in the direction of that kind of happiness. First, it asks you to compare your present position in life with the position you desire. Next, it presents a step-by-step career-planning process. Finally, it suggests a method for deciding which approach is the most likely to bring you to the state in life that brings you satisfaction and fulfillment. By the end of this chapter, you will have the means to make that all-important decision by and for yourself.

Looking Toward Your Your Future   With your commitment to self-discipline and a clear direction, you are ready to do whatever is necessary to advance from your present to your future. The question is, of course, specifically *what* is necessary? For the answer, we turn once again to a step-by-step process, approached this time from the viewpoint of time management. Some of the steps involved in this system, to be carried out in writing, follow:

1. Complete an objective *diagnosis of where you are now,* including your present personal profile, your missions, your capabilities, your strengths and skills, your accountabilities, the external and internal trends affecting you, your vulnerabilities, your opportunities, your weaknesses, and your problems. Include also the logical alternative actions that you might take to achieve your identified potentials.

2. Identify *the future you wish to achieve.* Profile that future specifically enough so that you can actually draw a picture of it—that is, an overview of it with its specific process within a specified time frame.

3. Detail not only the gap between present realities and future hopes, but also the *individual components and the "due dates" for tackling the opportunities and problems.*

4. Next develop *a detailed plan of action* with specific steps. Figure 2–2 illustrates this type of action program, which is used as part of the Career Planagement® and Planagement® systems.

5. Carefully *summarize the time* you require to accomplish your plan, clearly showing the priority and operating schedule with key milestones.

6. Effectively *plan and manage each day* in support of your plan, so that your schedule of actions is maintained or improved through a variety of time management techniques.

TAKING ONE DAY AT A TIME

This sixth step is one of the most troublesome for many people, because they do not have a system for planning and managing each day. In actuality, most people find themselves being managed by each day's changing, unanticipated events. Most people fail to manage the events in their lives and then determine the results achieved. They lack control over their time, as well as a sound, established priority of efforts to be expended.

To realize the future you desire, you have to create and consistently implement a disciplined system for effectively and efficiently managing each day, because that future is determined directly by how well you manage the days that lead up to it. The system we propose for "taking one day at a time" is extremely simple to understand and to execute, but to apply it consistently requires enormous

FIGURE 2-1. Advancing toward your future

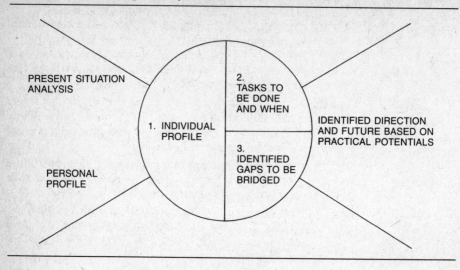

FIGURE 2-2. An illustrative career plan

Charles R. Composite   Career Plan Example
     PROGRAM SUMMARY

Programs and projects
should be developed for
each *major* action identified
throughout the plan.

	THIS	REPLACES
FILE:	7A1	
DATE:	3/1/XX	
PAGE:	1 OF 1 OF	

I. *ACTION PROGRAM* Name and Number _____ Career Plan—7A1 _____
   Write down my Career Plan, identify the right job and establish a plan
   of action to get it   0.5As and AI

II. *OBJECTIVE* (What by When) OBJECTIVE NUMBER (Most Important)
   To establish a Career Plan in writing by March 5, 19XX, and to start the
   right job by March 31, 19XX

III. *ASSUMPTION/POTENTIAL*
   A. That I will find a Planning/Management Method by 3/3/XX (Obj.
      0.5B1)
   B. The most important potential is that I will establish a sound direc-
      tion for my career and identify and get the right job.

IV. *STRATEGY* (How, Approach)
   To use the Career Planagement System to know myself better and
   establish a sound, written Career Plan in one day, and to develop a
   skill to do more in less time with better results on my next job and in
   the future

A. Projects (Action steps in sequence)	B. Schedule (When)	C. Responsibility (Who)
1. To apply Career Planagement System, which includes the development of a written job description which best fits my capabilities and supports my career plan.	By 3/3/XX	1. Me—with the Individual Development Center Program & the Planagement Career Counselor
2. To complete my written Career Plan (0.5A2); includes Personal Profile and Self-Development Program	By 3/5/XX	2. Me—probably will be complete on 3/3/XX
3. To schedule at least 5 interviews with companies most likely to have the desired job.	By 3/6/XX	3. Me—with suggestions by the Planagement Career Counselor
4. To send out at least 20 letters	By 3/8/XX	4. Me-use IDC Suggested Letter
5. To find the right job & be selected for it.	By 3/27/XX	5. Me

V. *RESOURCES REQUIRED*
  1. Money Cost of IDC Career Planagement Program, plus direct mail cost and the gas for the car to get to scheduled appointments
  2. Manpower 100% of my time for the next four weeks
  3. Materials/Other
     a. Career Planagement Program and supporting materials
     b. Direct mail letter & enclosures as provided by the Individual Development Center

VI. *COST/BENEFIT PURPOSE/RESULTS (Why)*
  1. Cost is reflected by the budget for this program, plus 4 weeks of my time 100%.
  2. Benefits include identifying and starting the right job, generating the needed income, and having a Planning/Management System that will assist me in doing more in less time with better results in the future, which should be the skill I'll need to get the job, both present and future, that I want.

VII. *ALTERNATIVES CONSIDERED* (Description and Disposition)
  1. To go into business for myself
  2. Take an immediate temporary job in order to get income sooner.

self-discipline. Used properly, its power is huge: Research indicates that those who use it can increase their productivity by up to 50 percent—and even more—each day. Here's how it works: Each day, list in writing the six most important things that must be done the next day in the order of their importance. Base their priorities on their relative benefits and results. Then accomplish those things one at a time (Figure 2–3).

FIGURE 2–3. Charles R. Composite—career plan example daily planning

Originator: Charles R. Composite
Distribution:

	THIS	REPLACES
FILE:	7D1	
DATE:	3/3/XX	
PAGE:	1 OF 1 OF	

SUBJECT: *PLANNING AND IMPLEMENTING ONE DAY AT A TIME*
LIST THE 6 MOST IMPORTANT ACTIONS YOU SHOULD ACCOMPLISH TOMORROW

Action	Benefit/Result
1. Appointment with personnel agency	1. Put myself on the job market & have more jobs to choose from.
2. Send out 20 letters to local firms. See list provided and suggested letter.	2. Direct contact—most likely prospects.
3. Personal interview appointments—at least 3, see suggestions provided.	3. 3 Best Prospects—possibly get a job sooner than forecast.
4. Review this Career Plan with my two best references & ask them for their suggestions and help.	4. Confirm references & obtain their support & ideas, possible referrals.
5. Obtain Lead the Field Program and listen to tape on Attitude & Better Time Management.	5. Self-understanding & improvement supportive to need & Career Plan.
6. Review want ads in the newspaper to see if there is a job that would fit (do this daily).	6. More jobs to choose from & possible earlier starting date.

PUT ACTIONS IN ORDER OF IMPORTANCE AND
COMPLETE THEM ONE AT A TIME

1. *4*
2. *2*
3. *3*
4. *1*
5. *6*
6. *5*

Don't overlook the specifics of this technique. Particularly, be sure to put your list into writing in order of importance. Some people list the things they want to do mentally, but these lists are often not in the order of identified importance. As a result, people do what is easiest first and procrastinate on the most difficult—and frequently the more important—tasks. They tend to get to those tasks "some other time," which often never comes. In that case, neither does the

desired future come. Procrastination, while a very human characteristic, is unfortunately still the "flab" of an undisciplined
mind—one of the greatest causes of postponing the desired future
into oblivion; hence, the Planagement® system's time management
tool for better daily planning and management, shown in Figure 2–3.
Experience has shown that this tool is of enormous benefit to those
who use it consistently—those very few people who develop the self-
discipline required to use it to its greatest advantage.

Can You Get There from Here? Assuming that you now work for an employer-organization, the
most crucial decision of your career is to choose one of the following
alternative actions:

1. To stay with your employer,
2. To go with another employer,
3. To go into business for yourself,
4. To change your career direction.

Many employees choose alternative 1 every morning that they show
up for work—without giving their "decision" much thought. Yet
doesn't a decision of such consequence call for more thoughtfulness
and deliberation?

You can approach this decision with greater organization simply by taking four steps. These steps did not materialize from a
crystal ball or a midnight dream. They are instead the hard-won
results of a decade of application, thought, and summation. For over
ten years, as of the publication of this book, the Planagement®
system has been implemented in all types of organizations, large and
small, as well as in a wide variety of industries and with people in all
sorts of work situations. The results have clearly shown these
methods increase peoples' work satisfaction. And the results also indicate that, when work satisfaction is increased, so likely are productivity and quality. The only element that seems to decrease is the need
for close supervision.

The Planagement® system has yielded six simple steps in making this decision:

1. Develop a written profile of yourself and of what you want
   in an ideal situation.
2. Write out the ideal description.

3. List the important aspects of that ideal situation. Then assign each aspect with a priority rating. Use the following grading system:
   5 "Must have"
   4 "Wanted"
   3 "A plus"
   2 "Less important"
   1 "Not very important"
4. Develop a decision matrix. Across the top of the matrix, place the four alternative actions (To stay with the employer, and so on). Down the side of the matrix, run the aspects of your ideal situation, with the grades that you have assigned. Then review the matrix, and make your decision. (See Figure 2–4.)
5. Develop a written plan to take you from where you are now to accomplishing your alternative.
6. Implement the plan as the top priority in your life.

FIGURE 2–4. Example

Factor	Priority Rating	Present Job	New Job	In Business For Self	New Career
No More Requirements	2	Yes	No	Yes	Yes
Work Satisfaction	5	No	No	Yes	Yes
Advancement	4	No	Yes	Yes	No
Compensation	3	No	Yes	Yes	No
TOTAL		2	7	14	7

Before Making Your Decision . . . In making this all-important decision, your personal philosophy, as well as that of the employer-organization, plays a heavy-duty role. You might, therefore, want to consider the conclusions that have resulted from years of applying the Planagement® system.

A POSITIVE PERCEPTION OF HUMAN NATURE

Of crucial importance is that you and the organization accept as truths the following perceptions of human nature:

- Applying physical and mental effort in work is as natural as it is in play or rest.
- Individuals employ the required drive, self-direction, self-discipline, and self-control in support of objectives to which they are committed.
- The size of the rewards to be achieved from accomplishing an objective determines the extent of a person's commitment to those objectives.
- Under the proper conditions, the average person learns not only to accept, but also to seek, responsibility.
- The vast majority of human beings *do* have the capacity to exercise a relatively high degree of imagination, ingenuity, and creativity in solving organizational problems and in improving their performance.
- Most individuals achieve less than 10 percent of their potential to produce at a higher level, in more important work, and with increased responsibility.
- The growth and development of the organization depend directly on the growth and development of the individuals who comprise the organization.

THE IMPORTANCE OF A SOUND MANAGEMENT PHILOSOPHY

Based on these insights, the organization should establish a management philosophy and approach that gets the following results:

- A positive direction and climate, along with a growth orientation, that keeps the opportunities in front of the growing human resource.
- A professional planning management system that may be used by the organization, by management teams, and by individuals for their jobs, careers, and professional development.
- Participative management by example—a supportive type of management style. Management by consensus is an additional strength of this approach.
- An imaginative compensation and reward system that is based on results achieved and that has no upper limit.

- A job structure that allows for job enrichment, job enlargement, and measurable standards of performance. Measurable standards are very important for objectively measuring performance and increasing work satisfaction. How so? People love games. Yet all games have standards of measurements such as your par in golf, your average in batting or bowling, your "stats" in football, and so on. Improving on the measurable standards in a job makes the job a game, and the work becomes a lot more challenging, satisfying, and fun.

- A formal human resource development system that maximizes performance, promotability, and work satisfaction. This is a system of selecting, placing, and "growing" the right person in the right job with the right supporting plan, as well as the right development and career path program.

- A commitment to excellence by seeing the best in individuals and by expecting the best from them. Performance can be measured by the quality of the person's plan and of the work in support of the plan, as well as by the quality and value of the results achieved.

THE IMPORTANCE OF ACCEPTING CERTAIN RESPONSIBILITIES

To achieve work satisfaction, you must meet at least the following responsibilities:

- Accept the fact that the responsibility for work satisfaction rests with you—that is, with the one doing the work. If you are not enjoying your work, it is your fault and not the fault of "external factors," such as the job itself, the boss, the organization, or the family. Certainly these factors may contribute to your unhappiness, but, if they are all that bad and won't change, then you can leave. Take your abilities and career plan where you'll find a better fit. If you stay to become increasingly unhappy, place the blame where it belongs: with the person who decides to remain miserable on the job. In a word, with you.

- Develop a written personal profile—an ideal job description—supported with a job plan for improving performance. In addition, make up a formal career plan, backed by a program for self-enhancement and professional development. Design this plan to bridge the identified gaps that reach from you, from your job, and from your company's needs for improved performance, to your individual needs as reflected in your career plan or your ideal job. Without question, your responsibility is to establish your own internal drive, direction, discipline, and development—everything that is required to achieve the desired future based on your own unique potential. Surely a strongly supportive family, a supportive company, a supportive boss, a properly structured job with a positive organizational climate and systems can all be enormously helpful. *But the responsibility ultimately rests with you and with no one else.*

All development is self-development. All true and lasting motivation evolves from within. Such motivation is based on an attitude that is internally generated, and it is supported with the drive to establish direction (motives) and the self-discipline to take the necessary action. It is a simple formula: motive + action = motive-action, or motivation. In direct support is a development program to help make advances.

- Develop the understanding and capabilities of a professional manager. Apply these capabilities to yourself, since you are the most important asset you have. Be able to answer objectively the following questions in a confident and positive manner:

  1. Are you professionally and formally planning, organizing, implementing, and controlling your life?

  2. Are you happy in your work? Are you excelling in performance (beating "par"—improving your average, standards, objectives, results) with constant, measured improvements?

  3. Are you measurably improving yourself in accordance with your present job and career plan requirements?

  4. Do you view your job and career plans as a business to be managed by a professional president? Such an approach to a job is a great contributor to increased job satisfaction, performance, and promotability.

  5. Are you willing to pay the price and to employ that needed self-discipline required to develop the self-confidence and

skills required to plan your work independently and to work your plan, thus achieving what you want out of life?

COMPARE...COOPERATE

Match the organization's plans for the future with your own. Make the best possible fit. Cooperate to develop a mutually supportive tailored program of training and development, along with a creative results-oriented reward/compensation system. By working in support of each others' plans, you and your employer establish a powerful and productive psychological contract.

The Choice Is Yours When the organization and the individuals that comprise the organization consistently evaluate before making a decision, they increase employees' work satisfaction, performance, and promotability. Best of all, over time, individuals grow to love their work. They come to understand that the quality of their work and of their performance on the job directly reflect the quality of themselves, which in turn determines the quality of their lives.

You know you have achieved success when you can spend time as you want to, not as you have to. You can quickly identify persons who have achieved success in their work when you hear them say, "Thank God it's Monday. Thank God for every irreplaceable day of a wonderfully productive and rewarding life!"

Are you such a person? If not, you *can* be if you so choose. And the choice is yours to make. You are the general manager of the most important asset in the world—you! Unfortunately, most people don't realize that they are, in fact, presidents of their own lives and that the quality of their lives hangs directly on how well they manage themselves. One of the most important insights gained from the Planagement® system is that *the same sound management techniques that apply to organizations apply just as productively to individuals.*

So all individuals have a crucially important decision to make in regard to how they manage their lives. They have basically three choices:

1. To manage life like an amateur,
2. To manage life in an inconsistent manner, or
3. To manage and to plan life professionally.

CHOICE NO. 1:
TO MANAGE LIFE LIKE AN AMATEUR

Tragically, most individuals, either consciously or unconsciously, do not choose to manage their lives at all. Instead, they allow others and circumstances to manage them. Over 90 percent of the population have to have their situations planned for them, and need to be supervised to accomplish their work. These individuals, normally the lowest paid, do not in general achieve very much.

CHOICE NO. 2:
TO MANAGE LIFE IN AN INCONSISTENT MANNER

All of us have met people who, at times, are tops, but who cannot be consistent in their performance. This inconsistent group comprise about eight percent of the population. These individuals do only part of their own planning and management, and they require some supervision to continue to progress. Individuals in this category use professional, disciplined management approaches, but only from time to time. At other times the discipline dissipates, and the amateur dominates. So their progress is compromised, and their mediocre results fall short of capitalizing on their recognized potential.

CHOICE NO. 3:
TO MANAGE AND TO PLAN LIFE PROFESSIONALLY

Only 2 percent of the general population plan their lives and work their plans. These rare individuals, usually the leaders in their chosen fields, achieve considerable success and satisfaction from what they choose to do.

Almost every person has the inherent capability to select and apply Choice No. 3. This ability has very little to do with background or education. But it has a great deal to do with ambition, with discipline, and with making the most out of life. It means doing what is required to identify and to manage professionally their own inherent potential.

Why bother? Why plan and manage your life? Everyone should do so because a sound professional management system is based on practical, *continually applied* common sense, available to everyone who has been blessed with a healthy mind.

3

CLIMATE:
PEOPLE ARE THE ORGANIZATION

This country's greatest unrealized potential lies with its people, who, as we know, utilize only a small fraction of their total capability. Yet we tend to ignore this expansive reservoir of potential. Few companies have developed systems for tapping this reservoir—many companies have actually created an internal environment and organizational structure that vigorously *wastes* the resource. Such policies seem perplexingly inconsistent. Few managers, if any, would accept the obsolescence of their machinery without attempting to extend its useful life through preventive maintenance, practical modifications, and modernization. Making maximum use of any resource makes excellent economic, as well as psychological, sense.

Why, then, waste the human asset? If managers could be persuaded to gain the needed understanding of the human resource—and such management involves many unfamiliar and unknown factors—and then to maximize its contribution, they would also enjoy maximum utilization of all their other assets—machines, dollars, materials, and space. Just as managers allocate time and dollars to the care and maintenance of these other assets, they should apply time and dollars to developing people.

Even when certain resources have been "used up," management takes great pains to recycle them: steel, paper, aluminum, glass, and even garbage! They do so, very rightly, not only to conserve our remaining natural resources, but also to meet supply and demand. Perhaps managers should begin to see the benefit in "recycling" the human resource too. Figure 3-1 draws an analogy between the benefits of recycling what we normally consider resources and those of "recycling" human resources.

The question remains unanswered: Why has so little been done in this most crucial area? The normal response is that most managers have been taught only the basic functions of business—marketing, finance, production, and so on—while precious few have learned much about human beings. Unfortunately, that answer might not be complete. Just as serious a problem—and perhaps a more basic one—relates to management's frequent failure to meet its single most important responsibility: to keep the company's growth and opportunities ahead of the capabilities and ambitions of its people. If management does not do so, the people either leave or stop growing; either way, the result is individual and organizational apathy with eventual atrophy.

Apathy is the rule rather than the exception. Very few companies have a clear direction with a supporting system for insuring continuous growth that is well understood and communicated. Consequently, most organizations are often managing only their momentum and not their potential. Becoming enraptured with the routine is very easy—so easy that, sometimes, even a change for the better is an unwelcome intruder in a sea of complacency.

Taking Steps Where are you now, as a person or as an organization? Ask yourself some key questions and objectively review your answers. Have other people in your organization tackle the same questions, just to see if you get a common view or a lot of different views. If the views are different, the question becomes, why? These questions might include:

1. If I (and/or the company) keep doing the same things for the next five years, what will happen?
2. What would be the most desirable situation five years from now? And how does this "ideal" situation differ from the one presently projected per the answer to the first question?

FIGURE 3–1. The benefits of recycling

Natural, Inanimate Resources	Human, Living Resources
1. Conservation of *limited* natural resources.	1. 90 to 98 percent of the human capacity is untapped, providing an opportunity for the virtually limitless "mining" of the human mind.
2. Extension of the life of materials through reuse.	2. A happy, challenged, growing individual not only lives significantly longer, but also is reborn many times through the opportunity to be creative and increases his productivity and personal satisfaction through moving sound concepts into reality.
3. Lower cost of utilizing reused materials, as opposed to locating, acquiring, and processing new raw materials.	3. Some of the major costs of business could be avoided through the recycling of present existing human resources. These costs include those associated with turnover, search, selection and hiring, training, adjustment, and other related costs. These probably total up to the largest, least measured and managed costs in organizations. In addition to the obvious benefits inherent in cost avoidance, you would also gain an earlier, more rapid, and larger productivity increase from tapping more of the untapped potential of existing people because of their experience and familiarity
4. Converting waste into usable product, thus favorably impacting on reduced depletion and environmental pollution.	4. An organization's growth and development of its people who comprise the organization. The organization's climate (internal environment) determines what kind of people are attracted to the organization and what kind of people stay in the organization. A "polluted" internal environment does not attract or keep living, dynamic, productive, creative, growing people. Without these people, an organization stagnates, declines, dies, and is eventually buried in its own mediocrity.

3. Do I (does the company) have a clear picture of what I could and should achieve during the next five years? If so, do the people who need to act in support have a common, clear understanding of the direction, together with the actions required of them to move the picture into reality on schedule?

4. What needs to be changed, learned, or mastered to make the desired future a reality?

5. What resources are required? When are they required to accomplish the plan? And what is the gain (total benefit less total cost) to be derived?

6. Do I have (does the company have) a defined supporting/planning/management/communications/coordination/development/control/update system to identify, expand, and work continually toward achieving as much of my (the organization's) potential as is possible?

7. What percentage of my (the company's) time, dollars, and other resources are being applied for improvements and for the "new"?

In trying to establish where you are now and where you want to be, you could, and probably should, ask many more questions. Very often, during the gap between now and then (and there should always be one), you can advance better by making better use of the human assets at your disposal. If you yourself have a clearcut mission, then you can give your best. And if you can provide an organizational climate that evokes the eager cooperation and support of others, then you can expect the best from them. By balancing these elements for the maximum benefit of all, you can keep the projected "then" always a little ahead of the ever-changing "now."

But where do you begin? Like so many areas in business, human resource development involves a number of steps, which we will pursue in this chapter:

1. Setting up the right jobs.
2. Placing the right people in the right jobs.
3. Linking compensation to performance.

Setting Up the Right Job

Structuring good jobs is one way of structuring a good company. The people doing those jobs want to know exactly what they are supposed to be doing, so that they can tell when they're doing well. The reason is that most people need their work to be meaningful. People want to be defined and recognized as individuals. People today are telling institutions and organizations to "stop defining me the way you need me to be—define me as I am." Such is the observation of one of the world's leading behavioral scientists, Dr. Frederick Herzberg, Professor of Management at the University of Utah. In his address at the University of Tulsa, he stated that the biggest problem of management today is realizing that work is not an instrumental act, that it has to be a meaningful activity, and that workers have to be defined by what their needs are, not by what management needs them to be.

So significant is Dr. Herzberg's work that his "Eight Ingredients of a Good Job" have been incorporated, along with several others, into a position description within the framework of the Planagement® System. Experience with this system has shown that these ingredients definitely help to create a good job that attracts and keeps good people. These ingredients, along with Suggested Actions, are shown in Table 3–1. Feel free to expand these ideas and the related Suggested Actions as the needs of your individual situations arise. However you do it, the structuring of a good and satisfying job within a good organization is becoming an increasingly important part of the manager's job. How well managers meet this key responsibility frequently determines their own success as well as their companies' future.

TABLE 3–1. Ingredients of a good job

---

1. Establish the *direct feedback of results.* Don't delay the feedback, because the longer the feedback takes, the less useful it becomes. Also, it should consist of objective measurement, not of personal evaluation. Finally, the feedback should be directed directly to the employees concerned, not to their bosses.

   A Suggested Action: Have employees develop written plans based on their jobs and then report by exception to their supervisors. In this way, the employees become the first auditors of their own performance. They also have the opportunity to make the needed corrections that might be required to manage change and accomplish the plan. In addition, by using an Exception Report to keep up with changes, the plan is kept up-to-date. Through this "living plan," the employees develop improved skills for managing change to advantage.

2. Every job should have *a client relationship.* Employees should recognize that they have customers to serve rather than just bosses, supervisors, or policies, rules, and procedures. The "customer" can be an area, another department, or any element inside or outside an organization. But the client orientation should go beyond reporting relationships to bosses and a requirement of pleasing just them.

   A Suggested Action: In the first section of their plans for their jobs, the incumbents should specifically define their customers. They might also list the key influences on the customer's decision to buy the products (reports, for example) and/or services (such as recommendations) that the incumbents offer through their jobs. In some companies, the staff departments are required to sell their services to the line organization

---

(cont.)

FIGURE 3–1. (continued)

in competition with outside consulting and service groups. Needless to say, this set-up has quite an impact on the attitude and performance of staff personnel.

3. Every job should entail a *learning fuction* and perhaps an outside training program. The job should be structured so that at least 15 percent of it requires continually learning something new.

A Suggested Action: Build this learning function into the job. Include the function among the accountabilities of the job and allow 15 percent of the time available to be spent on it. Convert this accountability into a specific objective in the plan. Support it with a written self-development and education program designed to accomplish the objectives(s).

4. Individuals should have *the right to schedule their own work* as much as possible. They usually know how to do the job and how to schedule it better than anyone else.

A Suggested Action: As part of their written plans, have the incumbents prepare an Operational Schedule that shows, in the order of their priorities, the objectives and supporting programs with key milestones. This schedule should be reviewed and approved as part of the plan. Once approved, it should be reported on by exception with the rest of the plan.

5. Every job should have its own *unique element of expertise,* so that the job holder feels that he or she has particular expertise and knows more about the unique element than anyone else. In regard to this special expertise, the incumbent could virtually serve as a consultant to others. Dr. Herzberg compares this to the pride of knowing "this is what I can do—I'm doing my own thing—I have a special talent that makes me unique and I can consult to others with this talent or skill."

A Suggested Action: As part of their plans and in the first section, incumbents should list the unique capabilities, areas of distinctive competence, key resources, and skills that are needed to do the best possible job to meet the job's requirements. In addition, the incumbents should list these same items as they relate to them personally. Any gaps that are thus identified should become the personal development gaps, which lead acquiring the needed expertise and skills.

6. Job holders should have *control over their own resources.* Let them have their own budgets, and let them manage those budgets for their operations. With expense accounts or approved budgets, they themselves control the expenditures of the resources approved for carrying out their jobs.

A Suggested Action: One of the last parts of the plan should be a section on the Budget and Resources that incumbents feel they require to accomplish the plans. Again, the resources requested should be reviewed, possibly modified, and approved as part of the plan. How

(cont.)

47

FIGURE 3–1. (continued)

those resources are managed and how the plan is implemented are then the responsibilities of the incumbent.

7. Incumbents should have *direct communication with client systems.* All employees should be able to communicate directly with each other and not be blocked by organizational lines. In most companies the organization chart, which represents lines of communication, frequently causes over-communication so that the important part of the communication is lost. Dr. Herzberg said many things in life are better left unsaid, so that frequently the more you communicate, the worse things become. All communication should be active and selective. It should pass on the important information and leave the rest behind. It should avoid swamping people with junk mail to the point that they miss the first class messages.

A Suggested Action: A Coordination/Communication Report makes this particular ingredient a practical and operational reality. In this type of report, incumbents write down their assumed support from others over which they do not have control or authority. They then go directly to these individuals and persuade them to agree to their assumptions and establish an objective in support as part of their plans for their jobs. Once agreement is reached, the objective is reported on by exception, like any other part of the plan. In this case, the reporting follows a horizontal or diagonal flow—across organizational lines—rather than just the vertical flow. Many additional advantages are achieved from using this powerful tool, which is based on the definition that, "Management is getting things done through other people regardless of the reporting relationships."

8. Assuming the presence of the preceding seven ingredients, you then may have the eighth ingredient, which involves *personal accountabilities.* It is important to hold persons responsible for their jobs and to measure their performance objectively against predetermined standards. Dr. Herzberg observed that frequently companies measure how well housebroken their individuals are, not how well they perform. He further states that you can't hold anyone responsible for an idiot job unless you have an idiot in the job. Otherwise, the person doing the job could perform only the idiot functions and would, therefore, appear to be an idiot.

A Suggested Action: First of all, write down a description of the job and its requirements so that everybody clearly understands what is expected. This job or position description should include general and specific accountabilities (responsibilities). These accountabilities, in turn, should have specific standards of acceptable performance that are clearly measurable. Without such standards, you have no objective way to appraise performance, and the job becomes about as satisfying as playing golf with no par. A suggested format for a sound position description would include:

Definition of the Job

(cont.)

FIGURE 3–1.   (continued)

Purpose of the Job, including Primary Results to be Achieved

Nature of the Job

Unique Capabilities, Resources, and Skills Required to do the Job

Products and Services of the Job

Customers Served and Key Influences that Cause a Decision to Buy

Organizations, Coordination, and Communication Responsibilities

Cost/Benefit Analysis and Summary

Accountabilities—General and Specific, including Performance Standards and time allocation

---

The Planagement® System: Placing the "Right" People in the "Right" Jobs

Establishing the "right" jobs is only one of a two-step operation. The second step is to fill those jobs with the "right" people—a task that seems to confound many a manager. Rare is the manager who is as well trained in the fundamentals of people as in the fundamentals of business.

Rare also is the firm with an effective system for matching its people with its positions. As a consequence of the hit-and-miss practices of most organizations in regard to hiring and promoting, employee turnover comprises the largest cost of doing business today, as well as being a leading reason for business failures. So dire is the problem that the government is becoming increasingly active in forcing equal opportunity programs on organizations.

Hence, the need for a system that places the right individual into the right slot. Among the criteria that such a system should meet is distinguishing those individuals with the ability to plan their work and to work their plans from those requiring a great deal of supervision and who do not know how to plan, manage, and control. In addition, this selection system should help to identify individuals who are ambitious and who want to progress to higher levels of responsibility. It should also provide insight as to whether these ambitious employees have enough self-discipline to pursue personal development programs and thereby to gain the needed knowledge, skills, and attitude for performing at a higher level on more important activities. The Planagement® Selection System increases the probability of correctly identifying not only the levels of job candidates, but also which candidates have potential for progressing into higher levels. This selection system involves five steps, as shown in Figure 3–2.

FIGURE 3–2. Planagement® selection system flow diagram

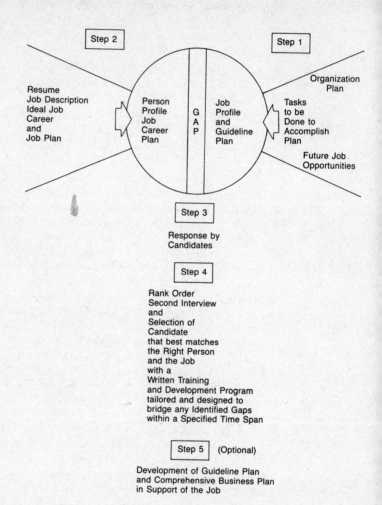

Step 2

Step 1

Resume
Job Description
Ideal Job
Career
and
Job Plan

Person
Profile
Job
Career
Plan

G
A
P

Job
Profile
and
Guideline
Plan

Organization
Plan

Tasks
to be
Done to
Accomplish
Plan

Future Job
Opportunities

Step 3

Response by
Candidates

Step 4

Rank Order
Second Interview
and
Selection of
Candidate
that best matches
the Right Person
and the Job
with a
Written Training
and Development Program
tailored and designed to
bridge any Identified Gaps
within a Specified Time Span

Step 5   (Optional)

Development of Guideline Plan
and Comprehensive Business Plan
in Support of the Job

STEP 1: DEVELOP POSITION DESCRIPTIONS

Develop *comprehensive position descriptions,* as described in the preceding section. These profiles should be done objectively, apart from consideration of any individuals.

STEP 2: GIVE OUT SELECTION KITS

Give qualified candidates *selection kits,* which include the following specific tools:

1. A *position description kit* makes use of the same format as the one used to develop the position description in step 1. By following this format, the candidates develop written position descriptions as to how they see either the actual jobs or their ideal jobs.

2. A *plan development workbook* guides the candidates in developing an abbreviated plan for the jobs and/or their careers.

3. Also included is a structured format for developing the persons' *backgrounds and work experiences.* Give careful consideration to EEO requirements when developing this resume outline. Focus particularly on the objective identification of the candidates' knowledge, skills and ambition, rather than on their age, sex, religion, race, or formal education, unless the job specifically requires an eduational achievement.

4. An *organizational orientation kit* gives candidates insight into the nature of the organization, along with its purposes and requirements. Should there be a mismatch between the person and the organization, it is best to identify this as soon as possible. As part of the selection process, the orientation section should invite the candidate to submit written questions with regard to the organization. A great deal can be learned about persons from the questions they ask and from their ability to establish open, accurate communications from the outset.

STEP 3: GET BACK SELECTION KITS

Candidates should complete all the required information in step 2 and submit it for review within one week (or less). Those who neglect to respond automatically eliminate themselves from further consideration.

STEP 4: RANK-ORDER THE CANDIDATES

Objectively rank-order the candidates. This ordering is based on the quality of the candidates' work. Specifically, it depends on the degree of correlation between their job description profiles—their questions, resume, and plans as developed in step 2—and the requirements of the job as described in step 1. Starting with the candidates at the top of the list, schedule second interviews until the final selection is made. Should any gaps exist between the job and person, clearly identify these gaps in writing to the candidate. Also, establish a written training and development program with dates of completion, so the gaps will be closed within a specified time span. A Planagement® program summary is frequently used to document this training program.

STEP 5 (OPTIONAL): NARROW RECOMMENDATIONS FURTHER

Make recommendations for key positions. Once you have narrowed the field to up to three candidates for each job, write up a guideline plan for each job. Do so independently of any candidate. Then request each of the final candidates to develop a comprehensive business plan in support of the job. Then correlate their plans with the guideline plan. Based on the correlation and quality of the plans, establish a rank order of preference and select the candidate based on this rank order. This plan also provides a basis for monitoring progress and for measuring performance on the job.

The Planagement® Selection System does not guarantee perfect accuracy in selecting the right person, and it is certainly no panacea, since it does require time and cost in providing the supporting tools. Experience has clearly shown, however, that this system increases the probability of selecting the right person and represents one of the best cost/benefit investments an organization can make.

A Practical Approach to Management Development

Once the "right" persons are situated in the "right" jobs, where do you go from there? Logically, the next aim is to develop those incumbent managers so that they contribute more and more to the organization's profits and growth the longer they are in their jobs.

The tougher question is, "How do you tap the potential that exists in your present managers?" The many answers and approaches to the management development question seem to fall into two general schools of thought. Members of the first school think that a program should be tailored to the specific needs of the company, as well as to the style of the company's managers. The other school of thought indicates that a logical and universal approach can be taken that will be productive in any company, at any time, and with all managers. Perhaps the most productive approach lies somewhere in between these two opposing views and borrows the best from both.

A GOOD FIT

Here is a simple and practical approach that works for most companies. This approach works just as well for developing your future managers as it does for increasing your present managers' performance. Follow its steps in Figure 3-3.

1. *The Practical Ideal Manager:* To develop managers, first identify the type of managers that will best support your company's plan. Without this logical first step, which is frequently overlooked, your management development program will lack specific direction, because it will lack a basis for measuring its own progress and contribution. So, to have an identified target to work toward, establish and document a specific profile of the "Practical Ideal Manager." Perhaps nobody will ever reach the practical ideal, but you will at least be able to measure progress toward this challenging goal.

2. *Documented Job Profile:* Once you have established the target, carefully and thoroughly document each existing and future manager's position description. Very often managers do not have a good understanding of their jobs. Frequently, in fact, the boss and the manager see the same job differently, a discrepancy that makes objective performance appraisal practically impossible. As a by-product benefit, these position descriptions also provide targets in the develoment of your existing managers for selecting the right per-

FIGURE 3–3. Steps of the management development program

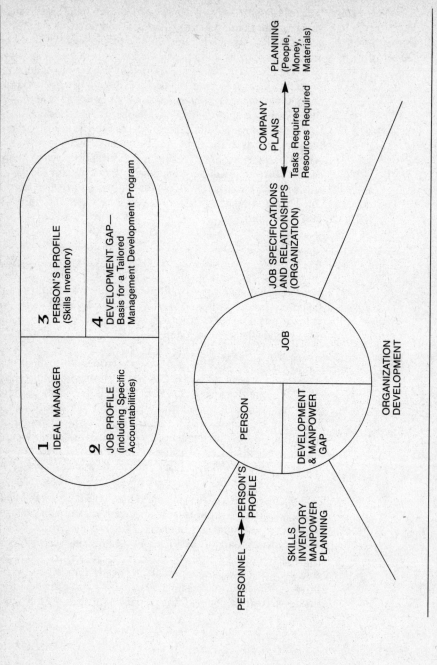

son for each job—whether you promote people within the company or recruit them from outside it. So make sure the managers understand their present jobs. Document an agreed-on position description (job profile).

3. *Skills Inventory:* Establish the profile of the managers: their strengths, weaknesses, skills, experience, and *ambition*. Then compare each manager's profile with the job profile. If there is a gap—and such is often the case—it becomes the basis for a formal, yet tailored, Management Development Program.

The growth and development of an organization depends directly on the growth and development of its people. Perhaps the greatest key to maximizing profits, growth, and satisfaction is to have the right person in the right place, at the right time, with the right skills, at the right cost, for the right job. The rapidly emerging field of organizational development is skillfully contributing to making this important concept a practical reality. Accordingly, establishing a sound management development program is one of the manager's biggest challenges and opportunities. Hence this type of effort can and should be managed as carefully and with as high a priority as any other tasks the manager performs.

Measuring and Rewarding Performance

The third area that is vital to a healthful climate is rewarding high performance. Of course, to reward performance, you have to be able to measure it, and there's the rub.

Of the many fuzzy areas of management practices, evaluating and encouraging performance is among the worst. Not only do most managers seem content to use subjective systems for increasing salaries or issuing bonuses, but some even feel such systems are part of their prerogative. In fact, several have flatly stated that they have the "power," as managers, to measure performance any way they choose and that their decision to reward or not to reward is based solely on their judgment and/or personal preferences. Consequently, their performance reviews are inconsistent, and they frequently surprise the parties concerned—sometimes favorably and sometimes not. But there should really be no surprise at all!

Without arguing the rights of a manager, most reasonable people have to agree that measuring and rewarding performance should be based on a clearly understood set of objective criteria. Performance reviews should not be surprise parties, because surprises are anything but constructive and serve only to violate the real purpose of performance reviews.

55

Professionals particularly *want* to be measured and *want* to improve their performance. But no one wants to be judged in the absence of clearly measurable standards of performance, which should be contained in position or job descriptions. So the all-important question is this: What precisely is your job? If you have a written statement of your responsibilities and functions, then your superior can determine objectively how well you are performing. And you can do the same for your subordinates, if they have clear-cut job descriptions. In fact, anybody can be evaluated fairly, as long as he or she has a job description that is understood and agreed on by the subordinate and the supervisor. Without such measurable standards of performance, you have no objective and mutually understood basis from which to evaluate work.

Such an understanding is not always the case. In frequent cases, we first ask subordinates to describe their jobs and on what basis they were being measured by their supervisors. Then we ask the same questions of the supervisors about the same jobs. Invariably, the answers differ enough that conducting performance reviews and establishing appropriate compensation have a built-in problem.

Another very common problem is that activity becomes more of a focal point for gauging performance than results. This orientation, which also causes frustration and waste, is frequently much more unproductive than identifying and concentrating on results.

So how do you go about developing an objective system for measuring and rewarding performance? To begin, review the following premises and try to accept them.

PREMISE 1: JOBS HAVE MEASURABLE STANDARDS

Any job or position can and should be measured through measurable standards of satisfactory performance.

PREMISE 2: MEASURE BY RESULTS ACHIEVED

Professionals want to be measured and compensated in accordance with the results they achieve, with no top limit.

PREMISE 3: CHALLENGE TO BEAT STANDARDS

For professionals, work becomes more fun and psychologically rewarding if they are challenged to equal or beat a measured standard through their improved performance. Enjoying games is just human nature, and all games have some standard that the players attempt to beat as they improve their skills.

PREMISE 4: COMPENSATE ACCORDING TO ACHIEVEMENTS

Professional managers possess and want to nurture an inherent entrepreneurial spark to manage their own business. In an entrepreneurial organization structure, each job is viewed as a profitability (measured-gain) center and run as a business, with compensation directly related to the gain achieved. Inherent in this approach is increased job/work satisfaction, which contributes to attracting, developing, and retaining top professional managers at all levels in the organization. Maximum performance is achieved with this approach.

PREMISE 5: EXPECT CHANGE

The future will be neither like the past nor like what we think it will be in the future. The rate of change increases constantly. Accordingly, professionals can grow and improve at a faster rate than anticipated, if given the opportunity and incentive to do so. Hence, any position/job description and its measurable standards of performance are subject to change, enlargement, and enrichment. In addition, peoples' performance, at least in part, should be based on how well they anticipate, favorably influence, and effectively manage change.

Many managers have great difficulty accepting this fifth premise. Why? Because doing so only makes their evaluating tasks harder. They can measure performance against criteria that are "standing still" better than they can against standards that are on the move. Their rationale is the same as that for hitting a stationary target. So they would prefer the performance standards set in concrete.

When those standards get rigid, however, a number of unfortunate things happen. For one, many individuals resent having their performance measured against what they regard as out-of-date or unrealistic criteria. Their reaction is typically to make their job-related targets as easy as possible, to insure their accomplishment and the related reward. Further, although rigid standards are justified by the reasoning that "compensation will be fair within the organization and competitive outside it," the frequent effects of this policy is to compensate mediocrity equally and to set upper limits of compensation on the job. In addition, when salary points are given for increasing the budget and the number of employees supervised, the economic incentive favors building empires, sandbagging budgets, and generating higher salaries in other counterproductive ways.

If you accept these five premises—especially the fifth one—you can then establish an effective system for measuring and rewarding performance. Here's how.

Linking Compensation to Performance

STEP 1: ESTABLISH A POLICY

Establish the policy that:

> All individuals with other-than-routine responsibility and/or other-than-routine ambition will have up-to-date job/position descriptions with measurable standards of performance, supported with a written plan summary, both of which are kept current through monthly exception reporting.

STEP 2: DESCRIBE EACH POSITION

Develop a comprehensive position description that converts accountabilities (responsibilities) into measurable, results-oriented standards of satisfactory performance, as shown in the following example:

Job Function
Manufacturing: Plant Manager
Accountability/Responsibility
To produce goods with high quality and at low cost
*Results-Oriented Measurable Standards of
Satisfactory Performance*
To maintain at least 95 percent quality level at a quality control cost that does not exceed 5 percent of manufacturing costs, less overhead.

STEP 3: SPECIFY STANDARD OBJECTIVES

Develop a supporting written plan to the job with sound measurable standard objectives, which relate to the accountabilities and standards of performance of the job.

To obtain at least a 7 percent quality level at a cost of 4 percent by 12/31/XX.

STEP 4: SPELL OUT THE GAIN

Assuming accomplishment of the objective, measure the gain (profitability) over the standard in dollar terms.

Profitability/Gain/Results
Based on a 2 percent improvement in quality, costs of returns will be reduced by $50,000 for each 1 percent improvement, for a total savings of $100,000, plus a budget reduction of an additional $25,000 through reducing quality control costs from 5 percent to 4 percent of manufacturing costs, less overhead. Total savings/benefit through accomplishing this objective will be $125,000.

STEP 5: ESTABLISH A COMPENSATION PLAN

Establish a compensation program related directly to the results achieved in step 4. This compensation agreement becomes either part of the job description or part of the supporting plan.

Agreement
That 10 percent of the gain will be granted as a bonus and that an additional 10 percent will be granted as a salary increase next year, if the gains are reflected as the new standards of satisfactory performance in the job description.

Bonus
Based on the above agreement, the bonuses for accomplishing the objective would be $12,500 (10 percent of $125,000 savings).

Exception/Update of the Job Description
Assuming the plant manager agrees to establish new standards based on the improvements obtained from accomplishing the objective, the standards of satisfactory performance would be increased from a 95 percent quality level to 97 percent, and the cost of quality control would be reduced to 4 percent from 5 percent of manufactured costs less overhead. Based on the ad-

option of these improved standards of improved performance, the salary for the next year for this job would be increased by $12,500 (10 percent of $125,000 continued savings over the original standards).

Carrying this entrepreneurial system to its natural conclusion, a failure to achieve the standard would become the basis for downward adjustment in compensation, unless the exceptions to meeting the standards were legitimate and had been approved as such by the supervisor. This approach to compensation appeals to professional, high-performance managers who want to be paid according to the results they achieve. The advantages to the company include a higher level of performance from its managers, while the salary costs become more of a variable and actually lower in relation to results. They no longer represent fixed costs that must be paid out regardless of performance and results.

Acceptance of these five premises and the implementation of these five steps lead to a fair and objective system for measuring and rewarding performance. In addition, organizations that have this type of system attract and retain the professional, high-performance types who are key to a high-performance company. Such a system also takes the "fuzziness" out of the measuring and rewarding task.

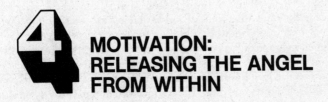

4 MOTIVATION: RELEASING THE ANGEL FROM WITHIN

Michelangelo Buonarroti, one of the world's most gifted artists, created many a masterpiece during his eighty-nine years on this earth. Among his most famous was a statue know as The Angel.

When The Angel was completed, an admirer asked Michelangelo how he was able to visualize The Angel from the original block of stone? The artist replied that he had not chipped away rock to create The Angel. He had merely released it from the rock.

One of the gravest responsibilities of managing is the development of people. That is, as a manager, you must see The Angel in each human being and somehow release it. In more practical terms, you have an obligation to show others how to achieve their own balance and how to develop their own unrealized potential.

You're motivated. But is everyone else? As much as productivity improves with the installation of the latest automated equipment or newest procedures, a motivated employee still remains the most powerful contributor to productivity. Employees must *want* to improve their performance and increase their output. As discussed already, a positive working climate and the integration of the individual's needs with those of the organization are about the only ways of stimulating others to become self-motivated. In fact, studies show that at least 90 percent of the ideas for profit improvement and growth flow *upwards* in the organization with a positive climate, open communications, a team approach, and a company-first attitude. Harnessing such enthusiasm for meaningful work, the untapped potential, the creative abilities, and the entrepreneurial spirit in most human beings is one of the most important requirements for productivity improvement.

But can you motivate someone else? Increasing evidence shows that, contrary to popular belief, motivation cannot be externally imposed—it is actually an internal process. The dictionary defines it as "the act or process of motivating, the condition of being motivated." Motive, a related word, is defined as "something (as a need or desire) that causes a person to act." Just these definitions seem to imply that motivation is indeed an internal process. It evolves from the individual's needs and gives rise to a motive powerful enough to cause the person to act. In reality, therefore, motivation is motive + action, which is generated by an internal process of human needs. External factors can influence motivation, but the intensity and direction of a person's motivation is exclusively internal.

If all this is so, then managers who believe that their primary function is to motivate subordinates have to be rendered less than fully effective by their misconception. Managers, on the other hand, who understand the real nature of motivation have to be more effective.

To gain this critically important understanding of motivation, managers should recognize a simple fact: To influence the depth of a person's motivation, they must first develop the skill of diagnosing the individual's needs, as well as the organization's needs. They must then establish a climate and management system that supports both types of needs.

So that is our next step too. Based on numerous Planagement® applications in all sorts of organizations, the following step-by-step formula has proved helpful in establishing a climate that prompts employees to improve their performance.

A Six-Step Formula of Motivation for Increased

STEP 1: BE A PARTICIPATIVE MANAGER

Develop a positive humanistic management style based on a belief in and understanding of human beings. Without this style, you cannot positively influence motivation, because you will be an autocratic rather than a participative, supportive manager by mandate. Douglass McGregor's Theory X (the autocratic style) and Theory Y (the participative and supportive style) describe the two opposite styles, based on the manager's view of human nature and motivation. If managers are convinced that they must motivate (that is, force) a person to work, then they tend toward an autocratic management style. Managers who believe that people are basically self-motivated—that is, they want to work and want to improve themselves and their performance—have a more supportive and participative style.

STEP 2: ESTABLISH CLEAR-CUT ORGANIZATIONAL DIRECTION

With a positive humanistic management style, you must establish a clear-cut organization, with a positive direction and discipline. Organizations and individuals that lack direction and discipline tend to decline into morbidity and despair. In such cases, management must turn to negative motivation.

STEP 3: BALANCE FREEDOM WITH DISCIPLINE

Initiate a positive organizational climate that balances freedom with discipline. Individuals require the freedom to develop their motives and to take action in support of the organization, but this freedom must be balanced with the discipline of the organization's direction, needs, and actions. A climate that constructively blends individual and organizational needs in synergistic, mutual support is one of the manager's most important responsibilities, because it provides one of the greatest opportunities for increasing performance.

STEP 4: PLAN FOR HUMAN RESOURCE DEVELOPMENT

Next create a system for sound human resource development. Here is the sequence of programs that gets you there:

1. Structure job descriptions (profiles) so that they meet the criteria of a good job.
2. Define the profile of the person who would be best qualified to do the job.

63

3. Identify gaps between the job and either the person presently in the job or a candidate for the job. The best way is to involve the person in diagnosing the existing gaps.

4. Develop a training and development program designed to advance each individual where necessary.

STEP 5: UNDERSTAND HUMAN NEEDS

Next you must understand and apply both the behavioral sciences and scientific management. Very few managers have been taught to understand human beings. Most business education focuses on the technical functions of business and management, which include finance, marketing, sales, production, problem solving, and the like. As a result most managers have a great technical knowledge of business, but only a limited knowledge of the human asset, which controls all the other assets of money, materials, time, and space.

One of the most important insights in the behavioral sciences is expressed by Dr. Abraham Maslow in his concept of the hierarchy of human needs. This hierarchy, which provides a key to motivation, is illustrated in Figure 4–1. Based on his research, Maslow concludes that, as each need is satisfied, a person is no longer motivated by that need, since it is satisfied. The person then "rises" to the next higher need, which then becomes the motivating need. This process repeats itself until the person reaches the top of the pyramid where "self-actualization" occurs. In other words, the person is living and achieving the ultimate dream. At this highest level, a person

FIGURE 4–1. Maslow's hierarchy of needs

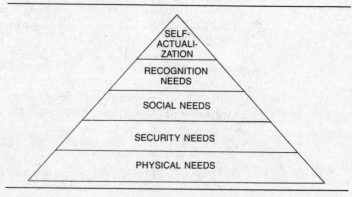

operates with the maximum degree of motivation. Life becomes a self-fullfilling prophecy, in which a person lives and performs up to his or her own individual potential.

STEP 6: GET FEEDBACK TO MEASURE MOTIVATION

At this point, you need a feedback system to measure the level of employee motivation. The many techniques for doing so include a formal climate analysis or attitude survey. An additional tool is the profile of motivation (Figure 4–2). With this tool, you can measure the motivation of yourself or of others. Simply place checkmarks in the left- or right-most columns, according to which entry better describes you or your subject. Then follow the directions for totaling and compare the results with the scale at the bottom.

This formula is the key to making your concept of motivation become an actual system for evoking motivation in people. If, through the feedback channel, you gain an insight into a person's personal priorities and individual level of need, you can relate assignments in such a way as to "turn that person on" to accomplishing the needed tasks. For example, suppose an individual wants to be mentally challenged and has a need for recognition. In such a case, you might structure a program that represents a chance for learning, accomplishment, and advancement. Since the program would then contribute to the person's development, it becomes a self-motivating force that contributes to getting the job done. On the other hand, let's say that the same program is offered to a person who favors a physical task and who has a strong need for security. This individual might be turned off by the challenging and possibly risky opportunity. In all probability, the subordinate would resist taking that particular job. Needless to say, if the right job is offered to the wrong person, or vice versa, the results are usually poor and the morale low.

This insight is just as important to those who are not necessarily managers. A salesperson, who is charged with the responsibility of making sales, needs such insight. And any individual who wants to get along well with others, and who may from time to time need to get things accomplished through the efforts of others, can make use of it.

This Power from Within   In our increasingly larger and more complex society, each individual seems to depend more and more on the efforts of others to get things done. We are becoming ever more interdependent. In light of

FIGURE 4-2. Profile of motivation

Check (✔) Which Applies	Characteristics of an Unmotivated Person	Characteristics of a Motivated Person	Check (✔) Which Applies
	Lacks a plan and direction	Has a plan and direction	
	Procrastinates—no goals	Has goals and gets work done on time	
	Must be supervised	Limited, if any, supervision required	
	Lacks drive—has no dream	Very ambitious—has a dream	
	Does the minimum	Does the most possible	
	Inconsistent	Consistent and dependable	
	Negative or "blah" attitude	Positive attitude	
	Complacent	Enthusiastic	
	Routine and facts-oriented; no risk taker	Action-oriented, synergy beyond facts, seeks the new and better, has entrepreneurial spirit	
	Poor time manager	Values time and manages it well	
	Total number of (✔)	Total number of (✔)	
−	Multiply Number of (✔) by Minus (−) 10	Multiply Number of (✔) by Plus (+) 10	+
	Subtract the Minus total from the Plus total. Place the difference on the scale below to measure the levels of motivation.		+
			−
			(+) (−)

Level of Motivation Scale

Rating	−100	−75	−50	−25	0	+25	+50	+75	+100
X Score									
Level of Motivation	None	Very Low	Low	Limited	Some	Fair	Good	High	

this trend, individuals who understand human beings, and who thus become better managers, are likely to end up as the leaders of their chosen fields. And the reason is primarily their understanding of and ability to manage the human resource. They understand the power from within human beings.

To effectively lead and to inspire others, as a manager, you must gain an overall understanding of individual human beings, as well as of their personal priorities and particular levels of needs. You cannot assume that all people are alike and that they all respond in the same manner to the same things. That's just not so. On the contrary, you must thoroughly understand each individual for whom you have direct supervisory responsibility. If so many people report to you that you cannot take the time to understand each of them, then you should probably take measures to remedy that circumstance. You might reduce your span of control. Or you might acquire the supporting tools that provide the needed insight into the individuals for which you have responsibility.

Give up the notion that you can motivate someone else. You can inspire, stimulate, and encourage others. You can provide a compatible and supportive organizational climate that contributes to an individual's self-motivation. But the motivation must come from within, not from you.

This is not to say that you cannot "access" that motivation. If you have a grasp on an individual's priorities and needs, you have an excellent opportunity to "push the right button." You're not doing the motivating. You're simply eliciting the individual's motivation to support you actively, as the leader. Motivation may be an internal process, determined only by the free decision of the individual. But that free decision is influenced in a positive or negative fashion by the external circumstances that contribute the necessary data for the decision making.

To answer the question posed at the start of the chapter, the primary function of a professional manager is to ensure that the external circumstances, the style, the climate, and the opportunities of the work environment all relate positively to the needs and desires of the employees. Implementing that formula maximizes employee job satisfaction and consequently increases performance.

Some managers carry this responsibility farther than others. In fact, most successful professional managers, who have established the best long-term performing organizations, have gone beyond their own self-actualization. These managers have developed a keen diagnostic skill for placing others in Maslow's hierarchy. They have then developed tailored supporting programs, so that these persons—if they have the required drive, ambition, direction, and discipline—have the opportunity to rise to their own level of self-actualization in jobs that provide the best possible fit. Many of these managers have adopted the philosophy that the best way to find yourself and to maximize your own performance as a manager is to lose yourself in the service of others, so that they may maximize their performance. These enlightened cause-and-effect managers clearly recognize that the growth and development of the organization depend directly on the growth and development of the people who comprise the organization. This view of the organization and of the professional manager's job is depicted in Figure 4–3.

FIGURE 4–3.   Hierarchy of needs of both organizations and individuals

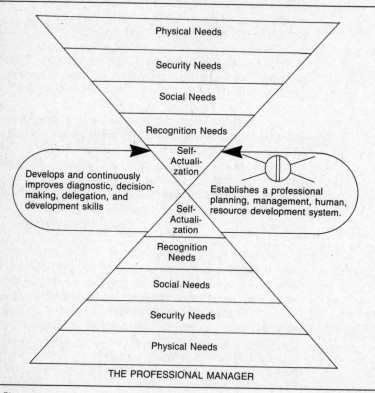

THE PROFESSIONAL MANAGER

Motivation Through Education

Sometimes assuming the teaching role is the only way to positively influence the management climate, careers, and performance of those around you. Yet all too many managers protest that they are managers, not teachers. They don't want to teach. Many become quite upset when confronted with the challenge of teaching someone else about their business or their job. They much prefer to delegate this responsibility to the personnel or training department—or let the other person "catch on" through observing and on-the-job training. Although experience is a valuable component of the total learning process, the "experience-is-the-best-teacher" approach is usually much more time-consuming, more costly, and poor in results than a more orderly approach. A thorough, organized program produces much better results in 40 to 70 percent less time.

So why do managers resist accepting the responsibility for teaching someone else? One of the most basic reasons is that managers often have not been taught how to teach, and so they avoid the task because they don't know how. In addition, many people who have had poor teachers have lost respect for teachers specifically and for education in general. So they do not want to be identified with someone or with a system that they themselves do not like very well. Another possible reason is the mistaken idea that you have to be an expert in a subject before you can teach it. Since many managers do not feel qualified as experts, they do not feel qualified to be teachers.

This last excuse is a particularly popular one. Who qualifies as an expert? What makes a person "educated"? The answers to these questions touch on an emotionally charged area of controversy. Some people are of the opinion that, to be educated, you must have received a degree that says you are now educated. Others feel that the academic approach provides, not an education, but rather only a smattering of fragmented facts and opinions that are rarely organized enough to be useful and productive on the job or in life. These individuals usually emphasize that a practical education can be obtained only from "The School of Hard Knocks." This age-old argument can probably never be resolved. The truth is probably that both the academic type of education and that gained from the "School of Hard Knocks" have individual value and, when combined, are frequently stronger than either approach alone.

Let's face it, we have all met clods from both "schools." We've shaken hands with arrogant ignoramuses whose only claim to fame is a degree—even if an advanced degree. By the same token, we have also met the pompous know-it-all graduates of the School of Hard Knocks, who constantly refer to their many years of experience, which obviously hasn't taught them a thing.

Then we have met those rare individuals whom we immediately recognize as being several "cuts above" the ordinary person. We recognize that they somehow have lived their lives in such a manner that they have acquired a superior education that can be clearly recognized and respected. Perhaps if we take a good look at some of the characteristics of an educated person, we may learn more about the process and results of a real education (Figure 4–4).

FIGURE 4–4. Characteristics of an educated person

---

1. The person has a sense of confidence, not in knowing all the answers, but rather in the acknowledged capability and self-discipline required to get the needed knowledge to make a sound decision and to take the proper actions.

2. The educated person is well aware of J. Carl Humphrey's definition of greatness as follows: "The potential for greatness lies within each of us—it is simply our best." The educated person constantly does his or her best, having developed an ability to see continually the best in others and to give the best as well.

3. An open, inquiring, growing mind is a readily identifiable characteristic of an educated person. In no way will this individual hold a prejudice, but will view situations and people with an open and objective mind that seeks only the truth, the best, and the fair.

4. Another characteristic is an ability to listen to all information and then apply the analytical discipline needed to develop an independent, objective conclusion.

5. An educated person never laughs at new ideas or says that something is impossible or that it cannot be done. The outlook is positive, with a faith that improvements can and should and will be made.

6. You are not able to sell an educated person on magic—that forward progress depends primarily on luck or happenstance. Rather, the educated person recognizes that progress depends on a consistency of purpose and direction, supported by the discipline and courage of taking the actions required to make the right things happen.

7. Perhaps one of the most important aspects of an educated person's makeup is the ability to do an objective self-analysis and correctly identify the most important strengths and then build on these strong points.

8. The educated person knows the value of good habits and understands how to form them on a continual, self-improving basis.

(cont.)

FIGURE 4–4. (continued)

9. Another vitally important skill of the educated person is the acquired ability to understand important differences. An example of this ability is reflected in the prayer, "Oh, Lord, help me to recognize those things that I can change and those things that I cannot change, and give me the wisdom to know the difference." An educated person also knows when not to think and when it is wise to call in the expert to do the thinking.

10. The educated person has a tendency to be imaginative, but also cross-examines his or her daydreams, selecting the good ones and making them a practical, productive reality.

11. A truly educated person understands the learning process and continually applies it in daily life. He or she understands that education is a never-ending, continuing journey, not a destination.

12. An ability to see and love the beautiful is another trait of an educated person. No matter how bleak a situation might be, the educated person is able to identify the best and the beautiful that does exist.

A number of additional characteristics could be added, but the twelve in that figure should provide us with a checklist to measure ourselves, as well as others, in relation to a truly educated person.

Regardless of their reasons and excuses, the fact remains that those who want to be professional managers accept the responsibility for teaching. This role has too high a priority and is too inherent in the manager's job to be ignored.

In fact, one important reason to take on the teaching role is inherent in managing. If management must get things done through other people, then managers must teach others what must be done and how to do it. Otherwise, they must continue to "do" rather than delegate. And any person who finds doing more comfortable than delegating is a doer, not a manager.

An even more influential reason for teaching is the tragic fact that our educational system frequently fails to educate. Many students graduate with few skills, with only fragmented facts and knowledge, and with overexpectations as to their value and ability to perform. These inadequacies, which then become the manager's problems, cost time, money, and effort to correct.

On one occasion, when speaking to over one hundred high school teachers and principals, I personally experienced the weakness in our educators and in our educational system. They were asked, "What is the most important thing that you are trying to teach your students?" After much discussion, the answer came back that they were teaching their students how to think. But when asked what thinking process they were teaching, not one was able to verbalize or to put on the blackboard any specific thinking process—their most important subject.

This trend seems to persist at college and graduate levels as well. One of the presentations I make at graduate schools of business has as its title, "What is an MBA?" The most frequent answer to this question that I get from these soon-to-be graduated masters of business administration is that it is a piece of paper worth several thousands of dollars more in annual salary.

Perhaps the greatest reason for becoming a teacher is the strengthening of that crucial quality of self-discipline, which separates the professional manager from all others. Thomas Henry Huxley noted this benefit when he wrote:

> Perhaps the most valuable result of all education is the ability to make yourself do the thing you have to do, when it ought to be done, whether you like it or not. This is the first lesson to be learned.

Taking Steps to Teach For these and other reasons, every manager must assume the responsibility and role of a teacher. As managers recognize this requirement more and more, they represent a growing demand for practical programs that can be taught easily by nonteachers without sacrificing the quality of the results.

Years of research and experience have led to an established approach that has helped managers overcome their reluctance to become teachers. The approach consists of five steps for sound teaching.

STEP 1: DECIDE WHAT CAN BE TAUGHT BY PRACTICE

Establish a concrete system for teaching whatever can be taught to others through practice. Unfortunately, lecture-oriented teaching is not very effective because human beings remember less than 10 percent of what they hear. To *write* something is to remember it, and to *live* it is to understand it. So, in a sound educational process, the thinking process is taught and applied in a conscious, tangible manner to the subject at hand or to an actual existing situation.

STEP 2: TEACH AT THE STUDENT'S LEVEL

Diagnose your "student's" level of knowledge, ability, and desire to learn. Then utilize the method of learning that best fits the student. Too often teachers communicate from their own internal knowledge bases, using methods of instruction that are most comfortable for them rather than for their students. This internal, teacher-oriented—rather than external, student-oriented—approach frequently results in a communication and educational gap that negatively impacts on the student, the teacher, and the entire learning experience. The ability to diagnose, listen, tailor, and communicate with empathy are all important skills for teachers to have and to use constantly.

STEP 3: ENCOURAGE FEEDBACK OF RESULTS

Clearly identify, communicate, and establish the value of the knowledge and the results you want to achieve. Use a feedback system that measures the learning experience and the gains achieved. Every student should ask—and often does ask—"What's in it for me? What's the value of this program? How will I obtain benefits and measure them?"

STEP 4: USE VARIED TEACHING TECHNIQUES

Use a questioning and multisensory approach in teaching a subject. If education can be defined as a never-ending series of questions that ultimately lead to other questions, then the active, inquiring mind is continually cycling through a kind of feedback loop. Such a mind first gathers and processes knowledge. Then it utilizes, reinforces, and adds to this knowledge, through measurement of the gains achieved. Therefore, as a teacher, you should use as many of the human senses as possible. The more senses you apply to a learning experience, the more the student remembers and understands.

Hence, professional educators use a combination of lecture, visuals, writing, discussion groups, and other techniques, all to oblige the students to use as many of their senses as possible.

STEP 5: IF YOU JUST CAN'T TEACH . . .

If you still do not feel able or comfortable with the first four steps, for whatever your reasons, then you have basically three choices:

1. Get some professional assistance and establish an internal teaching capability within your organization.
2. Utilize the services of a professional teacher to conduct the needed program until someone within the organization develops the necessary skills.
3. Don't develop a teaching capability internally. Just continue to use the watch-me-do-it, on-the-job, unstructured, inconsistent learning approach—and accept the relatively poor results.

Selecting this third alternative may be unfortunate because you sacrifice the opportunity to develop the crucially important management skill of teaching others. This teaching skill, so basic to being able to delegate through the training and development of others, is fundamental to being a manager. In addition, by electing not to teach, managers only reduce their own ability and opportunity to learn more, because one of the best ways to learn and understand a subject is to teach it to someone else.

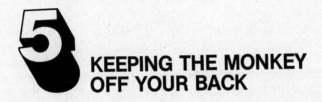

5
KEEPING THE MONKEY
OFF YOUR BACK

Exercising our will is not an intellectual act. It is a process for calling *to* our intellect a discipline that brings many things together and, along with the intellect, a direction is established.

Rev. John Wolf

Time is the Great Equalizer of all persons. Every individual has exactly sixty seconds in every minute, only sixty minutes in every hour, and no more than twenty-four hours in every day. Time is the only resource we can neither save, recapture, or manufacture. Once time has gone—be it a minute, an hour, or a day—it is gone forever. How well or how poorly it was spent becomes irrevocable history.

How well individuals manage their time also determines their progress and success. The same holds true, of course, for organizations, insofar as they consist only of individuals working together. Given the precious nature of time and the urgent need to use it productively, a great many books, tools, techniques, study courses, seminars, lectures, workshops, and various other opportunities have become available to help people use their time better. Yet few people take advantage of such opportunities. Wasting time seems to be a characteristic of our earlier years, as much as regretting doing so seems to be an earmark of our latter years. How many times have you heard others—or perhaps even yourself—say something like, "If I had only known that—or done that—years ago!" Whatever "that" was, the chances are that it was knowable or "do-able" at the time, but we lacked either the proper appreciation of it or enough willingness to find it out or to do it.

Now, we feel, it is "too late." Perhaps not. The key to making the best use of your valuable time is doing things systematically. Research shows that a systematic approach is always less time-consuming than a disorderly method. A sound planning capability gives you the direction to know which activities deserve your time—that is, which are most productive. Hence, how well you manage your time largely determines how productively you work.

Getting Started

So, in reality, it is never too late or too early to begin to use time wisely. Regardless of their chronological ages, all human beings have the inherent capability, spirit, and potential to do more, in less time, with better results. They need only want to. They need to be willing to apply self-discipline to leverage time management into a more abundant and satisfying life, rather than letting life pass into a gray mediocre history with flashes of "what might have been."

You also need a systematic approach that you can start to apply right away. Our systematic approach entails two prerequisites:

1. a determination to acquire the necessary self-discipline, and
2. a clear direction in your life.

SELF-DISCIPLINE

First, make up your mind that you will develop the *self-discipline* required to manage your time rather than allow it to manage you. No small or easy commitment, this determination is a must if you are going to use your time in the best possible way—it forces you to live your life in a disciplined manner. It forbids you to cop out with such excuses as, "I didn't have time to do it." This sort of rationale translates to, "I didn't take the time to do it, either because I had something more important to do or because I did not manage my time well."

If you make this commitment to managing your time and your life, you can never again lead the common life, where there is always time to do it over, but never time to do it right in the first place. You will develop the skills required to be not only more effective (doing the *right* thing), but also more efficient (doing *things* right).

DIRECTION

With this commitment, you need next a clear *direction* to utilize your time in the best and most supportive manner. Recall our earlier example of the jigsaw puzzle: Either you can work it by matching the pieces with the finished picture on the box top, or you can flip all the pieces over so that you cannot see how each fits into the final product. The second method is obviously the more time-consuming. In a very real sense, life is like a jigsaw puzzle. Ironically, most people—perhaps even you—try to put together their irreplaceable pieces of time without keeping in mind a clear picture of what they *are* working toward or, equally important, what they *should* be working toward. So you need to "look at the big picture." You need to establish your direction.

But which direction? That depends on your own unique self-interest, philosophy, mission, capabilities, skills, experiences, and potentials. As you might suspect, establishing a specific direction is difficult. Even with a sense of direction, many people have only a fuzzy and often incomplete picture of their future. Unless you can jot down on a piece of paper a clear picture of the future that you wish to achieve, so that you and others can understand it, then you are living your life without the precise direction required to use your time in the best manner. Hence, you need to master the diagnostic skill needed for an accurate and objective self- and situation-analysis.

In opposition to this approach, some individuals claim that they do not wish to establish direction because it is too demanding and too restrictive. These individuals say that it's a lot more fun to live one day at a time—with "serendipity" (the art of finding wonderful things not sought for). While they may certainly live their lives in this manner, rarely do such lives accomplish much more than a monotonous momentum of self-pleasures, which become increasingly boring as time goes by.

This is not to say, however, that your life has to be all work and toil. Actually, it can be very much like a game. But any game that provides satisfaction for its players usually has criteria for poor, good, and excellent "play." Because you can measure your own progress and success against a par, you enjoy the game, finding satisfaction in meeting a challenge. In the "game" of life, having a meaningful target or goal gives you a par by which to measure your satisfaction. It provides the zest and fun in life.

On the other side of the coin, the majority of individuals unfortunately seem content to live out their entire lives with a nagging feeling that they are living well below their real potential and that they are not able to go from where they are and to where they would like to be. They are haunted by the elusive hope of success, defined as reaching that point in life when you can spend your time as you *want* to, not as you *have* to. Very few people achieve this level of success, because they have never really figured out either what they want or what they need to do to get what they want. Many of these people who are unhappy to the point of suicide frequently emphasize that life has lost its meaning (direction)—that they are "bored to death." Others commonly try to offset this problem by keeping so busy that time will pass. Yet even these constantly busy people, without a clear-cut direction, are capable of despair. Psychologists have proven that an individual without a goal in life will dissipate into a state of morbidity and despair.

If you do not have the clear picture of the future that you would like to have, take the time to work one out. If necessary, work with a skilled trained professional who can help you establish a sound direction. This investment is probably the most important you will ever make because you will spend the rest of your life with whatever future you design (or don't design). The quality and satisfaction in that future depend entirely on you, on your self-discipline, and on your own unique direction.

As you make your crucially important decision and commitment to manage your time wisely, in support of the future you want to achieve, keep in mind the quotations on the first page of this chapter. They provide a valuable framework and reference. The fact is that most successful people relate the beginning of their achievement to when they made up their minds about what they wanted to do with their lives. Having made this decision, they consistently concentrated on the direction they established in support of their chosen goals, and they *made* the time they needed to achieve them.

Of the many important functions in an enterprise, one of the most important is sales. As a matter of fact, without sales, the enterprise goes no place! Regardless of the nature of the enterprise, if its products and services aren't sold, it ceases to exist. So important is this skill that many people regard selling as a profession—and as one of the most important of all the professions. Like any profession, sales consists of a group of individuals, organized around a body of knowledge, an agreed-on code of ethics, certain performance standards and methodical process. And, like any profession, sales has its amateurs and true professionals. Due to the special nature and importance of the selling function, no professional stands out more, and none is more appreciated, than a professional salesperson. Truly professional salespersons are the most sought-after individuals in the world. Due to the impact of sales "pros" on the success of an enterprise, no professional earns more than a top seller.

Beyond the sale of products and services, however, selling is a key skill for every manager and for every individual. Managers have to sell their ideas, and individuals have to sell themselves—to themselves and to others—if they are to succeed. Managers who are unable to sell their ideas are soon replaced by those who can professionally sell themselves and their ideas. Most people are fired not on account of a lack of expertise, but rather on account of their inability to sell and to get along with other people.

Given the importance of selling, everyone in an organization must be able to sell more—whether more products, more services, or more ideas—in less time. That responsibility is incumbent on every manager in the firm, not just on those in charge of sales. Further, those in a position to hire or to work with sales personnel must themselves be able to identify the characteristics of a real pro. The following step-by-step procedure enables you to maximize the use of your time whenever you are engaged in selling.

STEP 1: KNOW AND COMPARE YOUR PRODUCT

First, *know your product and service*—study them. Not only must you fully understand them, but you must also be able to communicate clearly their features in the form of customer benefits. Second, *compare the value of your products and services* against the competition's. Do a matrix of comparative features, benefits, economics, guarantees or warranties, and ease of use. This comparison permits you to insure that what you represent provides customers with the best overall value. If the products and services do not meet these criteria, professional salespersons will not represent them, since they are a disservice to the customer and a violation of their internal personal integrity and professional ethics.

STEP 2: DIAGNOSE CUSTOMER NEEDS

Diagnose your customer's needs. First, *identify your customer's present and future needs.* Insure that what you have to sell meets those needs equally or better than the competition's. At the same time, you must maintain the profitability required by your company to continue providing the best value. If your products and services do not measure up, communicate any shortcomings to your company's research and development department.

Second, as a kind of "field reporter," a professional salesperson serves as an excellent market research vehicle. So always maintain a *marketing orientation* that starts with the customer's needs, which provide the guidelines for organizing resources to meet those very needs in a superior manner. Amateurish salespersons have a sales orientation that focuses on their own needs and on the product or service. Their emphasis is on convincing persons to buy regardless of their needs. Such a hit-and-run approach may be economically rewarding in the short run. Over a long period, however, it is just not economically viable, because it communicates only dissatisfaction, fails to yield referrals, and eventually ruins the reputation of the firm.

STEP 3: CONCENTRATE ON KEY ACCOUNTS

Analyze the assigned territory and work it smartly, not hard. First, utilize *a key account approach,* which rewards you with the greatest dollar return for the time spent. Identify the customers you are now serving, noting the 20 percent who account for 80 percent of your total sales volume. Should you have a small percentage of these customer's total business, then spending 80 percent of your time with these key accounts should prove to be of great benefit. Sales amateurs spend an equal amount of time with all their customers without analyzing which are the cost-effective winners and which are the economic losers.

Second, develop *a "most wanted list"* based on your prioritizing customers according to their potential for business. Again, concentrate on the 20 percent of key accounts, in the order of their importance, that provide 80 percent of the total sales potential.

Third, utilize an account management approach with your key accounts. *A written profile* and an *account management plan* (AMP) for each key account. These tools provide the needed insight and guidance for maximizing your sales performance and economic results. Become part of your key accounts' planning for the future, so that you and your company may anticipate your customers' needs and act in support of their objectives. The result of this effort usually establishes you and your organization in a preferred supplier position.

STEP 4: DEVELOP A SALES PLAN

Develop a written sales plan to maximize your market penetration and share of your key accounts' total business. The sales plan should integrate all your targets for improved performance: both the long-range targets that may take several months or years, and the short-range projects that involve call patterns and schedules, supported with a time management system that maximizes daily productivity. All salespersons may be created equal, since each has the same sixty minutes in every hour and sixty seconds in each minute. Yet the distinguishing characteristic of professional salespersons is how well they plan, manage, and control their irreplaceable pieces of time.

STEP 5: CONTINUE TO LEARN YOUR TRADE

Learn and use the tools of the trade. Study the fundamental sales process and acquire superior selling skills through practice. Numerous sales training programs teach such basics as listening, prospecting, communicating, presenting, overcoming objections, closing the sale, and generating repeat business, plus referrals, which lead to new business. With the rudiments absorbed, to remain professional, you need to establish a continuing education program that bridges identified gaps, consistently adds knowledge, improves existing skills, and aims at new skills for constantly improving performance.

STEP 6: ESTABLISH A CAREER PLAN

Establish a Career Plan. We have already noted that the lives of people without direction and obectives dissipate into morbidity and dispair. For salespersons, the resulting negative attitude is tantamount to death. Hence, you need clear career aspirations, which provide daily challenges and long-term direction. The career target might focus on becoming the best possible salesperson or perhaps on advancing to sales manager and beyond. Regardless of the specific target, true sales pros objectively evaluate as their target the best job fit for maximizing their performance and work enjoyment.

Also, growing persons—and a professional is always committed to constant self-improvement and growth—are always identifying gaps between where they are now and where they want to be in the future. This ongoing process provides them with the challenge that assures the zest of an enjoyable and productive life. By comparison, amateurs are identified by their boredom, as well as by their lack of purpose.

STEP 7: PROVIDE FOR FEEDBACK

Provide a feedback system. A feedback system not only measures the cost of the effort in terms of the value of its results, but it also clearly establishes how well the job is being done. Such a system thus permits salespersons' compensation to be commensurate with their performance and with the value of their results.

Professional salespeople *want* their performance to be measured objectively and rewarded fairly. They gravitate to an incentive type of compensation system, because they want their scores kept. They want to reap the economic harvest from the seeds of superior performance that they plant.

Feedback also provides another invaluable benefit. It supplies the guidance needed for improvement and adjustment. It enables managers to achieve their plans and to manage changes to advantage. Constant improvement and managing change constitute a way of life for professional salespersons. Their commitment to excellence contributes in large measure to the consistent increases in sales volume and market penetration that real pros enjoy.

These seven steps comprise both a checklist and a process for becoming a sales professional. As persons master this process, they will be increasingly able to sell more and more in less and less time.

This ability will transform them into the world's most productive, valuable, respected, and highly paid professionals.

Delegation   Of the many skills a successful manager is required to master, one of the important is delegation. Yet few managers seem to understand how to delegate—and lack of delegation often works to the detriment of individuals and organizations. Although the term "to delegate" is properly defined as "to entrust to another," "to appoint as your representative," or "to assign responsibility or authority," managers avoid it because they feel they're "being dumped on."

While in theory delegation normally flows from the top down, the flow commonly works in reverse. Here is a typical example of this reverse flow.

> Sitting at his desk, the boss is trying to figure out how to reduce his workload. He has no time to plan, to manage, and to control, which are his primary responsibilities as a manager. The firm's expanding operating pressures are bogging him down. The entire organization is suffering. And business is starting to slip. The phone rings. At the same time Jane Tyler, the production manager, comes through the door with an unusually eager look on her face. It is only 8 AM, and the next nine hours will keep up about the same pace.
>
> As soon as the manager puts the phone down, Jane says, "Boss, I have a great idea on how we can reduce our costs." For the next fifteen minutes she enthusiastically explains in very broad terms her idea for reducing costs. When she is finished, she stands up and says on her way out, "Please give this idea some thought. When you work out the details, let me know what they are and whether you think we should use the idea."

The boss has just been delegated to. In fact, he has been dumped on. Jane goes out whistling a happy tune, confident that a raise will be forthcoming on account of the brilliant idea that flashed into her mind in about a minute. The boss, however, has been given the assignment of "thinking it over, working out the details, and finally reporting back to Jane as to what is to be done about it." He is more bogged down than ever. He is really doing the most important part of Jane's job—thinking out problems and opportunities to the point that they become practical. This work is the essence of management thinking and responsibility. Dealing thoroughly with this idea will take the boss several days, while Jane whistles a happy-expectful tune.

Nor does Jane win in this situation. She suffers, because she is not being challenged to think things out completely by herself. As a result, Jane remains a doer, not a manager, and her own ability to make good decisions is reduced, because she and the boss are content to let the boss do all the thinking. Jane does not mature into a manager, because she is content to think with someone else's brain and to be told what to do. Eventually, someone else will have to be brought in to relieve the boss of the responsibility for managing Jane.

Decide to Delegate If the human resources, all about you in your organization, are motivated and productive, then you should have no hesitation about delegating some of your responsibilities. But many managers are not sure how to do so. Here's a three-step method that shows how.

STEP 1: DECIDE WHAT TO DELEGATE

Decide what to delegate. Based on your insights gained by creating the business plan, you then have to free up time to do the more important things that increase your productivity. The key to doing so is delegation, which has, in our experience, consistently freed up from 20 to 40 percent of a manager's time. Basically, the delegation system includes the following:

1. List all the tasks performed in your job.
3. Estimate—on the average—how much time you spend on each task.
3. Divide the tasks into four columns:
   a. Must keep.
   b. Want to keep, but could share or delegate.
   c. Can share.
   d. Can delegate.

STEP 2: ASSIGN SOME TASKS TO OTHERS

Next, *make your delegations.* Assign the tasks that can and should be delegated to others, with particular consideration to one of the most underutilized resources in most organizations—the secretary or assistant. This person can often competently take over enough tasks to free up a good percentage of your time. The assistant thus makes a much greater contribution and is released from the secretarial routine.

STEP 3: EXTEND DELEGATION FURTHER

Then *extend the delegation system.* For secretaries to perform on a higher level, doing more important things, routine secretarial chores should, in turn, be delegated. Simply use the same delegation system that you employed to free up the needed time for yourself. Delegate such tasks primarily to individuals skilled in word processing equipment. Based on the experience of Planagement's Administrative Support Team Division, one skilled, soundly supervised word processing person should be able to do the routine work of two or more secretaries, depending on the type of work delegated. The result is not only a substantial cost saving, but also much greater accuracy and flexibility.

Delegation and Development

There is a strong interrelationship between delegation and development. Unless the boss acquires the skill of delegation, the organization will very likely never grow beyond the personal capability and whims of a "one-boss show." It will remain entirely dependent on the boss. Worse, the only people who will remain in the organization will be those who choose not to develop themselves and who are satisfied to depend totally on and to be dominated by the boss. In this type of organization, the flow of delegation is normally upward, whereas in a healthy, growing organization—with a sound present and good future—the flow of delegation is downward. (Figure 5-1). Obviously, an organization with upward delegation is very vulnerable, and it has at best a limited future.

The Planagement® practice experience has yielded an insight into the delegation process and has generated a step-by-step formula for delegating.

FIGURE 5–1.   The downward delegation grid

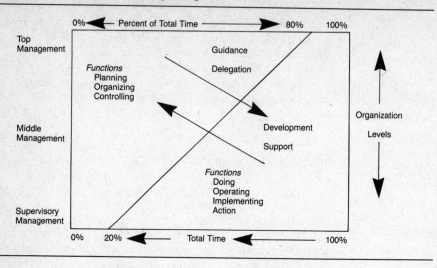

STEP 1: DESCRIBE YOUR POSITION

Develop a comprehensive written position description.

STEP 2: LIST DETAILS

List in detail *all* the tasks you perform in support of accomplishing your job.

STEP 3: ASSESS TIME

Put down how much time you spend on each task as a percentage of the total working time. Be as objective and accurate as you possibly can. Sometimes it is very helpful to have a close associate or your secretary do steps 2 and 3 independently. Then you can compare and combine, which contributes to a more accurate analysis.

STEP 4: CATEGORIZE TASKS

Now divide the tasks into four categories as follows:

1. Tasks you must do yourself.
2. Tasks you want to keep because you enjoy them or because you are comfortable with them and need them to occupy your time.
3. Tasks you can share with someone else.
4. Tasks you should delegate to someone else to contribute to their development and to free up your time.

STEP 5: SELECT APPROPRIATE PEOPLE

Select appropriate individuals to share and delegate those tasks that permit you to do so. Consider developing at least one or more backups for your job, recognizing that you will eventually need to transfer even many of the presently nontransferable items listed in step 4.

Give careful thought to using your secretary more: Secretaries are one of the most frequently underutilized resources in a company. This person, who often has the potential to be an administrative assistant or manager, could free up a great deal of your time, if allowed to do so.

STEP 6: NOTE TIME SAVED

Add up the percentage of total time you have freed through delegation.

STEP 7: LIST FUTURE TASKS

List the accountabilities and tasks that:

1. you would like to have,
2. you would like to be assigned, or
3. you need to do for the best interests of the job, the organization, and yourself.

STEP 8: PRIORITIZE TASKS

List the tasks enumerated in step 7 in their order of importance and/or preference.

STEP 9: ESTIMATE TIME

Establish the percentage of total time available that you estimate will be required to assume the responsibility for each task in step 8.

STEP 10: MAKE UP YOUR NEW LIST

Subject to the necessary approvals, as well as agreed-on delegation by others (if required), add on to your job list tasks from step 8 until the percentage of required time estimated in step 9 equals the time freed up in step 6.

STEP 11: PLAN THE DELEGATION TIMETABLE

Establish a written plan of action for delegating the tasks identified in step 4 to the people identified in step 5. Support your plan with a specific timetable; be sure people agree to the training times and timetable. Clearly establish measurable standards of satisfactory performance—and get mutual agreement.

As your time is freed up through this process, add specific tasks and the supportive training, as required in steps 8 and 9. A big blockade to delegation occurs when a person has not identified how to spend the freed-up time. When people are immersed in activity and always have more than they can do, they feel secure. Unfortunately, performance, compensation, and recognition often correlate more closely with how active and how busy they are, rather than with the results they accomplish.

STEP 12: DO IT! REDO IT!

Make these eleven steps a "living" process. Apply them formally at least once every six months, because most managers tend to underestimate how rapidly their people grow and learn to handle increased responsibility competently.

Planning   Planning—although all managers are expected to do it, few can explain how to do it. Business planning, unlike other essential business disciplines, has not evolved to the point of benefiting from generally accepted principles. In the *Guide for Bank Planning,* the statement was made that "it is not possible to describe a typical planning process." The vast majority of managers have no formal planning approach; they spend most of their time doing rather than planning. This situation is particularly sad, since, by nature, at least 80 percent of the manager's job consists of planning.

Why don't more individuals and organizations plan? Of the several possible answers to this question, the first and most basic is perhaps they do not know how! Our educational system does not teach us. And the ways that we typically pick up life experience do not include any real exposure to planning. As a result, most people don't understand planning and just cannot do it.

During the development of the Planagement® system, thousands of managers were asked what they expected from a planning system. What criteria did it have to meet for them to adopt it? According to their responses, the fifteen most important criteria are shown in Figure 5–2. They may be used either to measure the quality of your own planning management system or to guide the development of one.

Besides these criteria, you can do a few things to ensure maximum success with your planning system:

1. The plan should be tailored to the needs of the particular business, organization, and managerial style.
2. Ideally, a supportive policy should be established to insure that planning and management are indeed the responsibility of all participants and that they are important parts of their job. Such a policy might read as follows:

    All employees with other-than-routine responsibilities and/or other-than-routine ambition will have a written job description with measurable standards of performance, supported by a written plan for improving performance with a tailored training and development program designed to advance their skills. Both the job description and the plan will be kept current through exception reporting. This policy would be supported with written procedures for exception reporting, coordination, job description format, the information to be contained in the plan and in what order, and other elements that comprise the plan for planning.

3. The planning function should be established as a profitability center with a general manager assigned its responsibility. This manager of the planning function should:

   a. be an educator, not a consultant;

   b. not do the planning for anyone else;

   c. be the shadow of the substance and enjoy nurturing the growth and recognition of others; and

   d. act as a catalyst.

FIGURE 5–2. Fifteen most important criteria for planning

Criterion	The Plan . . .
1. Sound and systematic	. . . rank-order opportunities according to practical potentials and judiciously allocate resources in cost/benefit sequence. Both effective and efficient, goes beyond management by objectives and communicates the rationale that spawned the objectives. Based on the thinking/diagnostic skill, focuses on managing potential, not momentum, anticipative and problem-preventing in nature.
2. Universal and balanced	. . . provides a format that anyone can use individually and organizationally with a team approach. Based on common sense, balances scientific management with behavioral sciences, freedom with discipline, and operations with futures, profits, profitability, and growth.
3. Integrative	. . . orchestrates planning, management, control, communications, and development into a professional management system for increasing managerial and organizational performance.
4. Teachable	. . . provides a tangible plan for planning that is easy to learn and simple to apply. Utilizes reality-based learning where the education is the application, where the learning is in the doing for real.
5. Versatile	. . . works at all levels in an organization with unlimited focus on organization, job, function, career, program, project, opportunity, problem, product, new venture, acquisition, merger, family, and so on. Usable by anyone—from the

(cont.)

FIGURE 5–2. (continued)

Criterion	The Plan . . .
	highly educated to high school dropouts, from top managers to first line supervisors, from one nationality to another, and from one psychological bent to another.
6. Tailorable	. . . fits and adjusts to organization's needs and management styles. Maintains consistency, but its magnitude may vary from comprehensive to abbreviated and from many pages in a plan to a one-page plan summary.
7. Measurable	. . . produces results that are clearly measurable, both immediately and over a period of time, and in both quantitative and qualitative terms. Providing economic as well as psychological measurements, the system should provide an early warning capability so that opportunities may be exploited in a timely manner and problems may be prevented or reduced. Specific gains, losses, and behavior changes can be objectively and accurately identified.
8. Economic	. . . is oriented toward profit, profitability, and growth. Contributes to a constant gain. Its cost/benefit ratio must exceed a minimum of 1 to 3. For each 1 percent of working smarter, at least a 90-percent gain is achieved within 12 to 24 months. Focuses on asset management, tapping the greatest unrealized potential, and represents the best possible investment that can be made. Incorporates Paretos law of 20 percent controlling 80 percent of the results. Its consistent use will save significant time in dollars while maximizing productivity and results. Keys on results, not activities, and on the causes, not the effects. Goes beyond bottom-line management.
9. Feedback—closed loop	. . . provides the basis for managing by exception, the anticipation and management of change. Establishes a current living plan. Provides a system for control and updating, and allows for expanded span of control, consistently redefining an ever-changing situation that exceeds acceptable norms and established ranges. Contributes to the development of an anticipative skill and is the basis for an early warning system.
10. Flexible	. . . is firm enough to give direction and flexible enough to accommodate change. Provides a comprehensive system that may be applied for a multiplicity of uses and is adjustable to meet varying requirements. Selective parts may be used without losing the value of the discipline. May be shortened or lengthened, as the needs require, to deal with and to integrate long-range planning with operating man-

(cont.)

FIGURE 5–2. (continued)

Criterion	The Plan . . .

	agement, strategy with tactics, and the grand design with the supporting pieces that move it into reality.
11. Human resource development system	. . . results in identifying and placing the right person in the right job with the right plan to maximize performance, as well as the right training and development program to bridge existing and anticipated gaps. Integrates many fragmented, frequently conflicting programs into one basic system for planning, management, communicating, coordinating, consolidating, control, delegation, and development. Stimulates a positive attitude, work satisfaction, motivation, creativity, and the entrepreneurial spirit. Promotability and performance are increased.
12. Meets the five critical needs of business	. . . incorporates the key result areas, while focusing on the five critical needs for:

12. (continued):

a. a formal planning management and communication system,

b. a marketing capability and system,

c. a human resource development system,

d. a profitability control system, and

e. an identification and management of growth system.

13. Minimizes meetings and paperwork	. . . provides a manual management information system that may use the computer in support. Identifies, organizes, analyzes, and presents the minimum amount of information required to make sound decisions and the actions required to make the decisions happen. Provides the basis for managing by exception.
14. Easily understood and used	. . . readily signals users with its benefits and with the urgency for its use. Rapidly learned through application or workshop in a matter of hours. Organized so that each user may teach another. Includes self-instructional materials, and is organized with leaders' guide so that a "train-the-trainer" program may result. Constantly improved and upated, while remaining consistent and organizing knowledge in a common format.
15. Practical and implementable	. . . provides a basic professional management discipline and system that may be used for the organization, divisions, departments, functions, jobs, and careers by teams and by individuals with other-than-routine responsibility and/or other-than-routine ambition. In addition, a sound planning system should be based on the mind's natural process.

Strategy   Although strategy is a term we frequently hear and often use, very few seem to understand it. On the one hand, many leading businessmen and educators feel that sound strategy is essential to establishing a successful business. One study, in fact, indicated that strategy determined a least 70 percent of a business' future success and position in its field. Yet our experience with the Planagement® system has shown that few organizations have identified and documented strategies. Why not? The reason has not been a lack of desire or recognition of the importance of strategy, but rather a failure to understand the concept and the process for developing sound strategy. So, while dictionary definitions usually emphasize the military's use of strategy, the term is just as applicable to business organizations, which develop plans and goals to "meet the competition in the market place under advantageous conditions."

Let's begin with a working definition. First, since strategy is both an art and a science, it involves both judgment and a scientific process, as well as political, economic, and psychological factors. Strategy is the broad picture that includes how the goal will be accomplished, while tactics are the specific plans of action that will achieve the goal within the framework of the established strategy.

The following examples are not intended to be precise or based on extensive research. Rather, they are generally understood developments in business that might help you to gain a better understanding of what strategy is, what it does, and how it works.

EXAMPLE 1: MILITARY

During the second world war, as the story goes, General Douglas MacArthur was faced with the challenge of capturing fifteen islands in a chain that were infested with the enemy. It was estimated that several thousand American lives would be lost on each and every one of these islands, and that each island would require several months to capture, thus prolonging the war well over a year. The tactics were clearly understood. First, you bomb the island from the air and then from the sea. Next, you land the troops and fight for ground—cave by cave, hill by hill—until the enemy is killed or captured.

The best military minds were put to work to establish a strategy that would reduce the terrible cost in lives, time, and other resources, yet achieve the "must" objective of capturing the fifteen islands. Studying the facts (*scientific* analysis), they observed that the islands were in a chain. Their judgment (*art* of devising a strategy) was that, if you captured every third island, you could starve the other two into submission, thus neutralizing them and thereby eliminating the immediate need to capture them.

So the strategy was to take every third island in the chain and to fight only five battles instead of fifteen. The result of this strategy saved at least two-thirds of the originally needed resources, including men, money, material and time. Above all, the objective was achieved.

EXAMPLE 2: LARGE RETAIL BUSINESS

At one time in their histories, Sears and Montgomery Ward were close equals in the retail field. The two leaders of these companies made a judgment decision in regard to the United States economy. The Chief Executive officer of Montgomery Ward assumed that there would be a recession, and the company strategy became one of "nonexpansion" and of keeping their ample funds in a liquid state. Sears, on the other hand, assumed that the economy would grow, and its strategy became one of expansion.

Today the relative positions of these two giants in the retail field are due in large measure to the strategy adopted at that crucial time in their histories where it was determined that one of the equals was to become the leader in the field.

EXAMPLE 3: AUTOMOTIVE INDUSTRY

Ford and General Motors were co-leaders in the automotive field many years ago. As equals, each top management team set a goal of establishing a leadership position in the served market. But each made very different assumptions based on their research (and the lack of fact gathering), which in turn developed two entirely different strategies.

Ford assumed that what the public wanted was the best engineered, highest-quality automobile that could be built. Its strategy was to create the Lincoln Continental as the best built car in

America. Part of the reason for this decision was that the company was very engineering/production/sales-oriented.

General Motors, on the other hand, assumed that the public wanted prestige, and this strategy was reflected in the image created for the Cadillac. The result was that many more Cadillacs were sold than Lincolns, and GM became the leader in the field as measured by its share of the automotive market.

DEVELOP STRATEGY

You don't have to be the chief officer of GM or Sears, however, to need and to employ strategy. As a manager, you should be able to develop your strategy. And, like so many areas of management, this one involves a relatively simple step-by-step process, as shown in Figure 5-3. The process demonstrated in this figure, however, requires your commitment to three things:

1. a marketing (as opposed to sales) approach,
2. a profitability (as opposed to profit-taking) orientation, and
3. the 20/80—percent method for allocating resources.

Strategic Sequencing

History has demonstrated the importance of timing over and over again. The success or failure of an endeavor often swings on the sequencing of events. Something may happen now with no significant effect. But the same thing may happen later—in a totally different set of circumstances—with huge and long-lived effects. *When* something happens can be as important as, or even more important than, *what* happens.

When you try to time your endeavors so as to have the greatest effect possible, you are engaged in strategic sequencing. In its fully matured form, *strategic sequencing* is a process of effectiveness, in which you identify, prioritize, and integrate the individual's and the organization's opportunities in the order of their practical potentials. With this prioritization, you can then develop a sound strategic plan.

The next step entails a process of efficiency called *Systematics*©. In this process, you identify, design, prioritize, interlink, imple-

FIGURE 5-3. Process for developing strategy with an example

Step	Step Explanation	Example
1	*Science:* Gather the appropriate facts and analyze them to evolve the best possible situation that can be established with the facts available.	Fact: Company X is number three in the field with a market share of 10%. An analysis of the facts indicate that Company X has a superior technical capability and sales force.
2	*Art:* Apply judgment in the form of assumptions and establish potentials based on the facts in step 1 and the assumptions made.	The assumption is made that an improved product can be made and that the sales force has the capability to increase its market share with the improved product.
3	*Decision:* Steps 1 and 2 should contribute to your making a decision as to what you wish to accomplish by when. This is the statement of objective.	The decision is made to establish a leadership position in the field by obtaining at least a 50 percent share by December 31, 19XX.
4	*Strategy:* Develop and identify the strategy you will use to accomplish the objective—the general direction you wish to take.	The strategy established, based on the facts, judgment, cision made, is "to accomplish the objective through internal development rather than acquisition from the outside." A second strategy is designed to improve the company's profit position by and through "a greater participation in the markets it serves, and to optimize the use of all resources employed in the business through effective planning, organization, and measurement of performance.
5	*Action Plan:* *Tactics:* Establish the plan of action in the form of projects designed to accomplish the objective in the best way possible to maximize results. *Key Milestones:* These plans of action include: steps needed to be taken (what is to be done), by who, when and what resources are required (cost) and the results to be achieved (why; cost/benefit). These projects will be consistent with the strategy established.	Project sheets were then developed in support, an example of which might look like this: What: To complete the development of Product X Who: VP and RD When: 3/15/XX Resources: People: three full time, plus 70% VP time Money: $25,000 Material: ⅔ of the RD facility full time Why: To increase market share by at least 10 percent each of the next four years. This should result in our having price leadership, which in turn will increase profitability.

ment, and improve the systems required to support the strategic plans. These action plans or operating plans are implemented so as to effect the strategic goals in the most cost-effective way.

Thus, the two processes link effectiveness (doing the right things) with efficiency (doing things right), and lead to high-powered productive planning at all levels of the organization.

Bridging the Communication and Knowledge Gap

Few gaps between individuals are more frustrating than the communication gap. Four of the more important dimensions of this gap are these:

1. It is difficult for individuals to communicate objectively with themselves due to their built-in biases. This problem in communications is multiplied when we attempt to explain ourselves to others. An oft-quoted observation of our difficulty in communicating objectively with ourselves and with others expresses this problem well: "What you are speaks more loudly than what you say."

2. Due to our "built-in biases," we often find it easier to talk than to listen. We also frequently substitute our own interpretation for what was really said, which in turn causes us to say something different from what we hear. The common example is of people in a circle garbling the original message while relaying it in a whisper to each other. As a result, we usually remember less than 10 percent of what we hear. Our inability to listen well is a major contributor to the communication gap.

3. As human beings, we tend to make the simple complex. The 500 most commonly used words in the English language have over 14,070 definitions. Hence, even a common language provides ample opportunity for poor communications and a gap in understanding.

4. Human beings typically have an unstructured balance between logic and emotions. We often interpret a tone of voice much more than the words used. "How" something is said, coupled with the "physical expressions and movements," many times tells it like it is much more than words alone. Our own mood may block and prejudice our ability to believe what is being said, or we might just turn the other person off because we are not interested.

Bridging the communication gap is not easy. It requires a challenging combination of self-discipline and empathy, which to some extent are contrary to human nature. Yet overcoming these restricting tendencies yields a number of benefits, one of the most important being the ability more easily to overcome the knowledge gap. Thus, we more rapidly acquire and apply meaningful knowledge.

In fact, the knowledge explosion is so overwhelming that few individuals and organizations have developed systems for quickly identifying, obtaining, organizing, and presenting the minimum amount of information for making a sound decision. Consequently, a gap exists between useful knowledge and ability to use it. Increased communication and knowledge-acquisition skills become imperative tools to you as a manager. Figure 5–4 helps with guidelines for communication.

FIGURE 5–4. Ten guidelines for improved communication

1. Periodically obtain an outside, objective appraisal of ourselves. This can be accomplished in a variety of ways, including conducting an opinion and observation survey from those who work for us and with us, or utilizing a trained outside resource to give us some needed feedback and insight.

2. Document in writing our personal and basic philosophy and constantly monitor the consistency and compatibility of our actions as compared to our philosophy. Observed deviations will provide valuable guidance for us better to manage by example and convince others we mean what we say.

3. Adopt a basic principle that integrity is an absolute requirement to sound communication. If you don't believe what I say, you won't hear what I say. You will second guess me and we will not be able to communicate. Without communication, there cannot exist a sound and productive organization.

4. Accept as a basic law that the responsibility for communications is that of the *communicator.* In other words, if I do not communicate to you, it is my fault—not yours.

5. Train ourselves to listen well. There are several good books, presentations, and proven techniques for improving our listening skill. This is such a vitally important skill that several colleges have established courses in listening for full college credit.

6. Develop an open and inquiring mind. Learn to ask more questions rather than know more answers. Acknowledge in your own mind that I

(cont.)

FIGURE 5–4. (continued)

may have a better idea than you do and you will hear me out. If you ex-change one dollar with someone, you will have gained nothing; but if you exchange one idea with someone, you will be at least one idea richer. More often, your one new idea will synergistically react with your storehouse of knowledge with experience and will produce several new and valuable ideas.

7. If you are not sure what I mean, ask me to explain it again, and, if necessary, again. If I am the right kind of person, I will not resent your inquiry, but will probably appreciate it as an expression of your interest in what I am trying to say.

8. When dealing with a new or hard to understand thought, write it out as a supplement to your verbally expressing it. There are good reasons to believe that our brains are closer to our fingers than our mouths, as we can better remember and understand what we write as opposed to what we just say. While it is true that we remember less than 10% of what we hear, we can sharply increase this percentage through a multisensory learning experience. If we hear it, see it, touch it and say it, the chances are that we will comprehend and retain over 70% of what is being communicated, and it will always be a valuable resource stored in our minds the rest of our lives.

9. Another major contributor to improving communication is for us to develop a habit of "constant interest in the other person." This is not an easy habit to develop because of our very human tendency to be more interested in ourselves. Also, let's face it, some people are just plain bores or they have very little in common with us or few areas of mutual interest. Nevertheless, if we try to develop a habit of being interested in what the other person has to say, we probably will often be pleasantly surprised as to what we can learn. An additional dividend will frequently accrue to us in the fact that if we treat others with interest, they will become more interested in what we have to say, and the communications gap will be correspondingly reduced.

10. A tenth guideline to bridging the communication gap involves our continued self improvement in regard to using our own language better. There is a proven relationship between those who stand higher on the ladder of commonly identified success and their respective abilities to express themselves well, both verbally and in writing. This skill in effectively using the language is very basic to our being able to bridge the communication gap. There are, of course, notable exceptions to this guideline rule; however, they are the exception not the rule.

6 MANAGEMENT BY CAUSE AND EFFECT

Cause-and-effect management is founded on several building blocks: the careful application of the thinking process, the bridging of the Thinking Gap, the emphasis on a positive outlook, diagnosis, the 80/20 rule, and self-discipline. Such a managerial philosophy puts you in charge of, rather than at the mercy of, your working environment. It enables you to focus on the (usually few) critical factors that impact on a particular decision or even on your organization's overall performance. Its emphasis is on effecting fruitful change to prevent counterproductive situations, to foresee and avoid problems, and to minimize crises.

Unfortunately, most managers traditionally do not perceive their roles this way. They most commonly respond that their job is to solve problems. Some even maintain that a good manager should be able to resolve one crisis after another and survive along the way. The more crises, the more job security. Hence, their focus is on problems and the bottom line. Yet, from this point of view, both problems and the all-important bottom line are things that "happen to" managers, things to which managers react. The result is that "problem-solvers" or "bottom-line" managers generally magnify their problems, thus creating other problems. So, although this philosophy may currently prevail, it is erroneous and possibly even dangerous.

Professional managers must accentuate not crises but opportunities. They must focus not on problems but on the causes that enable them to capture profit and growth opportunities. They must anticipate and prevent problems, not wait for a crises to resolve.

The difference in the results achieved by these two opposed philosophies amounts to much more than most people think. Professional managers, as well as their organizations, become "thermostats," that is, sensitive to their environments and capable of effecting advantageous changes. On the other hand, reactive managers are better charactertized as "thermometers," which simply register, but not control, changes. Perhaps the best comparison of these two types of managers was noted by George Craig Stewart when he wrote:

> Weak men are the slaves of what happens. Strong men are masters of what happens. Weak men are victims of their environment. Strong men are victors in any environment. Strong men may not change circumstances, but they will use them, compel them to serve, and bend them to their purposes. They may not be able to change the direction of the wind, but somehow they will coerce the wind to fill their sails while they drive the tiller over to keep their course.

One Most Important Skill

At a presentation to a large group of experienced managers, I found myself in a question-and-response engagement that I hope proved as valuable to others as it did to me. Of the many challenging questions, the most intriguing was "What do you consider to be the manager's most important skill?"

At first, the skills most frequently emphasized in academic and management training and development programs came to mind . . .

1. decision making,
2. problem solving,
3. functional skills (such as marketing, selling, finance, production, and the like),
4. project management, and
5. technical skills (such as systems, engineering, mathematics, statistics, and so on).

101

The next group of skills that came to mind were the human relations skills, such as . . .

1. understanding and dealing with people through the use of behavioral science techniques, including psychology, sociology, philosophy, and other fields of study; and
2. the skills of listening, communicating, stimulating, empathy, team building, persuading, negotiating, and so on.

I thought also of the basic management skills, including . . .

1. planning,
2. organizing,
3. implementing, delegating, coordinating, consolidating, and
4. monitoring and controlling.

Finally, into my mind came that list of crucially important skills that might be referred to as the "fuzzy skills," which make management as much an art as a science . . .

1. analysis,
2. creativity,
3. entrepreneurial instincts,
4. judgment,
5. gut feelings, intuition, hunches, and guesstimates,
6. time management, a sense of timing,
7. thinking,
8. strategy,
9. sensing synergy and bringing it into reality,
10. maximizing profit, profitability, and growth,
11. establishing and using the authority of earned prestige,
12. general and professional management,
13. climate management,
14. management and development of the human resource, or
15. self-management.

You could probably add onto this list of fuzzy skills without end. Human skills that everyone has, they are virtually infinite in their number, intensity, quality, priority, and combinations. In fact, these skills are such a part of managing that many teachers and practitioners feel that management is so much of an art that it cannot be taught except through experience. While I sympathize with this viewpoint, I do not agree with it, because I have seen management skills taught successfully with outstanding, measurable results.

Itemizing these "fuzzy skills" in my head, I quickly hit upon the one skill that was more basic and important than any other. This skill is a basic part of every profession, including management. It is used by the most competent and effective educators. This skill is basic to all other skills, and its quality often has a major influence on the quality and productiveness of the others. Yet this same skill is among the most "fuzzy" and least taught. Happily, there is a growing awareness and increasing justification to recognize this skill as the most important one of all: Diagnosis.

Diagnosis   "This most important skill is *diagnosis*," I said in answer to the manager's question. Immediately other questions followed:

1. What do you mean by diagnostic skill?
2. How does the diagnostic skill work?
3. Can the diagnostic skill be taught and, if so, how?

WHAT IS DIAGNOSIS?

The *diagnostic process* is a series of carefully chosen questions that are asked in the proper order, at the right time, and in the right way.

This insight into the diagnostic process was generated in the research phase of the Planagement® system. At the outset, the hypothesis was that the most important management skill was good decision making. In an attempt to identify and understand the decision making process, several hundred managers, at all levels in a wide variety of businesses, were asked this question: "What is the minimum amount of information you consider in making a decision, and in what order do you consider this information?" Over a period of two years, the answers to this question were gathered and studied. The result was a series of questions, which formed a model for making sound decisions faster. This model consists of key questions in a sequence that provides managers and individuals with a practical diagnostic tool. This model has since become the basis of the Planagement® system and practice.

HOW DOES THE DIAGNOSTIC SKILL WORK?

The diagnostic process consists of a series of key questions that may be asked in any situation. Within the Planagement® system, the questions are asked, the answers are recorded, and sound decisions plus a written plan result. The answers develop the rationale in the manager's mind for understanding and making a sound decision.

CAN THE DIAGNOSTIC SKILL BE TAUGHT?

This skill can certainly be taught, and the best way to do so is to apply it on a continuing basis. The learning is the doing. In fact, tens of thousands of managers and individuals have been taught the Planagement® diagnostic skill, and they are applying it to themselves, to their jobs, to their organizations, and to their careers. This particular learning experience leads to a constructive change in behavior—results that are obvious and measurable.

AN EARLY WARNING SYSTEM

Why do some companies perform better than others in changing economic conditions? The answer is not luck, but rather a matter of good management instead of poor management. Picture two sailboats being blown by changing winds. One boat has no direction—no supportive hand on the steering mechanism—and so it is blown in any direction the wind chooses. In all probability, it will be sunk by the waves or dashed on the rocks. The other sailboat, however, has direction and a professional hand on the wheel. It takes advantage of the changing winds by organizing its sails in such a manner that, regardless of the prevailing wind, it maintains its course at its chosen speed.

But how do you know which way the wind is blowing? Part of "good management" is an *early warning system,* whose purpose it is to alert management to a changing situation far enough in advance to allow time for establishing the required programs that will produce the best results. Should the anticipated situation be

104

negative, then management can be prepared to make lemonade out of the lemon. Alternatively, if the situation represents an opportunity, then management can organize the required resources to capture the opportunity.

To establish such a system—to keep a guiding hand on the tiller—you have to establish and clearly communicate the direction of the organization in the form of a written plan. This plan provides a standard to measure not only the direction (good or bad), but also the magnitude of actual and anticipated changes. Without a plan, how do you gauge the impact of change? And how do you know what you should do about it? This plan provides the line of direction that threads itself through all the interim ups and downs of a business' life. (See Figure 6–1.) Additional benefits of having a plan include the increased ability to perform at a higher level due to your increased anticipatory skills, to prevent problems, to react faster, and to increase productivity through the application of a systematic approach. As a result you do more, in less time, with better results. Most important, because we live in an age of rapid change, a sound early warning system may well determine which organizations will survive and prosper in an increasingly unpredictable future.

FIGURE 6–1. Conceptual view of managing change

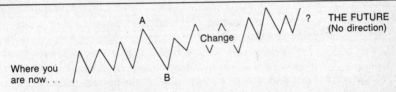

The situation without a plan with the magnitude of change represented from A to B.

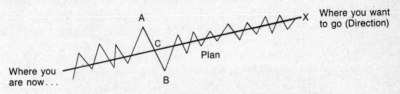

The situation with a plan reduces the impact of change from A to B to A to C (the plan line) and C to B. You know both the magnitude of the change, as well as its direction—positive or negative—and can therefore take the needed corrective action for managing change.

More than a skill, diagnosis must be considered a function of management—perhaps the most important one. With it managers can consistently make sound decisions, devise effective plans, and execute with a clear direction. In a very real sense, the diagnostic function precedes—and indeed makes or breaks—all others.

Discipline   How do you react to the word "discipline"? Is it a positive or negative term? Does it represent something valuable or something best avoided? Most people feel it is an abrasive, unpleasant word. This negative reaction probably stems from when we were children and "disciplined" for doing something wrong. Yet, oddly enough, the term "disciplined" has been employed to characterize individuals and teams who have excelled in their chosen fields. Even the dictionary defines the term in a number of confusing ways: as a form of instruction or training, as a field of study, as punishment, as control obtained through enforced obedience, as a prescribed conduct or behavioral pattern, as self-control, or as a rule or system of rules governing conduct or activity.

How can one word stand for so many things, both positive and negative? Perhaps the reason is that the word "discipline" is an aged term, whose older meetings are more negative than its current ones. These days, discipline has a positive and dynamic role in management and, for that matter, in life. Discipline is the price of becoming a professional manager, as well as a fundamental requirement for cause-and-effect management. In fact, the winners and leaders in every field have a discipline practiced in common. From corporations to football teams, from cab drivers to presidents, the ones who excel and who are obviously the top professionals in their activities—without exception—have a clearly identifiable discipline. The various types of discipline may differ widely in nature, but it is always consistent in its process and, frequently, although not always, in its practice. However fuzzy the concept, it provides an invaluable process and tool for the professional manager. And its benefit is the freedom you feel to be able to say honestly, "Thank God It's Monday!"

THE DISCIPLINE CHECKLIST

To reduce the concept's fuzziness and to make it more practicable, Figure 6–2 offers two checklists or questionnaires: one for the individual and one for the organization. The first part measures the

FIGURE 6–2. A discipline survey for you as an individual

1. Do you have a defined process for:
   a. developing plans?
   b. establishing clear direction?
   c. making decisions?
2. Do you accomplish your objectives and programs within the established time schedule and with the anticipated benefits realized? What is your on time percentage versus your percentage of procrastination?
3. Have you established sound priorities? Do you stick with them?
4. What method do you use to manage your time?
5. How do you objectively measure your actual performance against your forecast of progress and against its identified potential?
6. What written checklist do you use and for what purposes?
7. Do you have a written plan?
8. Can you draw a picture of your grand design with how and when you will achieve your goals and how you will measure its achievement?
9. Do you have a written self-development, improvement, or career program?
10. List your three most important purposes (missions in life), your three most important accomplishments (dates done), your three most important future accomplishments (dates to be done), and the gain between them.

For the Organization

---

1. Does the organization have a defined process for:
   a. developing plans?
   b. establishing clear directions?
   c. making decisions?
2. Does the organization accomplish its objectives and programs within the established time schedule and with the anticipated benefits realized? What is its time percentage versus its procrastination percentage?
3. Does the firm have established priorities? Does it stick with them?
4. With which method does the organization manage its time?
5. How does the organization objectively measure its actual performance against its forecast of progress and against its identified potential?
6. What written checklist does the organization use and for what purposes?

(cont.)

FIGURE 6–2. (continued)

For the Organization

---

7. Does the organization have a written plan?

8. Does the organization have a picture of its grand design, including how and when it is to achieve its goals and how it will measure its achievement?

9. Does the organization have a written self-development, improvement, or career program?

10. List the organization's three most important purposes (missions in life), its three most important past accomplishments (with the dates done), its three most important future accomplishments (with the dates to be done), and the gain between them.

11. Are the organization's missions and needs converted into objectives supported with written plans of action?

12. Are position descriptions in writing? And do they contain measurable standards of satisfactory performance?

13. Are the organization's objectives and priorities clearly and commonly understood?

14. What is the magnitude of deviation from established plans, including forecasts and budgets?

15. What is the monitoring and follow-up system? And how consistently is it applied?

16. Are key operating ratios, as well as the asset management concepts and tools, understood and utilized?

17. What percentage of the right people are in the right jobs? And what percentage of key employees have qualified backups? What is the percentage of promotions versus that of turnover?

18. What percentage of the programs of action are completed on time? And what percentage achieve the forecasted cost/benefit?

19. What are the organization's most important opportunities? Are they rank-ordered in accordance with their practical potentials? Are resources judiciously allocated in accordance with that rank-order?

20. What are the five most important written programs, in their order of importance? What will the gain be (cost/benefit), if they are achieved?

---

degree of your personal discipline, and the second gauges that of an organization. Note that the first ten questions for an organization are the same as those for an individual, but reworded. The reason is that the organization's discipline is merely a reflection of the discipline of its managers.

Many different kinds of discipline apply to a wide variety of situations. Here are some examples.

1. *Social discipline* means empathetic listening (as opposed to talking), remembering names, being on time, considering others' time, sensing others' needs, and assisting in meeting these needs.

2. *Self-discipline* consists of managing your time, establishing direction and priorities, consistently applying a physical fitness program, along with optimizing your living experience through a sound balance of the mental, spiritual or philosophical, social, and physical "whole person" elements. Additional examples include a formal program of self-improvement, honesty, dependability, consistency, and persistence. Also helpful is being results-oriented and as good as your word, with a positive outlook that supports your personal mission.

3. *Professional discipline* means having a written profile of the ideal job—the professional person/mission—that you wish to be/achieve. Supporting the written career plan, a gap analysis guides your self-development program so that it is cost/benefit justified to yourself and to the organization, in both quantitative and qualitative terms. You add dimension to your professional discipline by making sound plans and by making them happen consistently at a higher level on more important things with increasing results.

4. *Mental discipline* is consciously applying common sense through by using your mind's natural logical process. It means not only defining the situation, analyzing the situation, employing a judgment, making a decision, and taking actions. It also means avoiding procrastination, accomplishing the forcasted gains (cost/benefit), while consistently managing inconsistent situations (management of change) by redefining the situation and continuously reapplying the mind's process. The result is a plan for living, supported by a constantly strengthening mind.

5. *Learning discipline* requires you to define what is to be learned and why, to keep an open mind, to ask questions, to apply the knowledge or experience until it becomes a

skill, to remember knowledge by writing it down, and to understand it by internalizing it through repetition and by living it as much as possible.

6. *Organizational discipline* is comprised of establishing a clear results-oriented mission. The organization's purpose and philosophy must clearly state why it exists and what accomplishments it intends to make. With this sort of guidance, all the preceding five disciplines should be formally applied in concert through a formalized planning management discipline. The organization must establish a clear-cut direction based on rank-ordered practical potentials in support of its missions. It must insure that the resources are available to fuel the prioritized plans of action and thereby transform the missions and concepts of the organization into a practiced, productive reality. Essential to organizational discipline, therefore, is a formalized system that results in having the right professional person in the right job, with the right supporting plan and development program.

IS DISCIPLINE TOUGH, DEMANDING, AND WORK-ORIENTED?

The answer is yes, which is why so few people have plans and accomplish their plans: To do so requires discipline and work. Is it worth the effort? The following thoughts provide the answer to those who wish to achieve and live up to their own inherent potential:

Focus on
Discipline

No horse gets anywhere until it is harnessed.
No steam or gas ever drives anything until it is confined.
No Niagara is ever turned into light and power until it is tunneled.
No life ever grows great until it is focused, dedicated, disciplined.

—Harry Emerson Fosdick

THE DISCIPLINE HABIT

Frequently, discipline acts as a constructive catalyst for uniting drive with direction. It enables you to do what must be done to achieve successfully the objectives set. Each individual step has the capacity for self-discipline, but it must be consistently practiced so that it becomes a life habit.

This habit could be expressed as the conscious application of our minds to the following step-by-step logic (common sense) process:

1. Defining the present situation.
2. Analyzing the situation (relating the plusses and minuses).
3. Evolving alternative actions.
4. Making the best guess as to what the future will be.
5. Deciding on one action and establishing an objective (direction) of what is to be done by when.
6. Taking the actions required to make the objective happen.
7. Identifying the gain to be achieved from accomplishing the objective.
8. Managing changes by continually redefining the situation and adjusting accordingly.

FIGURE 6–3. Logic process of resurgence

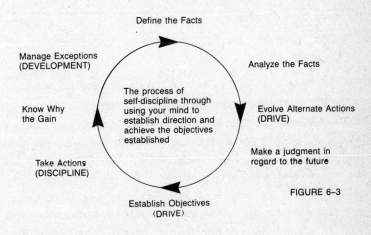

Define the Facts

Manage Exceptions
(DEVELOPMENT)

Analyze the Facts

Know Why
the Gain

The process of self-discipline through using your mind to establish direction and achieve the objectives established

Evolve Alternate Actions
(DRIVE)

Make a judgment in regard to the future

Take Actions
(DISCIPLINE)

FIGURE 6–3

Establish Objectives
(DRIVE)

111

FIGURE 6–4. The individual life cycle

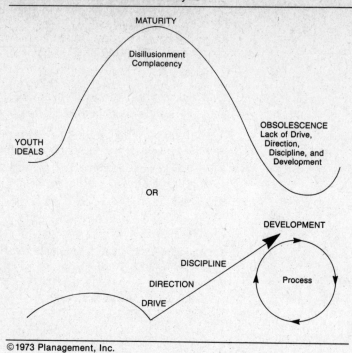

© 1973 Planagement, Inc.

This process of self-discipline, a modification of the logic process in Chapter 1, is shown in Figure 6–3. What happens when discipline isn't maintained in life is shown in Figure 6–4.

Implementing the Cause-and Effect Approach

With the proper diagnostic skills and self-discipline, you *can* transform the cause-and-effect concept into a powerful and productive management system, with three basic elements:

1. *Performance*—with the focus on the *cause.*
2. *Productivity*—with the focus on the *effect.*
3. *Profitability*—with the focus on *results,* as measured by the gain.

Actually, to put the system into practice, you have to satisfy five important organizational needs:

1. *Establish a formal management system* that integrates the functions of planning, management, organization, development, communication, administration, implementation, and control.

2. *Develop a marketing capability* that maximizes the organization's performance in its served markets.

3. *Make up a human resource development system* to tap the unused capacity in the human mind. Such a system is based on the philosophy that the growth and development of the organization depends directly on the growth and development of its human resources, since the human "asset" controls all the other assets of people, money, materials, time, and space. The human resource system should be designed so that the right person is continually selected and placed in the right job, with the right plan for job performance improvement and with the right training and development program to bring about identified individual and organization growth, now and in the future.

4. *Start up the administrative and control systems to maximize the individual's and the organization's profitability.* Measure profitability by the magnitude of gain from the activity. To draw a bead on and, thereby to control results, focus a profitability center on the most important standards of performance and key operating ratios in at least the following key areas:

   - *Customer satisfaction,* which you may measure by the increase in the share of profitable markets.

   - *Productivity,* which you may measure by the increase in cost effectiveness through the implementation of operations improvement programs.

   - *Innovation,* which you may gauge each year by the percentage of volume and profits coming from products and services developed the year before.

   - *Resources,* which you may manage through an asset management system. Such a system measures profitability by the increase in the return on assets employed (profit), while soundly increasing the assets employed (growth).

- *Management development and performance,* which you may quantify by merit increases based on improved performance, on bridging identified training and development gaps, on promotions from within, and on qualified backups for all key positions.
- *Employee attitude and performance,* which you may evaluate through, say, climate surveys or reduced turnover. You must know whether your formalized support of employees' career aspirations and plans is actually tapping the extraordinary potential of the human mind to work smarter, to increase productivity, and to enhance work satisfaction.
- *Public responsibility,* which you may appraise by the economic performance of the organization, together with how well its contribution meets the needs of its served publics, including stockholders, customers, employees, suppliers, community, industry, and the nation.
- *Communications,* which you may measure by an overall effectiveness index, which is based on an established profile of effective communications. Additional measurements include:
  - the cost of the time spent in meetings, compared to the value of their output,
  - the dissemination of information on a need-to-know basis,
  - the use of summaries to capture the 20 percent of the information that communicates at least 80 percent of the total meaning.

A formalized communication system enables you continually to identify, gather, organize, analyze, and present, in the most cost effective way, the minimum amount of important information required to make sound decisions, to take needed actions in their proper priority, and to control results through exception reporting.

- *Organization development,* which indicates the percentage of the right person in the right job.

5. *Establish a system that stimulates, identifies, and formally manages sound growth.* This type of system is frequently based on the management's philosophy to manage the or-

ganization's potential and commitment, as well as to keep the opportunities ahead of its growing assets, including the human resource. The primary function of this system is continually to identify opportunities, along with the priorities of their practical potential, and then judiciously to allocate and reallocate available assets to these opportunities within that order of priority.

These five critical need areas provide insights into the basic causes that most affect performance, productivity, and profitability. Analyzing these basic causes makes it abundantly clear to professional managers that the primary focus of the cause-and-effect management system should be on the individuals who comprise the organization.

Figure 6–5 shows the Cause-and-Effect Management System Brief Survey, a checklist designed to give you an idea of how much you are practicing cause-and-effect management right now. You can use this diagnostic tool now, as a pretest, *and* after you finish the rest of the book, as a post-test to measure your progress toward professional management. When you fill out the checklist now, you will likely have to answer no to several, perhaps many, of the questions. Don't worry if you must do so. The whole idea is to compare your results before and after.

If the benefits are not clear enough from such an analysis, they are certainly borne out by research and experience: When a professional management human resource system is successfully implemented, it *causes* at least a 1-percent increase in how "smart" individuals work, which *effects* at least a 90-percent gain in profitability and work satisfaction in the first twelve to twenty-four months of implementation. In fact, the cause-and-effect management system has achieved such superior advantages and outstanding results that it promises to become a dominant professional management system in the 1980s and beyond.

THE PRICE OF PROFESSIONALISM

The price of becoming a professional manager may be discipline, but the many benefits far outweigh the rigors of discipline. This book with its practical checklists, guidelines, and procedures will help make the discipline of becoming a professional manager orderly and enjoyable.

FIGURE 6–5. Cause-and-effect management system brief survey

	Yes	No
	(Check appropriate column.)	

1. Does your organization have a teachable professional management system for human resources development applied in all levels in your organization?

2. Do you know why management by objectives can be dangerous?

3. Do you understand the step-by-step process of diagnosis, which provides a checklist for making sound decisions?

4. Does your organization measure growth on the basis of increasing the bottom line?

5. Do you understand Theory X and Theory Y?

6. Do you understand Maslow's hierarchy of needs and their relationship to human motivation?

7. Do you have a time management system both long-term and daily?

8. Does your organization have a plan for the future that communicates a clear direction?

9. Do you feel your organization is achieving at least 50 percent of its potential for performance?

10. a. Do you understand the step-by-step process of thinking?

    b. If you answered yes to question a, list the seven steps of the thinking process.

      1. _____
      2. _____
      3. _____
      4. _____
      5. _____
      6. _____
      7. _____

                                    Total _____

	Yes	No

Multiply total Yes by 10 _____ and place this total on the effectiveness scale rating bar.

Cause-and-Effect Management System Effectiveness Scale

Rating Bar	Poor	Fair	Good	Excellent	Rating Bar
	0% 25% 50% 75% 100%				

As a professional manager, you must move against the tide of tradition and complacency. To overcome lack of discipline, failure to think, and negative attitudes toward work, you must be willing to take an active stand for the professional manager's philosophy or mind set. The next chapter addresses the need for the professional manager to be willing to fight for the important issues of the day.

The 80/20 Rule and Your Diagnostic Skill

At the heart of cause-and-effect management, then, is the skill of diagnosis. Professional managers must be able to isolate—that is, to diagnose—the 20 percent of causes that impact on at least 80 percent of the results. The next requirement is discipline—enough of it to bring to bear at least 80 percent of the availalbe resources on that crucial 20 percent. Hence, the two-way 80/20 rule.

This diagnostic skill provides professional managers with the ability to manage consistently inconsistent situations for a constant gain. Although this skill is dealt with extensively in a later chapter, suffice it to say that, in an age of ongoing change, anticipating and managing change are vitally important skills.

A GUIDELINE TO EFFECTIVE CONTROL

What is the minimum amount of information you need to make a sound decision?

In which order do you consider information?

The fact seems to be that 10 to 20 percent of the factors in your managerial jurisdiction tend to control 80 to 90 percent of the results. Put another way, if you can identify the key control factors of your business—the "minimum amount"—you can then exert better and more rapid influences to bring about acceptable results, even in changing times. Your job then becomes all the easier, because you have only ten to twenty things to control, rather than eighty or ninety. Such seems to be the unwritten law in one situation after another.

Despite its simplicity and apparent universality, this truism is commonly ignored. Perhaps the main reason is that, as human beings, we tend to make the simple complex, and the complex hopelessly confusing. Note our observation that the 500 most commonly used words in English have over 14,000 definitions! In the case of managers, this rule of thumb seems to flout their longstanding tradition that they be judged by the amount of their activity—even though they may be doing only some things right, rather than doing the right things. Ironically, managers who are "too busy" to consider their general positions usually have to work all the harder just to maintain their current success. They'd prefer to "keep chopping," rather than to stop and sharpen their axes.

The irony becomes even deeper when you consider that the 20/80 technique takes such little time and effort to execute. The process is nothing more than an extension of our own mental processes, by which the brain identifies, gathers, and uses information for "its own" decision making. All individuals have the ability to use the technique, because they all have the same fundamental thinking mechanisms. The differences among them lie in the varying degrees of personal self-discipline that people employ in "using their heads."

The technique itself is painfully simple:

1. Make a list of all the important elements in your job or in your business.
2 Then rearrange the listed elements according to the impact they have on your job or on your business.
3. Concentrate on the items that have the greatest impact, and treat the others accordingly.

The interesting and commonplace result, when we make a list of the eighty to one hundred things to be managed or done, is that the first ten to twenty items on the list often accomplish all eighty to one hundred easier and faster. Nevertheless, most managers seem content to be pressured by the one hundred and to try doing everything at once—usually with the result of taking five years to accomplish what might be done better in one.

Specifically, which elements are to be considered elements for such a list? A most productive listing was developed by Peter Drucker, one of management's leading educators. Dr. Drucker has identified what he terms the "Key Result Areas" of a business (Figure 6–5). Based on his own research and practice, he has concluded that, if managers manage these key result areas equal to or better than the competition, they will be able to increase profitability. If they do not manage these key result areas equal to or better than the competition, they will not achieve acceptable profitability.

Additional areas to be considered are becoming more and more important in being able to control results effectively. Many tools and techniques are being developed and applied with outstanding results

FIGURE 6–5. Some key result areas

1. *Customer Satisfaction:* This area involves marketing and sales, as well as some of its key operating ratios. Ways to measure your success in this area include the percentage of market share, the dollar volumes of sales to new customers, and so on.

2. *Productivity:* Gauged as the ratio of output over input, this element most often applies to manufacturing. Yet the concept works just as well in measuring all functional areas in a business. The key operating ratios to control the results in this area include sales and profit per employee, profit per payroll dollar, or tons produced.

3. *Innovations:* This element relates to the creative aspects of your business and to your ability to take a sound concept to commercial reality. The key operating ratios include the percentage of sales in new products and services, R & D expenditure as a percentage of sales, the number of new products introduced, and the like.

4. *Resources:* How well resources are developed and managed is measured by return on investment, return on assets employed, the percentage of annual increase in the assets employed, sales/inventory ratio, and several others.

5. *Management Development and Performance:* Increacing managerial effectiveness is one of the most important areas of potential for improved profitability. Some of the ways to measure progress in this key result area include development expenditures as a percentage of profit, management cost as a percentage of sales and of profit, the number of managers attending management development meetings, and so on.

6. *Employee Attitude and Performance:* Absenteeism is one measure of this area, along with employee turnover, the training budget, work stoppages (days lost), and several others. Other yardsticks include a measurable climate analysis or the results of an attitude survey.

7. *Organization Development:* The percentage of the right person for the right job is a key measurement here, along with the percentage of qualified back ups for all key positions, of effectiveness of one group, of effectiveness of the organization's structure to meet the needs of the business, of the number and magnitude of the gaps between the employees and their jobs (present and future), of effectiveness of the HRD System, Training, Development, Succession Planning, Hiring, dehiring, and Career Planning.

8. *Communications:* Measurements of the key result area would include the percentage of the Time Spent in Meetings, of effectiveness in communications, of effectiveness of the Management Information System, and of employees with written Job Descriptions with measurable standards of performance supported with a Written Job Plan kept current through periodic exceptions reporting.

(cont.)

FIGURE 6–5. (continued)

9. *Public Responsibility:* Measurements of this area include dollars for educational contribution and other contributions, the number of employees holding public offices or actively working in community programs, the number of handicapped or minorities employed as a percentage of the total employed, and so on.

10. *Profitability:* Defined as a continuing gain from the activity measurements would include the most important key operating ratios, such as the percentage of Return on assets employed, net profit at a percentage of revenues, cost of operations as a percent of revenues Debits to equity ratio and dates measurements such as percentage annual increase in assets employed, % unused in Market Share, % Revenue in Profit, and so on.

to the areas of communications, climate management, and organizational development. All of these key result areas together—and how well they are managed—largely determine the profitability of a company or the effectiveness of individual managers in their jobs.

Establish objectives in these ten basic areas, and give them a very high priority. In relation to these general areas, which apply to almost every company and to almost every key management job, you can identify up to twenty elements that are unique or most important to your own business. The chances are that these twenty areas will control at least 80 percent of the results you are after. If you are presently managing much more than twenty basic things, then your job should become easier by managing twenty or less, and you should be able to do more in less time with better results.

THE PROFESSIONAL MANAGER'S APPROACH™

Traditional Versus Professional Management

The top operating manager of the firm sat at a conference table with several of his subordinates. A traditional manager throughout his career, he had just gained an insight into what his firm needed to survive. Somewhat stunned to find that his life-long traditional techniques were *not* what the company needed, he responded by saying, "There are no chains tying me down. I can walk out that front door anytime."

After a weighty silence, one of his subordinates (a pro with real integrity) remarked, "Yes, you could. But your wallet won't let you get out of the chair." Obviously this subordinate was a professional manager who could tell the boss what he needed to know—not what he wanted to hear. This was the type of person I'd want in my company.

Tragically, however, the survival of such pros in a traditional company is at best doubtful, even though they are most needed in that sort of organization. So professional managers have to stand up and fight obsolete approaches. This fight is a difficult one, because the traditional methods that hold sway today have brought us to an unprecedented level of abundance. Yet everyone sees, with increasing clarity, that our high standard of living is deteriorating. Unfortunately, there seem to be more and more bureaucrats than builders in government, in business, and in education. Perhaps the new mandate given the government in the 1980 elections indicates that the period of laziness and complacency in the United States is over. Perhaps it means that the American people expect the public sector to be managed professionally. If so, an appropriate measure would be for the government to manage itself within an approved, sound, balanced economic budget, based on a limited and defined economic percent of the nation's gross national product.

In business too, professional management is just as much needed. With the domination of the traditional manager, many problems of the public sector exist in the private sector as well. In the private sector, bottom-line management frequently maximizes today's wealth at the expense of tomorrow's health. So it must be said: The traditional management practices that once made the United States the commercial wonder of the world will not get the job done in the 1980s!

If the United States is to reinstate itself as the world's commercial leader, then the traditional manager has to change. Today's traditional manager knows all the answers. The new breed of manager must know the right questions. Change is the only way, and it's almost too late for change now. Several aspects of "The American Way," however, are holding us back from this much-needed change. One is the current orientation of our educational insituations. Education is presently, in my opinion, a grab bag of unrelated topics—a type of nonlearning experience that generates reduced results. Carried over from the schools to business, these results were once described by a client, when asked to summarize his company, as a "hodgepodge of systems going nowhere." To make matters worse, they were bringing in a bigger computer to go faster in the wrong direction with a higher degree of assurance.

The compensation systems in most businesses today represent another inhibiting influence. Based on the same obsolete methods originally employed in our government, these systems reward managers for increasing their budgets and for enlarging their staffs. As a result of this uneconomic approach to compensation, each year the government takes more and more of our gross national product instead of its economic share. A well-known secretary of state once made the following statement:

Although the years ahead will be unusually dangerous, we cannot pursue peace at any price. There are things we Americans must be willing to fight for. This republic was formed by armed conflict for the freedom and the liberties we enjoy today—we must understand that. We must structure our policy under that credible and justifiable premise.

If a professional or consultant were to paraphrase this secretary of state, the statement would probably read as follows:

Although the years ahead will be dangerous for professional managers and consultants, their integrity will demand that the pursuit of peace and of pay at any price is unacceptable. There are things that we professional managers and consultants must be willing to fight for. The American economic system was built by entrepreneurial minds whose foundation of ethics greatly exceeded the size of their egos. These entrepreneurs of for-profit enterprises operated in a free market system that rewarded the competent. The system did not encourage the incompetent with government-sponsored economic favoritism, unemployment, and welfare. These entrepreneurial founders were the cause of our abundance today. This inherited abundance is being shamefully wasted today by the mindless bureaucratic traditional managers who prevail. The numbers of this populus must be reduced, and eventually the extreme traditional mind should cease to exist. We must understand this! We must structure and aggressively implement professional management systems under this credible and justifiable premise.

Confucius said, "Men who think in different ways do not plan together." But I say they can, as long as both are honest and have truth as their first priority. With this common foundation, traditional and professional managers can work as a team in support of the organization's best interest, which is to maximize the performance of the enterprise and the work satisfaction of its employees. In this case, the art of compromise is important and constructive. On the other hand, if there is no such common foundation, and if a sound compromise cannot be reached, then a constructive war of mind sets is probably in order.

Theory X and Theory Y The differences between traditional and professional managers are perhaps best defined by the Theory X and Theory Y schools of thought. These two extreme styles of management were described by Douglas McGregor in his book, *The Human Side of Enterprise.* According to McGregor, the Theory X type of manager lives by the following principles:

1. The average human being has an inherent dislike for work and will avoid it if possible.

2. Because of this human characteristic of dislike for work, most people must be coerced, controlled, directed, or threatened with punishment to get them to put forth adequate effort toward the achievement of organizational objectives.

3. The average human being prefers to be directed, wishes to avoid responsibility, has relatively little ambition, and, above all, wants security.

The climate resulting from this type of managerial style would probably be dictatorial in nature with stringent controls. Possibly, all the planning and management would be done by a "one-man show." Obviously, individual growth would be limited in this climate, and the motivating techniques used would probably be "hire-and-fire," together with the "small carrot and large stick."

The other type of manager, which McGregor describes as Theory Y, operates on the following basis:

1. The expenditure of physical and mental effort in work is as natural as play or rest.

2. External control and the threat of punishment are not the only means for bringing about effort toward organizational objectives. People will exercise self-direction and self-control in the service of objectives to which they are committed.

3. Commitment to objectives is a function of the rewards associated with their achievement.

4. The average human being learns, under proper conditions, not only to accept but to see responsibility.

5. The capacity to exercise a relatively high degree of imagination, ingenuity, and creativity in the solution of organizational problems is widely, not narrowly, distributed in the population.

*See Douglas McGregor, *The Human Side of Enterprise* (New York: McGraw-Hill Book Co.).

124

6. Under the conditions of modern industrial life, the intellectual potential of the average human being is only partially utilized.

In this type of organization, the climate would be considerably more positive than in a Theory X firm, simply because the boss believes in people and assumes they desire to grow and to have the ability to do so.

How important is it to understand Theory X and Theory Y? If McGregor was right, then it is vital to the organization's survival. McGregor felt that any manager who could not successfully practice Theory Y would probably, along with his or her organization, eventually cease to exist.

Is McGregor right? On the surface, it might seem not, since ironically, even today, the most common managerial approach leans toward Theory X. Yet the companies that have mastered Theory Y management have been able to attract and keep the best managers at a remarkably high productivity level. Their results show that Theory Y enables their members to make measurable contributions to the company's profit, growth, satisfaction, and position of leadership. A case in point: Robert Townsend, in *Up the Organization,* attributed his success at the Avis Corporation primarily to the implementation of Theory Y.

Perhaps the best test of the "practicability" of Theory X and Theory Y is to ask yourself which type of manager you would prefer to work for. The next step is to profile the climates generated by the X and Y styles, and then see which company you would want to be part of. While the choice is not as black-or-white as Theory X or Y would seem to be, you would still probably lean toward the Theory Y kind of approach and climate.

Profile of a Professional Manager

What is a professional? How are "pros" distinguished from amateurs? How can you become more professional in the conduct of your life?

As a professional manager, you should develop an approach to thinking, analysis, decision making, and action that sets you apart from amateurs. As a "pro," you are set off from amateurs by your distinctive characteristics, philosophies, views toward evaluation, and approaches to learning.

This is not to say that pros are stamped out of a common mold. They need not all look alike to qualify as professionals. For example, many of the most famous platform personalities in the world attend the annual convention of the National Speakers Association, along with the several hundred other speakers—some seasoned and some shiny new. Represented at this convention are all sorts of personalities, physiques, and perspectives. All races, religions, and ages are abundantly represented. Some of the speakers are good looking, some not so good looking. Others are tall or short, slim or plump. Both men and women participate in leading roles during the meetings, and everyone seems to participate actively in the challenging schedule of meetings and events.

Yet despite this great diversity, two basic groups became increasingly clear. Before long, you could identify individuals by which group they either belonged to or were moving toward. The two groups? The amateurs and the professionals. By reasons of some basic characteristic, each attendee quickly communicated a mental image, like a lighted sign, that flashed, "I am an amateur" or "I am a pro." Professionalism or amateurism is something from within the person.

Nonetheless, certain characteristics help to distinquish the pros from the amateurs. A listing of them can apply to individuals regardless of their type of work, their industry, or their profession. Such a list, in fact, can be a valuable tool for those who analyze themselves for self-improvement. In addition, it can also be formatted as a handy checklist for gaining insight into others.

The ten most common characteristics that separate the two groups are as follows:

1. Perhaps the most basic difference is that amateurs are anxious to tell you about themselves and about their activities, while the pros ask about you and show a keen interest in what you are doing.

2. The professional person realizes that our two ears and one mouth indicate that we should do twice as much listening as talking. The amateur does a great deal more talking than listening. By comparison to the professionals, amateurs have very little to say. Frequently they have had one year of experience twenty times instead of twenty years of growth. They excel in detailing the unimportant.

3. Amateurs focus on what they want or on what strengths they have. This sales orientation becomes particularly obvious when compared to the professional's marketing approach, which first diagnoses needs, and then organizes

and tailors the supporting conversation, services, and material to meet those needs. This outside/inside thrust enables the pro to be vastly more successful than the amateur in the marketplace, as well as in interpersonal relationships.

4. Amateurs are go-getters. Preoccupied with getting everything they can, they emphasize the help they need from you. The professional person asks, "How can I be of help to you?" The pro, as a go-giver, is recognized to be a generous person.

5. Amateurs have a win/lose competitive attitude. Professionals have a win/win philosophy, competing against themselves and not against others.

6. A pro favors a participative approach. Decisions are made primarily on a consensus basis by those who may contribute to the decision-making process or who are affected by the decisions made. An amateur will find security in an autocratic management style, with the emphasis on confrontation and management by clout.

7. Perhaps one of the most striking differences between an amateur and the professional is the absence or presence of a sound philosophy. A sound philosophy provides a positive self-image, which results in a positive attitude, clear direction, and a healthy balance of the whole person. In the absence of a sound philosophy, a negative attitude frequently translates into increasing morbidity and despair, due to a lack of self-respect and direction.

8. Amateurs don't have the self-discipline or objectives required to establish a consistent self-development program. The result is obsolescence.

9. Amateurs have only surface knowledge. Since their knowledge is not deep, they tend to be a jack-of-all-trades and a master of none. Yet the demand in any field is for master craftsmen of their trade. Professionals respond to such needs with a program of concentrated, continual self-development in a selected, focused field. As a result, they establish in-depth knowledge, capabilities, and skills through their standards of excellence, hard work, and constant practice. The pro knows that there are no shortcuts to excellence, only detours that dissipate their energies and results.

10. By reason of their commitment to excellence and dis-cipline, pros emerge as leaders in their chosen fields. To do so, they develop the skills required to plan their work inde-pendently and work their plan. As a result, they become superior time managers—able to manage change to advan-tage, while amateurs allow change to manage them.

This list of characteristics provides an excellent basis for areas to work on and to improve in, as part of a professional self-development program. All individuals have the capacity and oppor-tunity to become professionals, as long as they have the necessary desire, commitment, and self-discipline. Review Figure 7–1, and score yourself on your own professionalism.

PHILOSOPHY OF A PROFESSIONAL

Philosophy has been defined as a:

> love of wisdom or knowledge; a study of the processes govern-ing thought and conduct; the general principles or laws of a field of knowledge, activity, etc.; the mental balance believed to result from a study of human morals, character, and behavior.

The philosophy of either an individual or an organization sets the tone for all its activities, communications, priorities, and efforts. Professional managers, who look forward to Monday as an exciting challenge, must have a strong philosophical undergirding to develop the skills necessary for success in their chosen fields.

Yet a solid philosophy does not develop haphazardly. You need self-inspection, reflection, and understanding. Perhaps most impor-tant, a high self-esteem is the foundation of any reasonable, prac-tical, and effective philosophy. Those people who make progress toward the achievement of professional management can attribute a large portion of their success to their self-images. Why are self-images so important? As people develop stronger self-esteem, they are better able to accept change, to tolerate inconsistency, and to open themselves to innovation and growth. These are people who are "actualizing," that is, who base their lives and actions on awareness, personal development, honesty, and trust. This actualizing approach to life gives its practitioners great personal power—the power to put philosophy into action.

FIGURE 7–1. Ten common characteristics of a pro

Characteristics of an Amateur	Characteristics of a Professional
1. Is self-oriented.	1. Is oriented toward others.
2. Talks more than listens.	2. Listens at least twice as much as talking.
3. Sales oriented-inside/outside.	3. Marketing oriented-outside/inside.
4. Go-getter—helps self.	4. Go-giver—helps others.
5. Competitive—win/lose.	5. Supportive—win/lose.
6. Autocratic—confronts.	6. Participative—consensus.
7. Lacks philosophy and direction, resulting in negative attitude.	7. Has philosophy, direction, balance resulting in positive attitude.
8. Surface knowledge—no self-development program.	8. Deep knowledge—consistent self-development program.
9. Tendency toward obsolescence and being a follower.	9. Anticipates and manges change, pursues excellence, becomes a recognized leader.
10. No plan—poor time management—needs supervision.	10. Independently plans work and works plan—good time manager—strong self-discipline.

To measure your own or someone else's profile, add up the number of professional characteristics that you feel apply to yourself or to someone else. Then multiply this total by ten and place the total score on the following scale:

Amateur	Beginning Pro	Semi-Pro	Professional
0 points	25 points	50 points	75 points 100 points

A person's philosophy is therefore at the core of that individual's basic thoughts, attitudes, and actions, which all together comprise the personality. To some, philosophy is the expression of a person's very soul, communicated in the form of fundamental beliefs, ideas, and convictions, along with the grounds for them. You may have observed that individuals with similar philosophies become friends in a matter of hours, while others remain strangers all their lives, regardless of the time spent together. Perhaps you can see why people with radically different philosophies find it so difficult to get along and to work together. Their thinking processes are not different; such individuals just differ in their basic philosophies. Differing philosophies have contributed to the termination of employees, pushed along the dissolution of marriages, and even caused wars.

Yet a weak philosophy cannot lend support to a clearly defined plan. Without a clearcut philosophy, individuals, organizations, and even nations achieve only minimal accomplishments.

Yet, ironically, the government in the United States is founded on the tension between two diametrically opposed philosophies: the rule of the majority versus the rights of the individual. This type of government was born of the hope that a balance between these two opposing philosophies would produce better results than a favoring of one over the other. Today the trend toward big government, big education, and big organization, however, is increasingly apparent—as is its unfavorable impact on individuals. Many people in this country are now of the opinion that the country is declining, that it lacks leadership and direction, and that it has an apathetic attitude toward the basic philosophies that were the foundation for making the United States great.

Correspondingly, organizations often contain strong conflicts between opposing management philosophies. Yet despite the many apparent varieties of philosophies and of managerial styles, two very basic ones seem to prevail: the administrator's and the builder's philosophies. A profile of each, shown in Figure 7–2, could be continued indefinitely, but these ten characteristics provide ample insight into the opposing philosophies, as well as into the resulting styles of management that evolve from them.

The Traditional Versus Professional Manager

What sort of manager are you? Traditional? Professional? To make up a profile on yourself, review the following fifty characteristics of managers (Figure 7–3). Circle the entry number for the description that best fits you. Then add up the numbers circled under the right hand column and multiply your total by two. Compare the result with the ratings on the PMI Mind Set Profile Scale (Figure 7–4).

For example, if you circled 42 items under "Professional Manager/Consultant," you would have a rating of 84 (42 × 2). With that rating, you would be considered to have the professional manager's mind set, since you fall within the 75- to 100-percent range on the right-hand end of the scale. Within the range are included only two percent of American business management, only one percent of US government management, and less than one percent of US educational management.

When working with this profile, keep a few points in mind. First, the actual list of characteristics is much longer than fifty entries. Also, the list changes, and it will probably never be

130

FIGURE 7–2. Administrator's versus builder's philosophy

The Administrator	The Builder
1. Doesn't believe in people.	1. Has faith in people and deals with them as individuals and teams.
2. Emphasizes strong central control and decision making; expands bureaucracy.	2. Favors working through others with decentralized decision making and shared control.
3. Maximizes short-run profits; manages momentum; lacks creativity; resists change.	3. Maximizes long-term growth with optimum profits; manages potential; is imaginative; manages change to advantage.
4. Autocratic (Theory X) style of management.	4. particpative, supportive (Theory Y) style of management.
5. Utilizes win/lose approaches—demands the best deal.	5. Utilizes win/win approaches—works toward establishing a fair deal.
6. Depends only on self; does not delegate to others; self-centered.	6. Trusts others and emphasizes delegation and the development of others.
7. Does the thinking for others; feels superior to others.	7. Teaches others to think for themselves; uses team-approach.
8. Wants to be indispensable; activity-oriented.	8. Develops qualified backups; results-oriented.
9. Keeps information and plans to self.	9. Establishes systems for sharing information and plans.
10. Exploitative and opportunistic in nature; tends toward being a bureaucrat; reacts, fights fires.	10. A builder in nature with perspective, perseverance, and a desire to keep opportunities ahead of the growing resources; tends towards being an entrepreneur; anticipates, and prevents problems.

"complete." Second, like the list, the persons reading the list are changing all the time toward whichever end of the scale seems more advantageous and compatible. Third, you can rarely be productive while at either extreme on the scale. Finally, many individuals range up and down the scale, depending on circumstances, with the result that their behavior seems confusing to others because of its inconsistency. In reality, this irregularity reflects changes in life, changes in circumstances, and changes in purpose, as persons better understand themselves, their real situation, and their dreams for the future. This analysis provides the insight into the gap between where they are and where they want to be.

Keep in mind also that the traditional and the professional mind sets represent extreme views of the same situation. Neither type is a "bad" or a "perfect" person. Both may consider themselves ethical, and both may be equally sharp mentally. Both are merely the net products of their philosophies, intellects, experiences, and disciplines. In a sense, both mind sets have been conditioned to be what they are, to think the way they do. They just play the same game in different ways. Yet despite the polarity of the two mind sets, they can and should seek a way to work together. Although the resultant working realtionship may be difficult, each may learn from the other. And each may have the opportunity to gain a more balanced perspective.

The alternative to working together is, of course, working apart from—or worse, against—each other. This sort of extremism is at best myopic, because it is out of touch with reality. At its worst, it leads not to construction but to wars. Indeed, many business wars between managers arise from the differences between their mind sets. The conflict can be a contest of the minds (a win/win learning experience) or a mindless battle (a win/lose firing or resigning experience).

So, with cooperation and progress always as its aim, Planagement® research, development, and experience over the past quarter-century have led to one all-important conclusion (among many others): People can change if they so choose. Another complementary observation has been that certain behavioral patterns and results occur when people of different mind sets work together. For example, let's take the boss-subordinate relationship:

1. If both are in the 0- to 25-percent range, then very little progress is achieved, because one is a carbon copy of the other. About the most exciting time for these two bureaucrats is when they periodically check the carbons against the originals.

2. If a person in the 25-percent range works for a person in the 65-percent range, the relationship usually provides a good deal of learning from each other. These two produce very good results.

3. If a person with a 70-percent score works for a person with a 20-percent score, they have problems. The subordinate feels great frustration, and his or her results are limited at best. At some time the subordinate chooses to leave for a more compatible and supportive situation. If the subordinate stays, he

FIGURE 7–3. PMI© mind set profile number 1

Traditional Manager/Consultant	Professional Manager/Consultant
1. Tends to play the traditional and popular business game to maximize profit and compensation. Money is the name of the game. Put own best interests ahead of agreements made. Policy determines honesty.	1. Has integrity and will do what's right regardless of economic consequences. Honesty is the name of the game. Lives up to and beyond agreements. Honesty determines policy.
2. Focuses on the bottom line—manages effects.	2. Focuses on building the asset that controls all other assets—manages the causes.
3. Emphasizes short-term profits. Exploiter. Profit at the expense of growth.	3. Emphasizes perpetual profitability. Builder. Profits balanced with growth.
4. Builds with after-tax dollars. Maximizes taxes and growth of the public sector.	4. Retains earnings in the private sector and builds with before-tax dollars. Maximizes growth of the private sector.
5. Is a bureaucrat and breeds bureaucrats to manage momentum. Avoids risks. Seeks security, limited ethics. Lets external circumstances dominate. Survival is the name of the game.	5. Is an entrepreneur and attracts and retains entrepreneurial builders to manage potential. Loves a challenge. Has the ethics and guts to take calculated risks. Strives for excellence. Internal integrity controls external circumstances.
6. Profits are the end result. Measures success primarily in dollars.	6. Profits are the means to the end result. Measures success in freedom and work enjoyment, with dollars as a by-product.
7. Doesn't want to learn. Defensive with a closed mind. Not growing—a self-image of brilliance. Has learned all he or she wants to know. Moving backwards.	7. Eager to l(earn). Open mind. Constantly growing to a higher level on more important things. A self-image of being a student. Knows he or she has much to learn. Moving forward.

The living PMI Mind Set Profile is an expression of current thinking and attitudes as they relate to extreme traditional and professional views. This profile is proprietary to the Professional Management Institute and may not be reproduced in whole or in part in any form without the express written permission of PMI. This profile will be updated annually by PMI Founders, friends of the institute. Planagers® and PMI Consultants' consolidated input based on a combination of research, opinion and experience. The *PMI Mind Set Measurement System* © includes this profile, PMI's Mind Set Profile Scale, evaluation formulas, and annual update report. The system is provided to PMI members as part of their membership benefits and sold to others who wish to use this tool to evaluate themselves, their managers and employees, their organizations, and their industries.

FIGURE 7-3. (continued)

Traditional Manager/Consultant	Professional Manager/Consultant
8. Selfish. Self-centered. Wants all he or she can get. Sells what he or she has regardless of customer's needs. Political in nature. Sees power of job.	8. Wants to spread the wealth. Uses and is supportive of sound professional franchise and multilevel marketing approaches. Marketing orientation to provide what customer needs. Nature is to perform. Sees responsibilities in job.
9. Doesn't know difference between profit, profitability, and growth. quantity-oriented.	9. Has an organizational philosophy and structure that is designed to maximize profits, growth and profitability. Quality first, quantity second.
10. Finds pleasure and security in historical events and quantitative techniques based on history, such as extrapolative forecasting. Fearful of the future and uncomfortable with today. Fights change. Wants continuity.	10. Loves life and is excited about the anticipated future and manages it very well. Has a living plan supported with an ability and a management system to consistently manage inconsistent situations in a way that produces constant gain. Is regarded as a change agent. Demands challenge.
11. Knows what's wrong and exploits it. Sees the worst in others and exploits them, giving the least possible while doing it.	11. Identifies what's right and builds on it. Sees the best in others while giving the best he or she has.
12. Loves detail—80/20. May be efficient in doing the wrong thing well. Hodgepodge of systems going nowhere.	12. Has a system to identify and concentrate on the 20 percent of the elements that control 80 percent of the results. Is effective and does the right thing, as well as efficient in doing things right. Has clear, sound direction and priorities.
13. Uses only Systematics© . Manages by objectives. Tactical orientation.	13. Uses Systematics© with Synergistic Sequencing© Manages by judgment and toward objectives. Strategic orientation.

FIGURE 7–3.   (continued)

Traditional Manager/Consultant	Professional Manager/Consultant
14. Knows all the answers. Talks twice as much with one mouth.	14. Knows the right questions. Listens twice as much with two ears.
15. Talks about the profit system but doesn't understand it. Win/lose philosophy. Judges success on external trappings. Insists on the best deal.	15. Understands the profit system and actively supports it. Win/win philosophy. Determines success on internal factors. Establishes a fair deal.
16. Immersed in repetition and detail. Manages momentum. Opportunities fall behind resources.	16. Very Creative ©and concentrates on opportunities in order of their measured importance. Manages potential. Opportunities are always ahead of the growing resources, including the human resource.
17. Does the thinking for everyone. Puts limits on self and others. Discourages different ideas and approaches. "Not-invented-here" syndrome. Has to be author of everything. Plagiarizes.	17. Teaches people to think for themselves. A no-limit person. Builds others. Welcomes the new, the better, the different, regardless of source and ownership. gives recognition to authors. Researches.
18. Doesn't manage by example. Says one thing, does another. Do what I say, not what I do.	18. Does manage by example. Philosophy and actions are consistent and mutually supportive.
19. Management by clout. Autocratic style. a bully in a china shop. Must control. Mistakes are not tolerated. Tears people down. Pride only in own accomplishments.	19. Operates on the authority of earned prestige. Participative supportive style. Tough minded. Mistakes are tolerated as a recognized part of the learning process. Builds people up. Pride in others' accomplishments. Tends toward Theory 7.
20. Is the substance. Wants to be the focal point. Me-oriented. Takes credit. Makes working relationship decisions on external factors, such as sex, race, age, and the like. Must work with compatible but subor-	20. Shawdow of the substance. Operates as a catalyst. Others-oriented. Gives credit. Establishes working relationships based on mind set. Would prefer to work for a mind that would represent a learning and pro-

FIGURE 7–3. (continued)

Traditional Manager/Consultant	Professional Manager/Consultant
dite mind set. Wants people to be like him or her. Builds own self-esteem by reducing others' self-esteem.	ductive experience regardless of sex, race, religion, age, and so on. Wants people to be like themselves, and assits them to reach their potential. Enhances others' self-esteem.
21. Pyramid organizational structure and approach. Sees top jobs as power. Politician. Tells rather than sells.	21. Supportive organization structure, which turns the pyramid upside-down and focuses on entrepreneurial profitability centers at all levels of management. See all jobs as responsibilities. Statesman. Sells rather than tells.
22. Communications down. Manipulative in nature and communications frequently lack integrity. Believes truth is a matter of opinion.	22. Guidelines down, communications up. Open, honest communicator. Believes the truth is the truth.
23. Avoids measurement. Makes work work. Keeps plans a secret and not in writing.	23. Demands measurement. Makes work fun. Develops sound written plans and communicates them so they can be supported and improved.
24. Compensates according to activity and compatibility. Buys loyalty and respect. Gives salary points on size of budgets and number of people managed.	24. Creatively compensates based on results and performance. Earns loyalty and respect. Increased compensation is based on increased productivity.
25. Ego is larger than the ethical base. Only-if-you-win philosophy. Losing is unthinkable. Me-first priority.	25. The ethical base is so much larger than the ego that traditional managers think the professional manager is an idealist. Win/win philosophy. It's not whether you win or lose, it's how you play the game. Company-first priority.

The living PMI Mind Set Profile is an expression of current thinking and attitudes as they relate to extreme traditional and professional views. This profile is proprietary to the Professional Management Institute and may not be reproduced in whole or in part in any form without the express written permission of PMI. This profile will be updated annually by PMI Founders, friends of the institute. Planagers® and PMI Consultants' consolidated input based on a combination of research, opinion and experience. The *PMI Mind Set Measurement System* © includes this profile, PMI's Mind Set Profile Scale, evaluation formulas, and annual update report. The system is provided to PMI members as part of their membership benefits and sold to others who wish to use this tool to evaluate themselves, their managers and employees, their organizations, and their industries.

FIGURE 7–3.   (continued)

Traditional Manager/Consultant	Professional Manager/Consultant
26. Declining productivity with traditional bottom-line performance. Does the expedient. Must always be right. Looks for a scapegoat when wrong.	26. Increasing productivity with vastly superior bottom-line performance. Does the right thing. Must always be honest. Admits mistakes and takes blame.
27. Does the job because of good pay. Wallet feeds the mind. Maximizes the economic fruit of his or her labor.	27. Loves work and loves the job and consideres compensation as a by-product. The labor is the fruit far beyond the economics.
28. Says what he or she does. Doesn't say what he or she means.	28. Does what he or she says. Means what he or she says. Open communicator.
29. Understands the art of compromise and acts on it. Maximizes economic results dominates integrity.	29. Understands and seeks the truth and builds from it. Makes decisions based on the truth, the whole truth, and nothing but the truth.
30. Provides what is wanted. Popularity over performance.	30. Provides what is needed. Must perform with integrity. Performance over popularity.
31. Acts, then thinks. chops less and less wood, expending more effort with no time to sharpen the ax.	31. Thinks, then acts. Sharpens ax on a scheduled basis and chops more wood with less effort as a result.
32. Lack of a philosophy, which results in a lack of direction, in inconsistent action, and in confusion.	32. Has a strong philosophy and acts consistently in support of a clear-cut grand design.
33. Reacts to crisis and fires. Lives the life of a thermometer. Spends time as he or she has to with limited or no freedom.	33. Anticipates through the development of a strong diagnostic skill. Lives the life of a thermostat. Spends time as he or she wants to with ultimate freedom.

The living PMI Mind Set Profile is an expression of current thinking and attitudes as they relate to extreme traditional and professional views. This profile is proprietary to the Professional Management Institute and may not be reproduced in whole or in part in any form without the express written permission of PMI. This profile will be updated annually by PMI Founders, friends of the institute. Planagers® and PMI Consultants' consolidated input based on a combination of research, opinion and experience. The *PMI Mind Set Measurement System* © includes this profile, PMI's Mind Set Profile Scale, evaluation formulas, and annual update report. The system is provided to PMI members as part of their membership benefits and sold to others who wish to use this tool to evaluate themselves, their managers and employees, their organizations, and their industries.

FIGURE 7–3. (continued)

Traditional Manager/Consultant	Professional Manager/Consultant
34. Lacks a management system or keeps it internally for job security reasons. Wants to be indispensable.	34. Implements a teachable professional planning mangement system at all levels. Wants to be very dispensable.
35. Limited delegation, resists developing back-ups. Is insecure in job. Fears being replaced or passed by others. Works over others.	35. Wants to develop backups who can do his or her job better. Intelligent maximum delegation. Secure in job and wants to advance to next job. Works through and in support of others.
36. Fearful. Low self-esteem. Negative attitude. Know what's wrong. Focuses on problems.	36. Enthusiastic. High self-esteem. Positive attitude. Knows what's right. Focuses on opportunities.
37. Bored. Resources exceed ideas. May have good mind but does not use it well. Resists thinking. Does not apply common sense.	37. Excited and creative. Always more ideas than resources. Exercises and builds the mind through thinking. Applies common sense.
38. Does not trust people. Keeps them in their place. Sets up heavy-handed, tight controls.	38. Trusts people. Brings out the angel from within for unlimited growth of others. A light touch is frequently the right touch.
39. Hires weak people and pays the least possible. Works with turkeys.	39. Hires the best, pays the best, and does the best. Flies with eagles.
40. Likes dependent people who need a lot of supervision and their work planned for them. Manipulates parts of the person to self-advantage. Doesn't understand human beings and human potential. Thinks he or she can motivate others. Boss over others.	40. Demands independent people who can plan their work and work their plan with limited or no supervision. Deals honestly with the whole person. Understands human beings and the human potential. Knows that motivation is an internal process. Teaches others to lead themselves.

The living PMI Mind Set Profile is an expression of current thinking and attitudes as they relate to extreme traditional and professional views. This profile is proprietary to the Professional Management Institute and may not be reproduced in whole or in part in any form without the express written permission of PMI. This profile will be updated annually by PMI Founders, friends of the institute. Planagers® and PMI Consultants' consolidated input based on a combination of research, opinion and experience. The *PMI Mind Set Measurement System* © includes this profile, PMI's Mind Set Profile Scale, evaluation formulas, and annual update report. The system is provided to PMI members as part of their membership benefits and sold to others who wish to use this tool to evaluate themselves, their managers and employees, their organizations, and their industries.

FIGURE 7–3. (continued)

Traditional Manager/Consultant	Professional Manager/Consultant
41. Systems control the people. "Yours-is-not-to-reason-why" approach. Resists others' ideas. Follows past policies and procedures. cedures.	41. People control and improve the systems. Welcomes and encourages others ideas. Develops better policies and procedures.
42. The human asset is not on the balance sheet. Thing-oriented.	42. The human asset is on the management balance sheet. People-oriented.
43. Manages everything and hopes the results meet the extrapolated, rigid numbers forecast.	43. Uses a few key operating ratios and assumptions to control the desired results, which are three-level forecasted on a rolling basis that manages change to advantage.
44. Carrot-and-stick, Theory-X management (autocratic) style.	44. Understands human behavior and works toward Theory Y (participative supportive), while managing Theory B ©(a balance).
45. Thinks the management information system (MIS) is a big ego computer and never gets it working as a result.	45. Establishes a sound management information system manually. Then supports it, as appropriate, with as small computers as possible.
46. Tries to do everything. Ends up doing much less than was possible. Management by crisis.	46. Very selective, intelligent delegation. Focuses on the few elements that control most of the results. Management by exception.
47. Time and change dominate. Procrastinates, wastes time. Not considerate of others' time. Undependable. Not on time.	47. Time and change are managed. Gets more things done on time with better results. Equates time with life. Very considerate of others time. Dependably on time.
48. Prejudiced, makes people decisions on the basis of external factors such as sex,	48. Objective, makes people decisions on internal factors such as positive self-

FIGURE 7–3. (continued)

Traditional Manager/Consultant	Professional Manager/Consultant
age, race, religion, conformity, and the like. Judges by appearance.	esteem, sound philosophy, integrity, quality of mind, mind set, discipline, performance, and so on. Judges by internal quality and integrity.
49. Competes against others. Wants to fight and eliminate the pro.	49. Competes against self with a growing potential. Prefers not to work with the extreme traditional mind.
50. Typically typical. Won't rock the boat.	50. Dares to be different if it is the right thing to do.

The living PMI Mind Set Profile is an expression of current thinking and attitudes as they relate to extreme traditional and professional views. This profile is proprietary to the Professional Management Institute and may not be reproduced in whole or in part in any form without the express written permission of PMI. This profile will be updated annually by PMI Founders, friends of the institute. Planagers® and PMI Consultants' consolidated input based on a combination of research, opinion and experience. The *PMI Mind Set Measurement System* © includes this profile, PMI's Mind Set Profile Scale, evaluation formulas, and annual update report. The system is provided to PMI members as part of their membership benefits and sold to others who wish to use this tool to evaluate themselves, their managers and employees, their organizations, and their industries.

or she feels "sold-out" to the establishment. When this tragic event occurs, the mind set of the subordinate moves toward the superior's mind set because the wallet is feeding the mind. Eventually, both tell others in the higher percentages that they don't know how to play the business game. In the end, one bureaucrat retires and a carbon copy becomes the replacement. Tradition remains intact, and a continuing declining momentum is assured.

4. If two peers work together who are at the extreme opposite ends of the PMI Mind Set Scale, then normally the best thing is for them to ignore each other, if each is contributing to the organization.

5. If the boss and subordinate are at opposite ends of the mind set scale, then the result may be a war of minds.

Unfortunately, the resolution of such relationships is not always happy. On occasion, the usually outnumbered professional manager is unable to put his or her plan into action. In one such case,

FIGURE 7-4. PMI© mind set profile scale

1980 Estimate

	Traditional Manager/Consultant	Weak Trend Toward Professional Manager/Consultant	Strong Trend Toward Professional Manager/Consultant	Professional Manager/Consultant
0%	25%	50%	75%	100%
*13.13%				
*US Consolidated Position on Scale Based on Consolidation	60%	30%	8%	2%
**US Government	75%	20%	4%	1%
of	90%	9%	.8%	.2%

**US Management
**US Government
**US Eduation

*Consolidation of US management is 15.2%, of US government is 13.1%, and of US education is 11.1%.

© 1981 by Professional Management Institute. The PMI Mind Set Scale will be updated annually on July 4 and, together with an annual report, will be provided to PMI members and sold to others. This scale is proprietary to PMI and may not be reproduced in whole or in part in any form without the express written permission of PMI.

141

for example, the board of a client organization was extremely traditional, while its president was very professional. When the president submitted a plan to the board for maximizing the company's growth and viability, the board turned it down flat. It had other interests. Since they were already getting a good return on their investments, they really didn't care whether the company grew. The president fought the board for the survival of the multimillion dollar company and for the sake of its six hundred employees whose futures rested on the decision. The end result was that the president was fired in a traditionally cruel way.

Who was right? Who was wrong? Your response depends on your mind set. In my opinion, both the president and the board should have developed a plan together that would balance both views. This balance usually results in maximizing profitability, which produces twice as much on the bottom line.

So we end as we began. Managers must be willing to fight for the principles of professionalism. They must be committed to developing the skills and disciplines that allow them to tap the tremendous potential of the mind.

Inverting the the Top-Down Organizational Theory

To implement the professional approach, some of the traditional views of organizations and of supervisor-subordinate relationships obviously have to change. For many years, traditional managers have viewed their organization as a pyramid dedicated to insuring the survival of the fittest (Figure 7–5). This view frequently caused a

FIGURE 7–5. Traditional Organization View

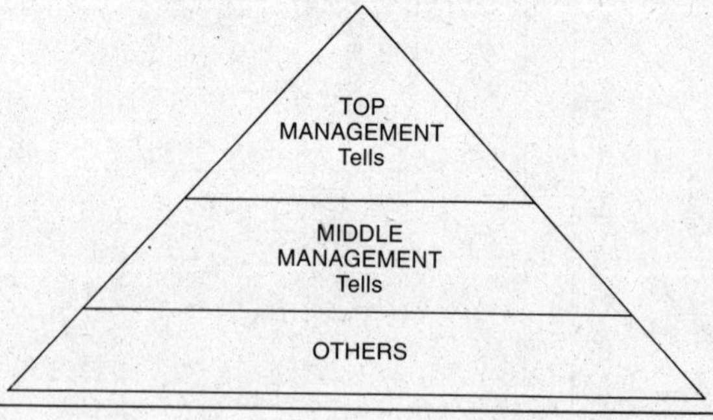

negative climate in which people were in competition with each other and the best politician often won the promotions. Managers viewed themselves as being "over" their subordinates, with a power to hire, fire, promote, and demote.

To create a positive internal climate, you need a different view of organization and management, illustrated by the inverse pyramid concept in Figure 7-6. In this view, each individual becomes a focal point of his or her own business and future. The primary role of managers is to act in support of those individuals for whom they have managerial responsibility. In addition, top management has a responsibility to the organization to allocate and reallocate constantly the organization's assets (people, money, materials, time, and space) according to the rank-oriented practical potentials of contributions to the organization's growth and profits. They have a simultaneous responsibility to the individuals who *are* the organization.

This supportive organization and management approach requires management's commitment to organizational growth and development, through the growth and development of the individuals comprising the organization. The overall results of implementing this approach are viewed as a managerial "masterpiece," created by releasing the many angels from within the individuals of the organization.

Taking Steps Toward a Positive Climate   Some managers are reluctant to teach, not because they don't know how, but because they don't see the reason for doing so. Their attitude arises from the same working environment that causes them to focus on weaknesses rather than on strengths, to criticize rather than

FIGURE 7–6. Supportive Management Organization Structure

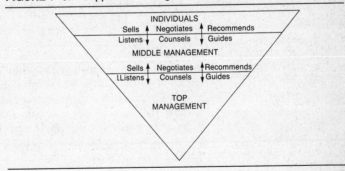

FIGURE 7-7. Entrepreneurial Organization Structure

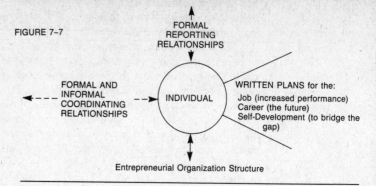

FIGURE 7-7

FORMAL
REPORTING
RELATIONSHIPS

FORMAL AND
INFORMAL
COORDINATING
RELATIONSHIPS

INDIVIDUAL

WRITTEN PLANS for the:

Job (increased performance)
Career (the future)
Self-Development (to bridge the gap)

Entrepreneurial Organization Structure

praise, and to seek out the negative rather than the positive aspects of any situation. Their attitude results from the same mind set that makes them think they can "motivate" people, rather than enabling people to motivate themselves. In short, they lack a truly positive organizational climate.

Here's a case in point. At a management meeting, one of the middle managers was asked for his definition of management. Without blinking, he said, "Management is watching a subordinate make a mistake and then giving him the devil for it." Everyone had a good laugh. The sad part, though, was that the manager was serious.

This sort of negative approach just doesn't work very well. In fact, it often destroys productivity. The far better approach, from the point of view of motivation, is to establish a thoroughly positive working climate. Following are a few steps you might consider as a means of creating that kind of climate for the sake of better teaching results. This five-step approach contributes toward establishing a positive climate supported with a sound management development system:

1. Adopt a positive philosophy and attitude toward other people. Always look for the best in others and believe that they want to improve their performance. Make every effort to identify the "angel" that exists in each person, and then work toward releasing that angel from within.

2. Create an organization that provides increased opportunities through a commitment and a plan for continuous growth, based on the practical potential of the organization.

144

3. Identify as clearly as possible each individual's career plan for the future. Almost every person has a dream for the future. This dream provides a primary motive for taking action. If the person's supervisor in particular and the organization in general will work to support that dream, then the individual becomes highly motivated (motive-acted) to work in support of the manager and the organization.

4. Frequently there is a gap between where persons are today and where they would like to be in the future. Profile that gap, so you can tailor a development program to overcome the gap. Here again, the person must be intimately involved in identifying the gap and in the consequent development program, because true development is self-development. Like motivation, self-development is an internal process. Both the career plan and development program should be put into writing and made part of the individual's personnel file.

5. Hold periodic performance and progress reviews with each individual. During these reviews, base the agenda on the exceptions to the job, career, and development plans. The supervisor and subordinate should work as a team in mutual support to make these plans a living reality, while managing changes or exceptions to the plans. In addition, having the right person in the right job is an essential element for successfully accomplishing this part of the system.

A professional management system must be based on the builder's philosophy—that is, on the principle that the growth and development of an organization depend directly on the growth and development of the individuals who are the organization. So in this system, the individual becomes the planning/management center for his or her own area of responsibility. And the objective of each manager is to do more, in less time, and with better results—through sound planning, improved communications, and control by exception. The system balances individual freedom against the discipline of the organization's defined direction and the management of its potential. As a result, management is better able to manage change, thus contributing to improved profits and to accelerated growth, as well as to increased job and personal satisfaction.

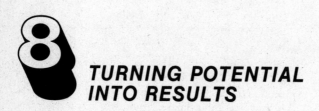

TURNING POTENTIAL INTO RESULTS

"Profitable" human progress requires translating goals into realities. Hence, the ultimate test of such progress is our ability to transform our plans into tangible results.

Yet managers and other individuals never fail to surprise me by asking, "What do you mean by 'potential'?" Let's be clear on what we mean: *Potential is the best or the worst that you can conceive in a given situation and that you could develop into actuality.*

Defined this way, potential may be considered the essential element in calculating payoff and risk. Most organizations have far more opportunities than they do resources. Since they cannot pursue all opportunities at once, they must decide which are the most likely to produce the greatest gain. Potential, as the best that could happen, is the gain. As the worst that could happen, it may be regarded as the risk. Therefore, the management that understands potential has the conceptual basis for gauging the gain versus risk in any opportunity.

The Three-Level Forecast: Simple but Productive

For some managers, taking the step from the conceptual to the actual is difficult. How do you establish a system for turning potential into actuality? One technique for developing such a system is the three-level forecast. This method is very simple and basic; yet it is very productive. Here's how it works.

STEP 1: GUESSTIMATE THE BEST

Guesstimate the very best that could possibly be achieved if everything went right. To that guesstimate, attach a probability of occurrence, which is really up to your feel for the situation. For example, perhaps your judgment is that you have, say, a 60-percent chance of the "best's" happening. The projection, then, would have a 60-percent probability of success. (See Figure 8–1.)

STEP 2: GUESSTIMATE THE WORST

Guesstimate the very worst that could happen if everything that could go wrong did go wrong. You have to be realistic in your appraisal of the momentum and inflation of the existing situation. To

FIGURE 8–1. The three-level forecast

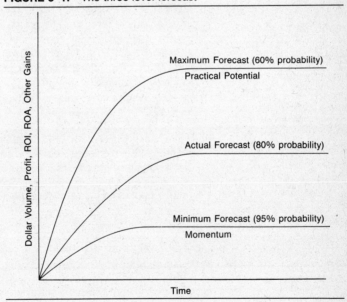

this analysis, you would then affix a projection of the possibility of failure. This judgment call could run as high as a 90-percent probability in some situations.

STEP 3: MAKE A PRACTICAL FORECAST

Based on these two extremes, the potential best and the potential worst, you are now in a position to *make a practical forecast* somewhere in between the best and the worst. Very often an 80 percent factor will be used to establish the practical or actual forecast.

BENEFITS

This three-level forecasting technique almost always produces three major benefits.

1. The actual forecasts are usually more accurate than they are with other methods.

2. In good (or at least stable) times, the outcome usually exceeds the actual forecast. The reason is this: when the potential best is identified, people can channel their efforts toward achieving it, and their results frequently exceed their expectations. Put another way, if people try to do better than what's expected, they almost always do better. The key is to identify something potentially better than what is expected.

3. In bad times, the three-level forecasting technique provides an anticipating capability, because the worst case has been identified before it happens. Such an early warning system can then be backed up with contingency plans, and you monitor and control outcomes by using key operating ratios.

The three-level forecast produces its greatest benefits when applied consistently to all situations, as opposed to one-shot applications here and there. While the gains in a very bad situation may be less than expected, the end result is still usually much closer to the actual forecast than the minimum forecast. Hence, the gain is almost always better with this technique than without it. In addition, if enough good potentials are achieved, they tend in the long term to more than offset the bad. The overall long-range result is that the actual forecast is achieved or even exceeded, even in poor times.

EXAMPLE

One three-level forecasting technique—actually used by an organization—has been proved to yield consistently forecasts within a 3-percent accuracy of the actual outcomes. Frankly, no one knows why this formula works, but, according to the management team as reported by their management consultant, the formula has worked consistently within this accuracy. Here's how it operates:

1. The *maximum* volume that could come out of a sales territory is identified as, say, $100,000.
2. Based on the existing momentum plus inflation, the *lowest* volume that could be produced—the assured volume—is established at, say, $75,000.
3. Based on these two guesstimates, the probable or actual forecast is $85,000.
4. The salesperson or manager who is responsible for the territory then guesstimates the probability of attaining each of the three levels of the forecast. These guesstimates are subjected to the calculations shown in Table 8–1.

TABLE 8–1. Three-level forecast calculations

Levels	Forecasted Amounts	Probability of Attainment	Related Calculation	Resulting Multiplier
Maximum	$100,000	40%	40%/205%	19.5%
Minimum	75,000	90%	90%/205%	44%
Probable	85,000	75%	75%/205%	35.5%
Total		205%		100%

5. Each forecasted amount is then multiplied by the resulting multiplier from this table. The sum total of the three resulting figures becomes the actual forecast:

$100,000 × 19.5% = $19,500
75,000 × 44% = 33,000
85,000 × 36.5% = 31,025
TOTAL $83,525

The actual forecast is $83,525.00.

For a number of years, the actual forecasts produced by this method have fallen within a plus or minus 3-percent accuracy of the outcome! A little skepticism about the validity of this formula is not surprising. Why it works may be difficult to understand but it does seem to work. Perhaps the reason has to do with logic of the inter-relationships.

THE LIVING-ROLLING FORECAST

The three-level forecast—or any single-level forecast for that matter—should be supplemented with what I call a "living-rolling forecast." For example, you start out with an in-depth forecast for five quarters. As time goes by, you update the forecast each quarter by dropping a quarter and adding a quarter. Thus, your forecast would always extend one year into the future, and it would constantly incorporate changing conditions.

The three-level rolling forecasting technique can be used by salespersons, by sales managers, and by general managers. In fact, it may be employed by any managers or any individuals who have the responsibility or inclination to forecast a continuing gain from their own activities and who wish to manage their potential, while controlling their results, in these rapidly changing times.

A Formula for Managing Your Future into Reality

Understanding potential this way is important for another reason with a larger dimension. There are two ways to approach the future.

The first—and probably the most common way—is to let the future take care of itself. Take what comes and hope for the best. Individuals and organizations that adopt this approach are usually satisfied to manage their own momentum, allowing change to manage them. Some include serendipity, which is the art of finding things not sought for, in their philosophy. These companies need the ability to react fast for them to continue—and sometimes to survive.

150

The second approach is just the opposite of the first. In this approach, companies use a formal planning/management method in a systematic way to project the desired future in clear visual form. Supporting assets are then allocated to make that future a reality.

Obviously, this second approach recognizes and capitalizes on potential, while the first ignores, and therefore wastes, it! The formal planning/management method *makes* human progress possible, while the serendipitous approach merely lets things happen.

The Planagement® approach involves using tailored systems, services, and materials designed to support organizations or individuals in making their future happen as soon as practically possible. This experience has shown convincingly that the future can be planned and managed. It has also proved that organizations or individuals who formally plan and manage their future are much better off psychologically and economically than those who do not.

The following formula is proof of these facts. But just reading it over will prove little, if anything. You should try to put this formula into action in your life, on your job. The only way to prove its value to yourself is through your own experience. Here is the step-by-step method, which you follow in Figure 8-2.

STEP 1: DEFINE GROWTH EXPECTATIONS

Make a basic philosophical decision about how you define growth. You have three basic choices: to decline growth, to stay the same (that is, to manage momentum), or to cause growth. Assuming you elect to grow, then the next step is to define growth as precisely and as measurably as possible. For example:

> To increase the assets employed by at least 15 percent each year, and also to increase the return on assets by at least 15 percent each year.

Assuming a compounded basis, the organization in this example has defined its growth as doubling its assets employed (its size) and quadrupling its profits in five years.

STEP 2: IDENTIFY OPPORTUNITIES

Identify (plan and diagnose) the existing opportunities in rank-order of their practical potentials.

152

FIGURE 8-2. Systems approach for managing the future

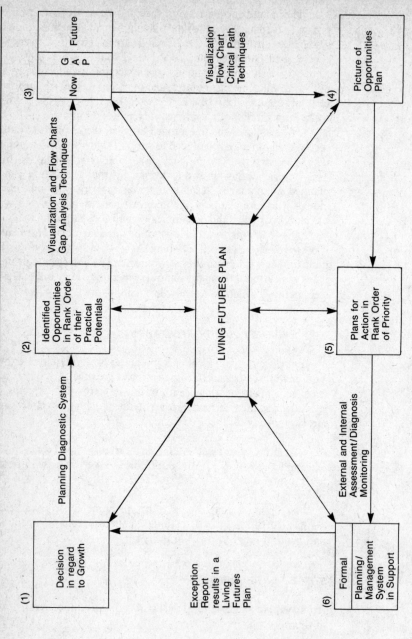

© 1977, Planagement Inc.

STEP 3: COMPARE PRESENT AND FUTURE

Clearly picture where you are now as compared to the future you desire. Identify the gaps you must bridge to capitalize on the opportunities and to achieve their potential.

STEP 4: CHART THE POTENTIALS

Make a picture plan of the opportunities, noting their values based on their practical potentials. Include the interrelationsips of these potentials, noting the timing (completion dates) and the assets (including skills and dollars) required to reach them.

STEP 5: WRITE A PLAN

Establish a written plan of action for each opportunity that you identify.

STEP 6: DEVELOP THE PLAN

Develop a formal planning/management system in support of your action plans. These plans should tell you when certain assets (resources) are needed. They should include a feedback system that anticipates, manages, and incorporates change on a consistent basis (exception reporting). You can employ many other supporting concepts and techniques in support of your futures plan, to measure precisely its gain, both qualitatively and quantitatively.

The Crescent Company Example

Here is an example of one organization's approach to its futures planning.

1. The Crescent Company is committed to sound growth, as measured by increasing assets employed by at least 15 percent annually and by increasing return on those assets by at least 15 percent annually.
2. Within the next five years, at least 30 percent of the company's volume and profit will come from sources that do not exist now.

153

3. The company's forecast is summarized in Figure 9-3.

4. To accomplish this growth profitability forecast, the firm will bridge the existing gaps through a task- and project-oriented organizational structure based on profit centers. One of the profit centers will be a futures division, under the control of a Vice President/General Manager. A summary of the futures division plan is presented in Figure 8-4, followed by the Crescent Company's commitment to sound growth.

FIGURE 8–3. The Crescent Company forecast

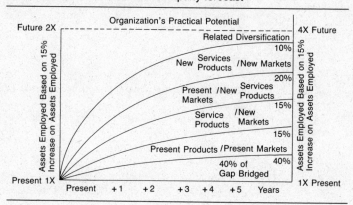

FIGURE 8–4. The Crescent Company's futures division plan

April 10, 19XX

Futures Division Proposal (one page plan summary)

Planagement
Plan Sec-
tions

(WHAT)   1. The *Futures Division* would be a *profit center,* as would each business area within this Division.

2. The *orientation* of this Division would be *"outside-inside"* due to the ever increasing magnitude, impact, and speed of external changes. The need to quickly take ideas to profits has also increased.

3. The *strength* of this Division would be in the creative services it provides and in the profits it generates. The

(cont.)

FIGURE 8–4. (continued)

weakness would be the possible duplication of effort. *Action* would be to generate a profit within this Division so that any duplication would be duplication of profits and growth.

4. The key *assumption* is that the needed personnel for this Division are presently within the organization and will be made available as required. This need will not increase costs, but is rather a reallocation of existing resources for increased effectiveness.

(WHERE) 5. The prime *objective* would be to prove the value of this Division by generating a recognized profit by December 31, 19XX. An additional objective would be to have by 19XX at least 30 percent of the organization's volume and profits come from product, services, and activities which are not now existing within the organization.

(HOW) 6. *Strategy* basic to generating a profit would be to sell services and establish one profit center of at least $XMM with an ROAEBT of at least X percent.

7. *Alternatives* would include: doing this at a Division level before Corporate; establishing it at a subsidiary level; or not doing it as a part-time responsibility of administrative services or of another staff component.

(WHEN) 8. *Schedule:* Approval 9/1/XX; Operational 12/31/XX; Profitable 12/31/XX.

(WHO) 9. *Organization:* Four people plus two temporary located in Chicago.

(COST) 10. *Annual Budget:* $250,000 exclusive of overhead. (Budget is the investment.)

(PROFIT)
(WHY)

(RESULTS)

11. *Results:* ROAEBT XX% or $XMM direct before-tax profit, plus $XXMM indirect profits through services, plus a pool of Entrepreneurial General Managers. This will be a key to providing Future Managers, in addition to profit, growth, and diversification contributions.

Crescent Company's commitment to sound growth

1. To have a management philosophy and organization mission supported with specific objectives and programs of action that will accomplish at least the following:

   a. Insure the healthy continuity of the organization through sound growth based on achievement of practical potentials.

(cont.)

155

b. Provide challenging, satisfying opportunities that keep ahead of constantly growing and developing employees.

c. Generate a return to stockholders that will provide as good or better an investment opportunity as any practical alternative available to them.

2. In order to accomplish the missions of the organization, it will be necessary to clearly identify and manage the practical potential of the company and continuously identify new opportunities so that sound growth will be achieved.

3. To support sound growth, the required systems will need to be developed and successfully established. These systems include the following:

a. A sound, living/planning/management decision making/control/update system.

b. A system for managing and developing the human resources, resulting in having the right person in the right job with the right plan and right skills at all management levels, including top management.

c. Work in support of subordinates so that their career plans will be achieved within the framework of the organization guideline plans and needs.

d. Provide a positive organization climate that will stimulate creativity, spark the entrepreneurial spirit and maximize motivation, growth and development within each employee.

e. An asset management system that will attract, allocate and reallocate the assets required to identify and exploit an ever-increasing list of sound growth with improving profitability.

4. To possess the needed personal discipline and commitment required to put the organization's best results constantly ahead of your own.

For those who aspire to be top managers, the above—admittedly incomplete—list of standards should start to provide an insight into the rigorous, demanding requirement of a top management job.

For those in top management, the above standards provide a beginning check list to objectively measure your own understanding of and achievement in meeting management's awesome responsibilities.

5. The company's basic strategy in support of this commitment to sound growth will be as follows:

a. To utilize the Planagement® system throughout the organization with individuals (career plans), jobs (other than routine), and all organizational units.

b. To adopt asset management, with assets (resources) defined as people, money, materials, time, and space.

c. To create a creative compensation program that is directly related to contribution and results, supported with both "hard" and "soft" dollars.

d. To follow the before-distribution concept rather than profit before tax, to provide before-tax dollars in support of our futures plan. These dollars will fuel our growth much more rapidly than after-tax dollars. Sound formal plans are a must for successful accomplishment.

e. To invest primarily in the human asset with development and training programs, supported with a Planager® of Human Resource Development function and in-house capability. The rationale is that such a focus offers the greatest leverage in both psychological (positive internal climate) and economic terms. While the human asset cost may be "depreciated" 100 percent each year, the company benefits with that 90-percent gain in productivity for a small 1-percent improvement in effectiveness and efficiency.

f. To keep the job and business opportunities ahead of available assets in general and ahead of the growing human asset in particular. This is the primary responsibility of top management and the Futures Division.

g. Input into the futures plan will be made from all plans within the company with the communication flow as shown in Figure 8–5.

FIGURE 8–5. Communications flow for the Crescent Company

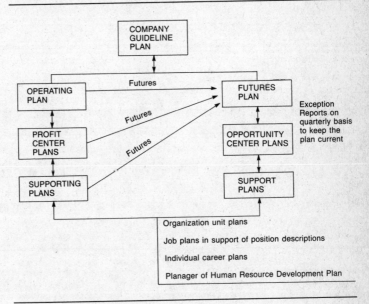

157

From Potential to Results

Understanding potential is a fundamental requirement for good management. If you do not recognize the best and worst possible cases in your undertakings, then you are working blind. Further, if you do not attach priorities to potentials as you see them, you can easily dissipate your efforts by pursuing either too many or the "wrong" opportunities. On the other hand, if you grasp the magnitude of the techniques and systems in this chapter, you become able to plan your own future, as well as that of your organization and, in perhaps small but concrete ways, of your country.

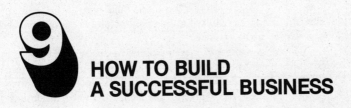

HOW TO BUILD
A SUCCESSFUL BUSINESS

Most career-oriented individuals have had thoughts about going into business for themselves. Very few ever convert this dream into actual practice because they are well aware of risk. If you have a step-by-step formula, however, for creating a business of your own, you not only reduce the risk of failure, but you also start to build the confidence, commitment, and direction required to make the business a successful reality.

While the formula suggested in this chapter may be employed in the start-up of a fully autonomous enterprise—what we normally think of when we "start a business"—it may also be used within the context of a going concern. Many an enlightened organization is creating a futures division and opening up venture team opportunities for its entrepreneurially oriented employees, so they will continue to contribute to the growth of the organization. The employer's rationale is that, in the absence of such opportunity, such individuals may feel they have to leave to build their dreams and their futures. So, applying the entrepreneurial formula within an established enterprise greatly reduces risk because of the inherent strengths within the concerned company.

STEP 1: BE SURE YOU'RE COMMITTED

This first step is perhaps the hardest: *Make sure you're an entrepreneur,* because you'll need the commitment. Over a ten-year period, for each hundred enterprises that started up, ninety-nine failed. Of those failures, 95 percent were ascribed to poor management; because the persons starting these enterprises were not entrepreneurs in the first place.

Do you have the characteristics required to be an entrepreneur? A myriad of organizations, books, workshops, seminars, articles, and tests are designed to help you determine your answer. Check yourself out. See if you *really* want to build an enterprise and if you have the strengths required to do so successfully. Finding out early is well worth the investment.

The Planagement® system, which has been applied with many established entrepreneurs, takes a simplified approach. It presents a profile/position description of an ideal entrepreneur (Figure 9-1). As a preliminary step to an entrepreneurial venture, you should write a profile of yourself and compare it to the ideal profile. Your purpose is to see how high a correlation exists between your personal profile and the ideal. If this entrepreneurial profile does not "fit" you, then the following steps to building an enterprise probably do not apply to you. On the other hand, should you have a high correlation with the entrepreneur's profile, and if you feel confident that you can handle the job (position) of being a business-starter, then you should implement the following steps:

STEP 2: BECOME A QUALIFIED MANAGER

The next step is to become qualified as a professional manager. The business arena has less and less tolerance for amateurs, including gifted amateurs who are not willing to pay the price required to join the elite group of successful entrepreneurs. In today's constantly changing times, if you do not have a professional management system and capability at start-up, then your venture's probability of failure is greatly increased.

FIGURE 9–1. Entrepreneur's profile/position description

Summary Statement: A person who is willing and able to assume the risk of planning, managing, controling, and building an enterprise.

1. This person should be a generalist, capable of understanding and implementing the functions of research and development, marketing and sales, financing and accounting, production and employee relations, and general management with supporting systems and controls.

2. The scope of this position involves generating sound ideas and concepts through all the steps required to make them a successfully operating reality and consistent practice.

Purpose (Mission) of an Entrepreneur:

1. This person should have a focused commitment to building a dream into reality. The purpose of this person's life at times is such a powerful, encompassing driving force that all actions subordinate and act in support of the entrepreneur's "grand design."

2. The results of the "grand design" vary with individual entrepreneurs, but the common characteristic is that the entrepreneur clearly knows the results to be achieved and clearly communicates them to associates.

Nature of an Entrepreneur:

1. Strong-willed, demanding of self and others, independent, demands freedom.

2. Able to see the big picture and the pieces that comprise it.

3. Unlimited energy, constant stamina.

4. Total dedication to the dream, to the enterprise, and to the people that build it.

5. Self-disciplined in the critical areas that contribute to the progress of the enterprise.

6. Sensitive to time, timing, and time management.

7. Doing, action-oriented.

8. Ability to make needed, timely decisions.

9. Flexible with the ability to handle many different things well.

10. Persevering, does not give up.

11. Physically and psychologically able to handle stress, pressure, risk, and failure; constant bounce-back capability.

12. A high tolerance for being alone.

Capability/Resources and Skills:

1. Capabilities:
   a. able to plan, manage, control and build;
   b. ability to get along with people; and

(cont.)

FIGURE 9–1. (continued)

    c. ability to manage consistently inconsistent situations in a way that produces constant gain.

2. Resources:

    a. a good mind;

    b. a sound body; and

    c. a firm faith in something, whether that something is God, themselves, an idea, the future, or the power of positive thinking. Whatever it is, the faith must be strong.

3. Skills:

    a. diagnostic, analytical, planning, and control;

    b. general management of all basic functions;

    c. time management;

    d. people skills;

    e. communication, including listening; and

    f. delegation and development.

Products/Services Produced by the Entrepreneur:

1. Products:

    a. a written plan for the enterprise;

    b. building the organization and systems required to accomplish the plan of the enterprise; and

    c. accumulation of the assets (resources), including the people, dollars, materials, machines, space, systems, and the like, all needed to accomplish the plan of the enterprise.

2. Services:

    a. a general management of the enterprise; and

    b. providing the center for decision making, communications, coordination, consolidation, and control.

Markets Served by the Entrepreneur and the Needs of These Markets:

1. The enterprise's publics comprise the markets served and include:

    a. *Stockholders,* who need security of investment and to be kept informed.

    b. *Employees,* who need security, recognition, and knowledge that there is a good future with the enterprise, which is supportive to their career and financial aspirations.

    c. *Customers,* who need a reliable source of supply that meets their present and future needs with maximum value based on cost/ benefit and ease of doing business.

    d. *Suppliers,* who need to be paid on time and to serve a growing enterprise.

    e. *Community,* which needs to have more jobs made available and increased revenues from financially healthy companies.

(cont.)

FIGURE 9–1. (continued)

    f. *Industry,* which needs to be supportive with active participation in associations, plus ideas for improving performance.

    g. *Private enterprise,* which needs to have new businesses established and soundly growing with a long-term future.

2. The entrepreneur needs to establish and to build an enterprise that provides the vehicle required to move the concept into reality.

Customers Served and the Key Influence That Causes Them to Buy:

1. The principal customers of the entrepreneur are those individuals and situations that are supportive to the entrepreneur's purpose and dream.

2. The key influence that causes them to buy is a clear understanding of and compatibility with the purpose and the dream.

Performance Standards of an Entrepreneur:

1. to move the concept into reality,

2. to achieve the missions of the enterprise,

3. to develop and accomplish a written plan for the enterprise,

4. to attract and accumulate the required resources (assets) to accomplish the plan,

5. to establish the organization and systems required to accomplish the plan for the enterprise, and

6. to be able to spend time as you want to, not as you have to.

Organization Relationships:

1. The entrepreneur *reports* to self and to the concept.

2. *Supervision* responsibilities may or may not involve other people, but they always involve supervising the functions required to build an enterprise. Sound, continuous supervision of self is one of the most demanding requirements of a successful entrepreneur.

3. The entrepreneur *coordinates* with the enterprise's various publics.

4. Although frequently a loner, the entrepreneur serves on *committees* that are supportive to the progress of the enterprise.

Accountabilities:

1. The *guidelines* are provided by the concept's requirements to become a reality.

2. *General accountabilities* including the following:

    a. visualizing the concept,

    b. developing and accomplishing the plan that makes the concept reality, and

    c. establishing, managing, and building the enterprise that provides the vehicle for moving the concept into reality.

(cont.)

FIGURE 9-1. (continued)

Specific Accountabilities	Standards of Satisfactory Performance	Percentage of Time
a. Concept and enterprise development, communication, and establishment	A written plan presented and attracting the required resources for implementation.	20
b. General management of the enterprise	Implementation and accomplishment of the written plan kept current through exception reporting.	70
c. To self	Consistently enhance the original concept and add better ones. To be able to spend time as you want to, while achieving personal and professional career plans and a self-development program.	10

How do you know when you're ready? Professional managers can be readily identified by the substance, quality, and professionalism inherent in their practiced system of management. Another objective (and excellent measurement of professional managers) is having a sound formalized planning process, which generates written plans and actions within the constraints of organizational discipline; and the plan must include developing the people required to implement the plan. The Planagement® system provides the entrepreneur with the methods, tools, and a professional manager's approach for maximizing the performance of the business and enjoyment of the work required to build a successful business. The Planagement system is detailed in the book *Planagement®* Moving Concept Into Reality, published by Professional Management Institute, Tulsa, Oklahoma.

STEP 3: MANAGE EACH PHASE

You must be able to understand and manage each phase in establishing a business. See Figure 9-2 for a flow diagram that illustrates these phases.

FIGURE 9-2. Business establishment flow diagram

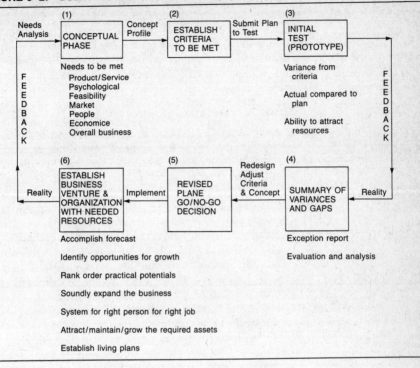

Needs Analysis

(1)
CONCEPTUAL PHASE

Concept Profile

(2)
ESTABLISH CRITERIA TO BE MET

Submit Plan to Test

(3)
INITIAL TEST (PROTOTYPE)

FEEDBACK

Needs to be met
  Product/Service
  Psychological
  Feasibility
  Market
  People
  Economice
  Overall business

Variance from criteria

Actual compared to plan

Ability to attract resources

FEEDBACK

(6)
ESTABLISH BUSINESS VENTURE & ORGANIZATION WITH NEEDED RESOURCES

Reality   Implement

(5)
REVISED PLANE GO/NO-GO DECISION

Redesign Adjust Criteria & Concept

(4)
SUMMARY OF VARIANCES AND GAPS

Reality

Accomplish forecast

Identify opportunities for growth

Rank order practical potentials

Soundly expand the business

System for right person for right job

Attract/maintain/grow the required assets

Establish living plans

Exception report

Evaluation and analysis

STEP 4: ESTABLISH A RESOURCE BASE

As a kind of life-support system for your plan, you must establish a resource base and system that constantly allocates and reallocates the assets appropriately—people, money, materials, time, space, and information. The criterion for professionally managing your assets should be maximizing profitabilty, defined as the gain from the activity—the profit and/or achievement of the mission, balanced with the sound growth of the enterprise. Work satisfaction is also a worthy standard, assuming that the right person is in the right job and that the rewards are based on the specific role played and the contribution made.

To establish such a system, you have to understand that any venture is comprised of five equally important functions, which can provide a sound basis for role identification and the distribution of gains on an equitable basis (Figure 9–3). To maximize profitability and to survive, you must perform and professionally manage all five interest areas: financial investors, entrepreneurs, salespeople, laborers, managers.

Balancing these functions is difficult, because each of the persons representing the functions often feels as though his or her role is the most important and, therefore, entitled to most of the revenues and control. This "must-have-control" syndrome is particularly conspicuous in the financial investors, who want the dividends or high earnings per share to protect their investment. They often use the "lever" of their backing to try to get their way: That is, without financing in a capitalistic society, no venture can get off the ground. This pressure conflicts directly with that of the innovative, freedom-loving entrepreneur who wants to protect and control the dream that the business is built around. The salespeople contend that, without a sale, nothing happens, while the laborers say that, without their function, the product and/or service cannot be delivered. Finally, managers argue that the quality of their management makes the real difference in the quality of enterprise's performance and in the magnitude of the results achieved.

If these functions remain conflicting and competitive, then the chances are excellent that the venture will come to nought and that the entrepreneur's dream will remain only a dream. If the venture is commenced with conflict, it will probably fail in the long run due to the built-in devisiveness.

FIGURE 9–3. The five functions of a venture and the 20/20 formula of distribution

Sequence	Basic Functions	Relationship	Percentage of Distribution*
1	Creative	Inventor, entrepreneur	20
2	Financial	Investor, stockholder	20
3	Marketing	Seller	20
4	Application/ doing	Actual work per- formers, Laborers	20
5	Administration/ management/ operating budget	Managers and staff	20

*Including equity, profit sharing, salary, bonus, dividend, interest, royalty, and so on.

STEP 5: ADOPT A BALANCED PHILOSOPHY

As an entrepreneur, you should adopt the philosophy that all five functions of a business are equally important. You must insure that each of these five critical needs of business are professionally managed and balanced.

Although these five steps provide a guideline, success depends most on the entrepreneur's quality, competence, commitment, determination, persistence and discipline.

Eagles Beware: Ten Reasons Why Companies Fail

Although most top managers realize that their first responsibility is the survival of the enterprise, few formally manage the venture away from the common pitfalls. The following ten reasons for failure—the most common ones—provide you with some guidance, and could actually become a kind of checklist. Unless you manage to avoid making these critical mistakes, you could find your business dream converted into a financial and often psychological nightmare.

1. POOR MANAGEMENT

The most common reason for business failure is poor management. Many entrepreneurs (risk takers) focus on their own unique skills and ideas, with the belief that their commitment is all they need to make their businesses successful. Unfortunately, this belief is a mistake, because you need sound management if the business is to survive and grow. Occasionally, a person gets lucky, and the idea "takes off." But the lucky case is very much the exception.

To live and prosper, you must consistently apply the fundamentals of good management. These fundamentals include:

1. planning and organizing,
2. implementing through disciplined doing and follow up,
3. communications,
4. coordination,
5. delegation,
6. consolidation, and
7. control, with management of change through replanning (closed loop living system).

167

You can learn each of these basic elements of management, developing them as a system through constant practice and eventually acquiring them as a skill.

2. INADEQUATE CAPITAL

Capital shortage, another frequent cause of business failure, is often due to poor planning and poor financial management. A good accouting system is essential, not only for tax purposes, but also for providing you with needed and timely information so you can make sound decisions as required. Almost every business has its good times and bad times. In the good times, the wise manager establishes the financial strength required to move the business forward, while insuring its continued viability when times are tough.

3. INADEQUATE BACKUP

The lack of a qualified backup can doom a business. If the business depends totally on one person, it cannot survive if something happens to take the person away from the business. In addition, few investors are willing to make capital available to a business that depends on just one person for its continuance. A "one-man show" finds borrowing funds almost impossible, unless the business has accumulated tangible and salable assets that can be mortgaged, usually for a fraction of their value.

Another serious problem with a "one-workhorse" business is that the person becomes trapped by the business: The business then controls the person, instead of the person controlling the business. When the enterprise is a person's total life, the real danger is that it will become too demanding. The founder may then find that all his or her time is spent in keeping the business alive, which in turn is slowly sapping the life of its creator.

To avoid this trap, develop at least one qualified backup. Developing backup is often the key to creating a healthy business with a potential for continuity, instead of a personal service enterprise that is the reflection of one person. One of the most crucial decisions a founder must make is whether to create an enterprise that earns one person a living or to build a business that grows and becomes self-dependent, apart from its founder. Most entrepreneurs never let the business grow beyond themselves, and consequently the business' success and life do not extend beyond the capabilities, attention, and health of its founder.

4. LACK OF DELEGATION

Another reason for business failure is that the owner/manager is forced to wear too many hats. Rarely is a person that good at everything that a business requires. An excellent engineer may be a poor salesperson. The outstanding salesperson may have a low tolerance for detail or for the financial aspects of the business. In addition, operating a business these days requires an increasing amount of paperwork and complexity, a great deal of which is caused by constantly expanding government regulations. This paperwork does little but dilute your time and effort. Wearing too many hats often leads to consistently long days and many nights for the owner/manager. Also, some of the fundamental needs of the business may not be met due to a lack of time, a lack of interest, and perhaps a lack of knowledge or competence.

In this situation, delegation becomes essential. A common problem, particularly in the early stages of the business, however, is that you might not have anyone in the organization to whom to delegate. The "too-many-hats" syndrome has caused many entrepreneurs to give up in frustration, after trying to manage a very real overload situation.

5. LACK OF SOUND BUSINESS ADMINISTRATION

Poor internal support systems also contribute to business failures. For example, perhaps an inadequate filing system wastes a lot of time in searching for needed information. Or a weak follow-up system to inquiries results in turning customers off, with the resultant lost business and poor reputation. You have to devote the appropriate amounts of time and money to these and any internal systems, because they are crucially important to successfully operating a business. The consequence of not doing so is a business that is frequently in trouble and at best marginal.

6. LACK OF MARKETING ORIENTATION

The absence of a marketing orientation eventually contributes to creating an obsolescent business that is increasingly unable to compete effectively in the marketplace. With today's rapid changes, an originally good idea may soon become obsolete. A marketing orientation must continually anticipate and identify the needs of the served market, so that the business may organize its resources to meet those needs as well as or better than the competition with acceptable profitability. A business that does not establish this marketing capability may well be a dying entity that finds sales and competition increasingly difficult.

7. LACK OF INNOVATION

A business must have the capacity to come up with always new and better products and services. A product's life cycle used to average over seven years. In today's age of change, it is unusual when a life cycle exceeds three years. Hence, a business must always be developing and improving its products and services. Managers must be able to balance present operations and futures (the new and better). They must allocate time and dollars to stimulate and manage creativity, an acquired skill. All this they must do, even when they are busy and when the business is doing well with its present products and services.

8. POOR TIME MANAGEMENT

Poor time management is probably one of the primary reasons that a business fails. Entrepreneurs are commonly "doing-oriented." Unfortunately, they tend to become so busy chopping wood that they have no time to sharpen their axes. The result is often reduced performance by the manager and the business. Burnout, another real danger, can also change what used to be fun into never-ending work and drudgery. Here again the manager has the opportunity to learn about time management and, with practice, develop the skill to do more in less time with better results.

9. INADEQUATE INTERPERSONAL SKILLS

Unsatisfactory interpersonal skills have killed more businesses than has a lack of technical knowledge. The ability to understand and to get along with people is mandatory if the business is to prosper.

The cost of this shortcoming shows up the greatest in the area of personnel. When you select and place the wrong person in a job, the effects are high turnover and inadequate productivity. One way or the other, whether the personnel go or stay, the losses can be staggering. A newspaper article once reported that, based on a study, more than $482 million are lost by United States businesses every day due to inefficiency. Additional research had indicated that less than 15 percent of an organization's potential is being obtained. This greatest unrealized potential exists, of course, in the human asset, which controls all of the organization's other assets.

Matching the jobs with the people pays in hard dollars. One estimate is that, if all the employees of an organization work just 1 percent smarter, the "bottom line" can be increased by at least 90 percent in twelve to twenty-four months. What you need is a sound human resource development system that places the right person in the right job, with a written job plan for performance improvement and professional development.

10. LACK OF DISCIPLINE

Why would an entrepreneur or focal point manager not give a business the attention it deserves? Why should a business be "ignored" to death? Among the more common causes, perhaps, is that the business has made the owner so wealthy that he or she is no longer motivated to support the business. Boredom is another possibility. Also, if success is being able to do what you want, rather than what you have, to do, the owner of a successful business may no longer *want* to pay a lot of attention to running it. As a success, the owner may choose to do something else.

Whatever the reason, a business that is not tended soon suffers and dies. Establishing, managing, and building a business is hard, demanding work. Unless you are very dedicated to the business, you probably will not have the self-discipline and supporting actions required to keep the business living and healthy.

With an understanding of these ten reasons for business failure, you have a kind of early warning system, which should be helpful in avoiding these common pitfalls to business continuity and growth. You may take positive actions to insure that these causes of business failure are not let go to the extent that the life of the business is threatened. If you accept the challenge of establishing and building a business that grows beyond the capabilities and life of its founder, then you should also accept this primary responsibility.

Making the Going Business Go

You may be a manager for a large corporation or the founder/owner of a small business. Whatever your situation, the elements that go into making a business organization successful are fundamentally the same. Only the details change from case to case.

Concepts and procedures that have worked in numerous situations include:

1. changing over to a participative management style,
2. making meetings more productive, and
3. managing the Synergistics way.

Each suggestion draws its strength from the natural needs of people, as well as from the natural flow of events. Participative management, for example, makes the management team work more efficiently as a whole than it could as isolated individuals, because each member participates or "owns" a piece of the firm's success. Poorly conducted meetings waste not only the individuals' time, but also time that could be used for real cohesiveness and united action. Hence, the waste of time is compounded. When meetings are properly conducted, those same destructive forces turn around and compound the advantages of coming together. The difference is in the planning. Strategic sequencing sets events into motion at times when those events can have their greatest effect—and it prohibits endeavors when circumstances would minimize their results. Finally, the game of Synergistics keeps opportunity always a little ahead of the organization and its constituent individuals, thus using people's natural incentives to achieve to keep the organization at the leading edge of its potential. All these methods have worked over a number of years and with a high degree of success, because they rely on the natural inclinations of people and of events.

Let's look at them one at a time.

Changing Over to Participative Management

Company presidents and founders frequently ask, "How do I build a management team?" Many of these individuals are strong entrepreneurs who have an overpowering tendency to be a one-man show. Somewhere along the way of building their successful business, these hard-driving, forever-working individuals begin to realize that they are starting to run tired. They ask themselves, "Why am I knocking my brains out in this business, just as I was many years ago when I started it?" Unfortunately, they were so busy building a company that they never took the time to build a management team—the backup that could take some of the operating load off the boss. Eventually these top dogs begin to feel a strong need to slow down and to develop a capability within the company that assures its continuity. At this point, they raise the question, "How do I build a management team?"

This is a tough question, not because there is no answer, but because it requires a change in the management style by the top officer. Usually, such a change is very difficult for businesspeople of this kind. The very strengths of entrepreneurs—the drive, the need to be always doing—tends to work against these individuals, against their people, and their companies. Hence these "one-man shows" are frequently unable to meet the toughest challenge they ever faced—that of changing themselves. Yet if they do not face up to it, the chances are that they will work themselves to death and that their companies will often be buried with them.

To build a management team, the entrepreneur must make several basic changes. These changes are difficult, because many of them require of the top manager totally different styles and practices. For example, instead of being a doer, the person at the top has to delegate to key subordinates, so as to develop them and spread out the work. As another example, a reorganization might oblige some of the people who used to report only to "the boss" to report to subordinate managers. In general, this is a frustrating time for one-man operations, because no one is going to manage or do things the same as they do. Furthermore, they are not quite sure what is going on, since they no longer have their fingers in everything. They may wonder if they are losing control of their own companies. Even worse, they may feel that their companies don't need them as much as they once did.

Perhaps the most difficult change to accept takes place in the company's management style, or more particularly in its decision-making process. Up to the point of changes, entrepreneur/founders make all the decisions and take most, if not all, of the needed actions. But then, to build a management team, they must change their style from single deciders (and frequently autocrats) to more of a participant in a larger decision-making procedure. This change in style not only slows down the decision-making process, but it also sometimes yields decisions that are not the ones the boss would have made as the solitary decision-maker. So these ex-autocrats find that supporting these decisions is difficult and even painful, but they need to do so if

173

their new teams are to grow through experience with increased responsibility. To achieve the desired results, entrepreneurs need successfully to establish the proper climate based on mutual trust, respect, and confidence between themselves and their teams, as well as among the team members.

Frankly, many—and perhaps most—entrepreneurs never master the requirements of being leaders instead of bosses. This unfortunate fact is a major reason why only one business out of a hundred continues after its tenth year and why, perhaps, only one out of a thousand celebrates its fifty-year anniversary.

Due to the nature of this change, however, an experienced outside professional counselor or consultant is frequently used to insure the success and smoothness of this crucial transition. In many cases, as the team grows in strength and competence, its members begin to make more decisions and more changes in the company. It becomes increasingly obvious that the company no longer is dependent on one person. As a result, that one person often feels a mixed emotion of pride and loneliness, not unlike seeing a child leave home. There is no question that a management team can be built if—and only if—the top officer is committed to doing so and willing to make the necessary changes.

Assuming that the top officer has made the commitment and is willing to undergo the changes, the following four-step process can be used to ease the pain of this transition from a "one-man band" to a management team approach. While many different approaches might be taken to build a productive management team, our experience has been that this four-step approach gets the job done and produces many measurable benefits to the company, for the entrepreneur, and for the management team.

STEP ONE: SELECT INDIVIDUALS

First, select the individuals who will be part of the team, and establish a formal planning/management team who will meet on a regularly scheduled basis.

STEP TWO: WRITE A COMPANY GUIDELINE

Develop a written company guideline plan. Based on our own Planagement® practice, the average time required to develop this plan is two days of the team's time.

STEP THREE: DEVELOP INDIVIDUAL SUPPORTING PLANS

This is a very important step: Have each member of the team develop a supporting plan based on his or her job. The usual time required to get this done, including the development of a comprehensive position description, is from one-half to one day. This supporting plan should include:

1. the individuals' personal career aspirations,
2. any identified development gaps that may exist between themselves and their present jobs, and
3. any gaps that will exist between them and their future jobs.

Once these gaps are identified—and assuming they can be bridged in a practical way—design and implement the appropriately tailored training and development programs. This third step might also include a professional evaluation of the individuals, to insure that the right person is in the right job now and in the future.

STEP FOUR: CONSOLIDATE AND INTEGRATE

Consolidate the individual plans, and then integrate the consolidated plan with the original company guideline plan. Thus the team itself establishes a sound company plan. Each member of the team has a specific responsibility within the plan, and all its members have a shared responsibility for making the plan happen.

Productive Meetings
One of the most frustrating and costly wastes in organizations arises from unproductive committee meetings. Whenever management reviews its committee practices—in almost any firm—the inevitable complaint is "What a waste of time and money." Why does management tolerate this enormous waste? The best explanation seems to be that managers are so busy with their jobs that they do not apply professional management methods to their committee work. Unproductive committees present a serious problem. An ineffective, inefficient manager who produces poor results is an obvious cost to a firm; but when these managers work together as a committee, then their costs are compounded and mutiplied many times. But that adverse affect can be "flipped," so to speak, to compound in the favor of, rather than against, the organization. Committees, when properly man-

175

aged, can not only be highly supportive to the participative style of management, but they can also produce measurably better results than could individuals working independently. Well conducted committees also provide the organization with the occasion for spontaneous management development, each member learning from the others on the team. Functional thinking is supplemented with team thinking, and all the thinking is based soundly on an increased understanding of all the members' functions.

Like so many other areas in business, meetings can be made more productive simply by following a simple procedure. In addition, however, you can sidestep all the poor connotations associated with the term "committee" by replacing the word with "team." Most people consider a *team* as a group of individuals organized for a particular purpose of achievement—a concept that should be inherent in any committee, but that often is not. The "team" concept brings that message across. Here are the steps for making meetings more productive:

STEP 1: ESTABLISH A TEAM CHARTER

Establish a team charter. This charter should answer three questions:

1. What is the purpose of the team?
2. What are the results to be accomplished?
3. Can those results be justified on a measured cost/benefit basis?

If these three questions cannot be answered affirmatively, then the team should not be formed, because its cost will exceed its benefit. Assuming the answers are all positive, the resulting charter should be published in writing and referenced frequently.

STEP 2: SELECT TEAM MEMBERS

Select team members. With a clear-cut team charter, you should be able easily to identify candidates for team membership. Questions about each candidate should include:

1. Why is this person needed?
2. What will be the person's contribution?

3. Can the team function without this individual's participation. If not, why?
4. What is the cost/benefit of this person's participation?

Again, if the questions do not generate a favorable answer, the person under consideration should probably not participate on the team.

STEP 3: ESTABLISH AGENDA

Establish results-oriented agendas. Each meeting of the team should be supported with and guided by a formally written, results-oriented agenda. This agenda should clearly communicate the timing of the meeting, the subjects (or topics) to be covered, and the results to be achieved. Planagers® and their clients have used the results-oriented form show in Figure 9–4.

STEP 4: SELECT CHAIRPERSON

Select a competent chairperson. While the results-oriented agenda assists in structuring and timing the meeting, the leader influences its pace, flavor, and productivity. Surprisingly, very few individuals have been taught how to organize and manage a successful meeting, even though the skill is extremely important to the professional manager. The team leader has considerable impact on the results achieved from the meeting.

Specifically how to manage a successful meeting, a subject in itself, is well beyond the scope of this section. Many books, written courses, and workshops are available on this subject, including some developed by Planagement®, Inc.'s Individual Development Center. Suffice it to say that a skillful chairperson needs to master several basic and important skills, which are not only invaluable when managing a meeting, but which are also of crucial importance in being a good manager. One good way to develop these important skills among the team members is to have rotating chairpersons.

STEP 5: DOCUMENT THE MEETINGS

Document the meetings. Insofar as human beings remember less than 10 percent of what they hear, meetings must be carefully docu-

FIGURE 9–4. Planagement® results-oriented agenda form

PLANNING DATA

	This	Replace
File:		
Date:		
Page:	of	of

ORIGINATOR:
DISTRIBUTION:
SUBJECT: __RESULTS ORIENTED AGENDA__   TEAM: _____
Date of Meeting _____ Time _____ to _____ Location _____
Chairperson _____   Documentor _____
Reference:

Time From To	Subject	Results to be Achieved	Actual Results	*Reference Minutes

Comments:

mented by written minutes. The results-oriented agenda helps in this respect, but is only one small step. For full records of the meeting, a skilled documentor should be appointed to take down meeting highlights. Minutes notes in the margins should indicate action items, along with the names of those assigned and the agreed on dates of completion. In addition, a results-oriented agenda for the next meeting should be attached to the minutes; this new agenda is developed by the team at the conclusion of the current meeting.

When properly applied, these five basic steps contribute to making teams and meetings more productive. They also offer the occasion not only for a professional management system, but also for a vitally important skill-building program in the development of professional managers.

The Management Game of Synergistics©

Success might be defined as getting what you want, and *happiness* might be equated with wanting what you have. But is success or happiness a state or a process? Can people achieve success and happiness once and for all? For some people, the answer is yes; they reach a comfortable stopping point in their lives. They have all they want.

Or do people *maintain* success and happiness through an ongoing effort? For those who say yes, the game of Synergistics provides the opportunity for the growth that these people need. For these people, *growth* means continually setting achievement targets at successively higher levels and with respect to more important matters. In this respect, growth makes success and happiness a never-ending journey—not a destination. When such people achieve success and happiness, they become frustrated and bored. When the challenge of growth ends, so do their lives. So for them, synergistics can be a life-saver—a new lease on life. Synergistics can cause a person to be reborn. It can make an old or retired person "young" again. It can rapidly replace despair with an insatiable zest for life. It can awaken a mind long asleep.

Properly played, synergistics can also produce enormous gains in profit and growth in organizations. Even in a nonprofit organization, synergistics lend an expanded purpose and an increasingly larger contribution through the achievement of a consistently higher purpose. The reason is that organizations, like individuals, have a hierarchy of needs, which are illustrated in Figure 9-5. The game of Synergistics represents the fulfilment of an important phase in this hierarchy.

FIGURE 9–5. Organizational hierarchy of needs

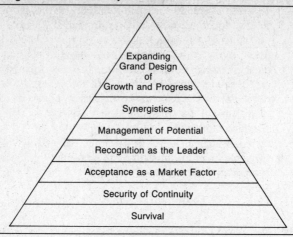

From what, specifically, does the game of Synergistics derive? It takes its name from the term "synergy," which is defined as "independent parts working together in such a manner that the whole is greater than the sum of its parts." In way of analogy, synergy is like the pearl created by the grain of sand that becomes imbedded in the meat of an oyster. Synergistics itself is a management process that insures that the whole will always be increasingly greater than the sum of its parts. The result of synergistics is the creation of an expanding grand design of growth and progress.

How exactly does this game work? Perhaps the easiest way to answer that question is by means of several examples. The following situations provide insight into how synergistics was applied in a number of situations, from that of a small local manufacturer with less than $10 million in sales to that of a large multibillion-dollar global conglomerate.

EXAMPLE 1: A SMALL BUSINESS

The president of a small family-owned manufacturing company, who had been in his present business all his life, was bored. He had inherited the business from his father, who had inherited the business from his father, who had founded it in the early 1900s. With his extensive experience and good mind, the president had done a superior job in running the business. The firm was not only profitable, but it was also respected by its customers and suppliers as a leader in its field. The family had earned a good living from the business, and the family tradition assumed that loyalty would insure business continuity from father to child. Although the current president was close to his fortieth birthday, he wanted no celebration, because he was unchallenged in his work and consequently a very unhappy person.

Desperately bored, he sought a new challenge. To improve further productivity and to develop stronger second-level managers, the president elected to implement the Planagement® system in his company. During the implementation, the client related his unhappy dilemma and asked if anything could be done about it.

The Planager® in support of this account assured the president that his was not an uncommon problem. He further assured the president that the application of Synergistics had not only solved this type of psychological problem, but that it has also been the basis for expanding financial success. The president elected to adopt Synergistics with the result that he is creating a proprietary professional management system for manufacturing companies, which can be sold as a package in the form of workshops, supporting implementation programs, and self-instructional materials. The business plan for this product line has a forecast that greatly exceeds the revenues of the president's manufacturing company.

In addition, the president is training a qualified backup to run his company, which obviated the need for his most qualified manager to leave the company and go into business for himself. This manager, who was also bored in his job and who felt that his growth was limited, was about the same age as the president and would also have a son entering the business in less than five years.

At this time, the president is very enthusiastic about building and managing this new business, which meets one of the greatest needs of his industry, while providing a new and potentially larger income stream to the family business. He proved the merits of the management package in his own company, which has contributed to solving some long-time problems and to making the company more profitable.

Another Planagement® client is a very large global firm with several billion dollars in sales and over one hundred thousand employees. Management was increasingly dissatisfied with their marginal results, despite a tradition of over one hundred years. Although they were one of the first companies to implement the management-by-objective approach ten years earlier, it was failing. Due to an increasingly dangerous debt-to-equity ratio, the new president had declared that he wanted a professional management system that would rapidly turn this sleeping giant around. After researching and testing over forty management systems from all over the world, they selected the Planagement® system.

Within two years, over ten thousand of their managers were using Planagement®, from the president to the foreman in the plant and the salesperson in the field. In addition, the firm's management has decided to supplement its operations improvement effort for increasing productivity and organizational performance with Planagement's® program of Synergistics. With the results they experienced, which increased profit performance by 90 percent in the first twelve months of implementation, they made a movie about this professional management system entitled "The Pursuit of Excellence." The implementation of Synergistics also produced several new business opportunities with profit and growth potentials far in excess of some of their traditional, mature businesses. In addition, the firm has coupled its acceleration in new product development to its participation in new markets with its present products, all to great advantage.

The company's managers, who gained creative confidence and skills through applying Synergistics, became committed to having at least 15 percent of their volume and profit every five years generated from new capabilities, new businesses, new products, and new services—none of which existed in the year prior to the five-year span. The company formed a Corporate Development (Futures) Department at the Executive Vice President level in support of their expanding grand design of growth and progress.

HOW IT WORKS

The Synergistics process focuses on four primary areas:

1. management philosophy,
2. job responsibility,

3. organizational structure, and

4. formalized systems.

1. *Management Philosophy*. If top management does not want to accept the challenge of managing the company's potential and if they are satisified with the financial rewards generated from the company's established momentum, then they will not be receptive to the implementation of Synergistics. A satisfaction with the status quo brings about an organizational environment that does not tolerate individuals and management methods committed to growth and progress. On the contrary, only a management philosophy that encourages challenge and growth will support the implementation of Synergistics.

2. *Job Responsibility*. Assuming that the managerial philosophy is supportive of the Synergistics process, the next requirement is to make improvement and creativity parts of every manager's job unless the job is strictly routine.

On an individual level, this integration can be accomplished by including productivity improvement and innovation as part of the job description under accountabilities. The job description could also contain:

1. measurable standards of satisfactory performance, stated, for example, as an annual increase of at least 10 percent in productivity and measured by at least a 10-percent decline in the department's budget;

2. a gauge of the manager's accountability in regard to innovation, such as a requirement to introduce at least one new product, service, or idea every six months; and

3. a minimum standard of performance, such as a rule that within three years the new input will be contributing at least a 5-percent income stream (as defined by multiplying 5 percent of the company's last-year total volume and profit).

On an organizational scale, job responsibility is also enhanced by top management's approach to opportunity. One of top management's most important responsibilities is to keep opportunities ahead of the growing assets of the corporation, particularly ahead of the human asset. If management does not "pay attention" in this respect, the strongest managers—those with an entrepreneurial bent—will outgrow the company and in all probability leave it, perhaps even adding to competitive pressure. Synergistics provides top managers with a step-by-step formula for stimulating, identifying, and managing the company's opportunities in the order of their practical potentials. It then provides the techniques and tools for allocating and reallocating assets to these opportunities in the proper order of priority.

On a national level, American business has an obligation to the country's economy. A growing school of thought holds that one of the most important public responsibilities of for-profit companies is to maximize their economic performance and viability. By meeting this responsibility, firms in the private sector enlarge their contribution to achieving a higher standard of living, while providing more and better jobs. The process of Synergistics provides a sound and productive method for meeting this important responsibility and need.

3. *Organization Structure.* Implementing a program of Synergistics in an organization that is not structured properly is difficult. One organizational structure that has proved to be very supportive to managing an organization's potential is shown in Figure 9–6.

FIGURE 9–6. A favorable organizational chart

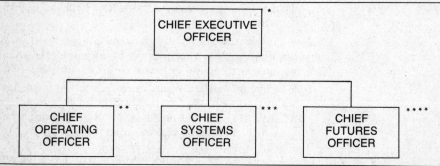

* CEO has the primary responsibility to optimize profitability by allocation and reallocation of assets to the best opportunities prioritized by their practical potentials.

**COO has the primary responsibility to maximize profits as measured by increasing the return on assets employed.

***CSO has the primary responsibility to provide and establish the required management systems for maximizing the organization's performance.

****CFO has the primary responsibility for maximizing growth as measured by increasing the assets employed.

But organizations are not structured in a vacuum. They grow out of the individual needs and interrelationships of the humans who make up the organization. For example, some individuals favor creating new and different systems or products, while most are more comfortable with implementing the existing systems and selling the established products. Those who are thrilled to develop new machines are normally very unhappy if they must also operate and maintain those same machines. Another common human tendency is to favor the familiar. Hence, managers sometimes become so immersed in operations that they have time only for meeting the many operating pressures of their jobs. This reaction is typical among managers, who consequently have little or no time for developing the new and the better.

So a sound approach to organization recognizes the differences among people. It strives to match the right person with the right job so as to take advantage of the individuals' strengths, while meeting the company's needs for increasing both profits and growth.

Several characteristics, however, facilitate the implementation of Synergistics. Open-minded, supportive managers are important, to take advantage of good ideas as they come along. Research and experience has shown that 90 percent of the ideas for operations improvement and growth flow upward, now down. In addition, companies that have successfully delegated at least 80 percent of their operations to level-two and/or level-three managers have generally out-performed companies that are operated from the top. Finally, serendipity, the art of finding wonderful things not sought for, also has a role to play in support of synergistics. And brainstorming techniques frequently contribute to stimulating organizational creativity and the creative skills of the managers.

4. *Formalized Systems.* Synergistics requires formalized systems, such as planning, management and control systems, management information systems, financial systems, administrative and operations systems, human resources management and development systems, productivity improvement systems, marketing systems, product development systems, results-oriented compensation systems, acquisition and divestiture systems, and other systems that meet the needs of the business and those of the managers in the business.

One of the most important systems is a formalized mind development program, whose purpose is to enable all key personnel consistently to work smarter. In reality, one of the primary objectives of Planagement® is just that—to teach people to think and work smart.

The results are greater productivity, a higher degree of promotibility, and increased work satisfaction. By introducing a system of measurement and rewards based on results, work becomes a very productive game in which improvement is the yardstick of accomplishment.

THE "PAYOFF" IS HIGH!

Organizations that have chosen to play the management game of Synergistics have achieved at least a 90-percent bottom line improvement in the first twelve to twenty-four months of implementation. In addition, these organizations' managers have not only experienced rapid growth, but they have also had a lot more fun in their work—to the point that some say, "Thank God it's Monday!" For these high-performing organizations and for their growing individuals, Synergistics is the only game in town.

PROFITABILITY

Profitability is a key to human progress. Although this statement may seem contrary to the popular idea of "obscene profits," we owe our high degree of personal freedom and abundant standard of living to the economic freedom we have experienced in this country. Accordingly, the profitability that I mean is not a short-sighted type of "bottom-line" profit making, but rather the total long-range utilization of important resources.

The difference between short-term profit making and long-term profitability is in managerial emphasis on a balance of profit with growth. To make an immediate profit, managers can do many things that may be detrimental to their organizations in the long run. They manage effects rather than causes, and let causes "manage" them. For true profitability, however, you have to concentrate your efforts on those factors that bring about the balanced results you desire—that is, the causes. Exert your managerial influence on these high-impact factors, and you can achieve both short- and long-term benefits. In effect, you are working for a bottom line, but you are using a much grander balance sheet, which includes such entries as conservation, social responsibility, innovation, risk-taking, human development and stewardship. In general, the quality and magnitude of bottom-line results depend directly on the quality of the organization's management system, as well as on the foresight and planning ability of the managers themselves. Worst of all, our long-term profitability must necessarily suffer if we allow the slump to continue for very long. Hence, productivity is at the root level of the whole urgent issue of profitability and progress. The vital importance of increasing productivity applies to nations, industries, and companies of all sizes, as well as to departments, jobs, projects, and—most of all—individuals.

Truth to tell, at least some individuals have been singled out for productivity improvement. These are blue-collar workers, who have been subjected for years to measurements and planning of the industrial engineer. And, to a large extent, these approaches have worked well. Yet right now, most agree, the United States is in a productivity slump. As a result, our standard of living, which is determined by our productivity, is beginning to slump.

Ironically, in the face of this presently slow-fused disaster, we tend to ignore the productivity of an area that has the far greater potential: that of the white-collar workers, the managers. Why hasn't management been subjected to the industrial engineer's yardstick? One reason is that the managerial job involves dealing with unpredictable people, doing many jobs that are difficult to quantify. Another reason is that management simply does not understand many of the tools and conclusions of the engineer, thus regarding them as suspect.

Managerial Productivity

With so much of the short- and long-term responsibility on their shoulders, you would think that managers' first objective would be to have everyone—themselves and all other personnel—putting out 100 percent. Yet the estimate is that United States businesspersons lose about *$482 million a day* as a result of obsolete work methods and practices. Efficiency in American offices has been estimated at less than 60 percent. Remember that this figure applies only to efficiency—that is, doing things right. Even though we are efficient only a little better than half the time, this estimate says nothing about our effectiveness—that is, whether we are doing the right things!

Yes we are in an overall slump. Perhaps the biggest reason for our general failure to act is the fact that managerial productivity, which is at the heart of the challenge, is so hard to gauge, much less quantitatively increase. Productivity is generally defined as a measurement of efficiency of production—a ratio of input to output, such as ten units produced per hour. It is the amount of benefit compared to the cost of producing that benefit. How do you then measure the input of management? How do you quantify the specific gain? And how do you compare that input to that gain?

There is no one-line answer to these questions. The fact is that quantifying a manager's efficiency and effectiveness is most difficult. Sometimes you have to wait for results to show over a longer period than if you were to install an improvement on the assembly line.

All this is not to say, however, that productivity improvement is impossible for managers. It is quite possible, and in some ways even easy. Naturally, productivity starts with the individual. If managers make the best use of their time, they not only set a good example, but they can then reasonably expect others to follow their lead. Perhaps most immediately important, their personal input/results ratio improves dramatically. Over many years, the Planagement® approach with quality control has frequently generated a one-to-nine cost/benefit ratio—or better. When used with a licensed Planager® in support, it can effect even greater savings and profit.

Let's take each area of your managerial responsibilities and deal with them one by one.

Orient Yourself to Growth

Establish a positive and growth-oriented mind set. To improve productivity, you must be dissatisfied with the status quo—continually seeking a better way. With a positive philosophy, you welcome challenge and view change as an opportunity for improvement. With such a mind set, you embrace the commitment to growth and profitability, which becomes a spontaneous, continuing, and accelerating gain from your activity. This concept is essential for making increasing productivity a continual process, as opposed to a start-and-stop exercise.

Create Your Own Position Description

If you have not already done so, develop a sound comprehensive *position description*. Most managers, surprisingly, do not have a thorough understanding of their jobs and standards of measurable performance. This step, which usually takes two to three hours, has proved to be well worth the time. Very quickly you know exactly what you are supposed to be taking care of—and what not to be concerned with. Next, develop a *supporting job plan* that maximizes your performance based on the practical potentials for improvement in your job. Including the writing of the job description, an abbreviated plan can be developed in a half-day. A comprehensive business plan would take about one full day.

Adopt an Asset-Management Approach

If the assets of an organization include its human resources, and if that particular asset controls all the others, then obviously that asset becomes one of supreme importance. Your approach must focus on the growth, development, and productivity of the people comprising the organization. Such an approach, in fact, goes hand-in-hand with our original definition of profitability—that is, a balance of profit with growth—as opposed to take-the-money-and-run philosophy, which soon runs down the organization's long-term potential. Profits and return on investment can be rapidly increased by selling or spinning off the organization's assets until the company disappears up it's own balance sheet.

For a productivity program to succeed, therefore, you have to define certain standards of performance—for every manager's job and for the organization as a whole—and measure the results. In a phrase, the key is cause-and-effect management (Chapter 6).

GENERATE POSITION DESCRIPTIONS AND COMPENSATION PROGRAMS FOR OTHERS

Do the same for all those who report to you as you did for yourself—give them clear descriptions of what they are supposed to be doing, and compensate them well for doing those things well. Make it clear that the results you expect constitute the economic justification for their jobs. Include those results in their job descriptions and express them as the minimum measurable standards of acceptable performance. Should the person exceed these minimum standards, then you have tangible reason for additional compensation—perhaps a bonus or a merit raise.

This type of compensation approach allocates economic rewards in concert with objectively measured increases in productivity. High performers with an entrepreneurial bent are attracted to such a results-oriented compensation system. And these high achievers accelerate the pace of productivity improvement and thus rapidly increase the organization's overall profitability.

GET THE RIGHT PERSON IN THE RIGHT JOB

Assuming you are the right person for your job, the next step is to match those under you to the right jobs. Why? Gaps in their productivity may be traced to gaps between their capabilities and the requirements of their jobs. Overall productivity depends on the success of the organization's human resource development system, which includes diagnoses of the gaps between those persons and their jobs. A primary purpose of such a system is, therefore, continually to select, place, and retain the right persons in the right jobs at the right cost and at the right time.

This type of program also provides job support plans, which support the development of individual potential, so as to improve performance and grow into more responsible jobs. In response to this analysis of individual needs, a training and development program must be tailored to meet the needs of both the organization and the individual.

In brief summary, the effective human resource policy states:

> Every manager with other-than-routine responsibility and/or other-than-routine ambition will have a written job description with measurable standards of performance. This job description will be supported with a written job plan that is designed to improve performance, while overcoming development gaps. Both the job description and the job plan will be kept up-to-date and performance will be measured through scheduled exception reports.

Hence, the integration and mutual support of the organization's and the individual's plans and objectives are achieved. This is the basis for a positive internal climate, improved morale, and a reduction of turnover, all of which are basic requirements for increasing productivity.

TAKE CONTROL AND GET FEEDBACK

Control and feedback constitute the basis for management by exception, a very productive management approach. To take control, you must establish your standards and set your direction. To get feedback, you must continually measure and manage deviations to stay on your course and to accomplish your plan.

High-performance managers use control and feedback to diagnose and to manage consistently inconsistent situations in a manner that produces a constant gain. They are problem preventers, not problem solvers.

ADOPT A PARTICIPATIVE STYLE

Management style, which is most frequently successful when it assumes a participative approach, involves all the managers and potential managers. It generally yields superior productivity, better decisions, and a dedicated support that grows out of a consensus of the participants.

DON'T LET OPPORTUNITY RUN OUT

Keeping opportunities ahead of the growing assets, particularly the human asset, which is another way of saying never let anyone be stifled by a lack of opportunity. Ongoing organizational improvement—productivity and profitability—depends greatly on the continual improvement of every individual's performance. The firm has to attract and retain the best managers. "Companies" don't compete, managers do! The company with the most competent managers will out-perform all the others.

Lead the Way The overall productivity of the organization can be enhanced in a number of other ways, which are perhaps best presented as "leadership techniques." These are simple points of managerial style that enable you and your firm to stick to the charted course.

THINK PLANNING

Increased productivity in the organization depends on "quality" thinking before taking action more than it does on a "quantity" of immediate action, necessitating many corrections along the way. More specifically, the burden is on *you,* the manager, to do that thoughtful planning. In other chapters, we have explained how most people tend to keep chopping wood without sharpening their axes from time to time. Over 90 percent of the population must have their work planned for them, and they require almost total supervision to get their jobs done. Only 8 percent—usually lower- and middle-level managers—are able to plan their own work even partially. The rare individuals who are the top managers, as well as the leaders and high performers in their fields, number fewer than two out of every hundred individuals. These individuals have developed the ability and skill to plan their work independently and to work their plan. So as a leader and top manager, your role includes teaching others how to plan, which is in effect, paramount to teaching people how to think. Thinking is the basic skill for working smarter and for increasing productivity.

Whatever your planning system, it should provide others with the process and tools to identify the company's opportunities in order of their practical potentials and then to support these opportunities accordingly with the disciplined allocation and reallocation of resources. Such a system is a fundamental requirement for increasing productivity.

FORMULATE A SOUND STRATEGY

By providing the guidance for effectively implementing activities, strategy plays a major role in increasing productivity. It establishes the priority of activities—what needs to be done when—so that everyone is working for the most important gains while using the least amount of resources.

ORGANIZE FOR SIMPLICITY

The most productive organizations apply the "KISS" principle: "Keep It Simple, Stupid." Specifically, they focus sharply on the 20 percent of the factors that control at least 80 percent of the results. Undisciplined organizations and individuals tend to make the simple complicated and the complex impossible. Simple goals, simple directions, simple controls, simple organizational structure, and simple communications all contribute to an effective and efficient management system.

USE PROJECT MANAGEMENT

Project management is a key to efficiency. At the heart of productivity is the need to maximize the gain from the organization's activities, which is one of the effects of project management. A primary objective of project management is carefully to think out and to record plans of action designed to maximize the benefits while minimizing the cost. By installing a project management system, an organization establishes a rational basis for allocating and reallocating assets to the most profitable projects in their order of importance.

KEEP YOUR MIS SIMPLE TOO

Create a management information system (MIS). A formalized MIS should rapidly identify, gather, analyze, organize, and present just enough of the important information required for making sound, timely decisions.

ENCOURAGE THE COMPANY OVER EMPIRES

Develop one basic management system. One of the primary causes for reduced productivity consists of fragmented and duplicated responsibility and efforts. In the most popular type of salary administration programs, managers are given salary points for controlling larger budgets and for managing more personnel. Naturally, in such an environment, managers tend to build wasteful empires, which results in conflict and duplication between departments and their managers.

Empire building also defeats a fundamental aim of any business: to keep expenses down. This aim is far better served by establishing one basic results-oriented management and compensation system. In such a system, all managers—operating as a team with a "company-first" attitude—help to overcome the blockades to productivity caused by internal competition, conflict, fragmentation, duplication, and the uneconomic expansion of organizational components.

Practice Professional Management

A professional management system is not just another "thing to do," not just another method. It is the living system that professional managers put to work every day of their working lives. It draws upon the concepts of human resource development, of a positive climate, of a growth-oriented mind set, and of all the other things we've talked about. And it puts all those things into operation.

The question is, how do you know whether your system is a professional system? How effective is it? Is your system working for you? As in so many areas of management, all you need is the proper diagnostic equipment. In this case, the Planagement® system proposes five steps, as follows:

STEP 1: ENHANCE YOUR UNDERSTANDING

First, you must objectively evaluate your own understanding of professional management and formalized planning, as well as of management, control, and development systems. Your clear understanding is crucially important in establishing planning and management systems, while developing better professional management capabilities. Let's, therefore, define two key terms:

1. *Formalization* which means that your modus operandi is written in the form of definitions, purposes, flow diagrams, objectives, systems, policies, procedures, strategies, programs, projects, and supporting financial documents, including forecasts, budgets, profit plans, cash flows, and balance sheets. These are the tools of professional management.

2. *A structured and systematic approach,* which means that you need a plan for improving your basic skills of sound planning, organizing, implementation, and control needs.

Now answer the questions in Figure 10-1 with total honesty. Once you have this questionnaire filled out, review it with the same self-honesty to see where you might improve your understanding and knowledge. As necessary, refer to the relevant parts of this and other books to get the insights and information you need.

STEP 2: RELATE TO THE FIVE BUSINESS NEEDS

The next step is to relate your present management system to what we call the five critical needs of business. Part of this evaluation is to measure how well the existing system meets these needs according to the scale laid out for you in Figure 10-2. In this figure, the scale and totaling mechanisms enable you to identify which of your plans and systems are working, which are not working at all, and which are not working as well as they could. The end-product of the evaluation is a prioritized listing of the needs that require improvement. Now you know what, if anything, you should be working on.

FIGURE 10-1. Questionnaire to measure your understanding of professional management and formalized planning management systems

	Yes	No
1. Do you have a written plan?	____	____
2. Do you know why management by objectives (MBO) can be dangerous?	____	____
3. What influence does strategy have on your future success?	____	____
4. a. Do you have a written strategy?	____	____
b. Do you understand how to establish sound strategy?	____	____
5. Do you have a checklist for making a sound decision?	____	____
6. Do you have a clear picture of the future you wish to achieve?	____	____
7. Do you have a method for planning, both long-term and daily?	____	____

8. What is the first step of the planning process?_____

9. What percentage of your total potential do you feel you are achieving?   ____%

10. Where is your greatest unrealized potential?_____

11. How do you tap your greatest unrealized potential?_____
_____

| 12. Do you have a system to do more, in less time, with better results? | ____ | ____ |
| 13. Do you understand the step-by-step process of thinking? | ____ | ____ |

(If you answered yes, list the seven steps of the thinking process [or what-ever you choose to call it: common sense, mind's process, seven-step Planage-ment® Process].)

a. _____   e. _____
b. _____   f. _____
c. _____   g. _____
d. _____

14. a. What steps do you go through to make a decision?
1. _____   2._____
3. _____

15. What is your most important:
a. strength?_____   d. problem? _____
b. weakness? _____   e. action to be taken?_____
c. opportunity?_____

16. How do you measure growth?
a. Your own:_____
b. An organization's:_____

17. What is the most important management skill?_____
_____

© 1978 by Planagement, Inc.

196

FIGURE 10–2. Evaluation of How Well Your Organization Is Meeting the Five Critical Needs of Business

On the scale for each of the critical needs (listed on the left), place an "X" in the appropriate box—that is, the box that best describes the status of the plan or system.

Critical Need	0% Nonexistent to Poor		25% Inconsistent to Fair		50% Satisfactory but Needs Improving		75% Excellent— Doing the Job	
Formal Planning, Management, Control System								
Organized Marketing Function and Plan								
Human Resource Development System								
Maximizing Profitability and Controling Results								
Definition and Management of Growth								
	0%	10% / 20%	30% / 40%		60% / 70%		80% / 90%	100%

SUMMARY OF OVERALL EFFECTIVENESS:

Add the percentage of each item to get the total of five needs: _____%
Divide by five for your average score: _____%

PRIORITIZE NEEDS TO BE WORKED ON:

1. _____ Score: _____%
2. _____ Score: _____%
3. _____ Score: _____%
4. _____ Score: _____%
5. _____ Score: _____%

STEP 3: IDENTIFY GAPS

Identify the gaps between what you have now and what you want. In this case, perhaps you've identified a need for a better fit of people to their positions in the firm. A better human resource development system might be in order. Or maybe your marketing plan seems ill-defined and random in its aims. Generate ideas for more specific markets or for greater emphasis on marketing and sales. You need not bridge any gaps yet, simply identify them.

STEP 4: TAILOR A SOUND MANAGEMENT SYSTEM

Now you can start developing specifications and answering the questions necessary to tailor a sound management system to your organization's needs. Figure 10–3 lists specifications that you should keep in mind as you put together this system. Review this list and refer to it often. Make it part of your thinking.

FIGURE 10–3. Specifications for a sound management system

1. The system should be simple to understand, easy to apply, and structured in a readily teachable form.
2. The system should tailor to the organization's needs, not vice versa.
3. Firm enough to give direction, flexible enough to manage change.
4. Results should be measurable.
5. Comprehensive in that it integrates planning/management and control into one system.
6. Provides a common approach and format at all levels of management.
7. Minimizes paperwork.
8. The system should measurably increase performance.
9. The system should be practical.
10. Provides a basis for managing change.
11. Problem-preventing in nature.
12. Provides a plan for planning and management.
13. Encourages operating management to plan.
14. Contribute to improved communication.
15. Establishes sound priorities.
16. Teaches time management.
17. Provides a project management system.
18. Contributes to the development of the human asset, as this asset controls all other assets.
19. Provides an early warning system with increased anticipation ability.
20. Should maximize profit, growth, and job satisfaction.

STEP 5: DEVELOP AN ACTION PLAN

Now that you know where you want to go, develop an action plan and program to establish your management system. The checklist in Figure 10–4 contains a number of key criteria (on the left), along with a line or two for each that provides a measuring standard of performance. You should compare your system against these standards point for point. Such a comparison serves to fine-tune your system very quickly, thus side-stepping the many booby traps of the hit-or-miss method.

STEP 6: MEASURE COST-EFFECTIVENESS

After putting your fine-tuned system into operation and monitoring its results, the next step is to measure its cost-effectiveness on an ongoing basis. The ever-asked question is this: Is the system bringing about the short- and long-term results that you desire? If so, fine. If not, you might have to repeat all or some of the other steps as necessary.

FIGURE 10–4. Assessing your planning/management system
(Place a checkmark for each item in column HAVE or NEED)

Standard or Criteria	Measure of Performance	Have	Need
1. Tangible system	1. Provides documentation and a plan for planning.		
2. Teachable	2. Can be taught and applied by all individuals with other than routine responsibility and/or ambition.		
3. Learned through rapid application	3. A written plan can be developed in one or two days.		
4. Documented benefits and results	4. Easily measured and monitored. Gains are clearly identified.		
5. Provide a single integrated planning management system	5. a. Long-range, operational, strategic and tactical planning. b. Establish sound objectives. c. Balance operations and futures.		
6. Communications	6. Guideline plan moves downward and supporting plans upward with coordination device provided.		
7. Implementation	7. Provides sound project management.		
8. Coordination	8. Means of coordinating the various plans.		
9. Commitment	9. Develops internal process and discipline.		
10. Resource	10. Supports achievement of the goals of the organization and individuals.		
11. Control	11. Provides management of results under conditions with operational schedule/key milestones and reporting by exception under changing conditions.		
12. Professional Management	12. Integrates scientific management with the behavioral sciences in a practial, productive way.		
13. Common format	13. Applicable to all levels of management and functions.		
14. Reduces paperwork	14. Rapidly gathers, organizes, analyzes, and presents the minimum amount of information required to make a sound decision.		
15. Coordinates individual and organization goals	15. Establishes a balance of individual freedom within organization direction and discipline.		

FIGURE 10–4. (continued)
(Place a checkmark for each item in column HAVE or NEED)

Standard or Criteria	Measure of Performance	Have	Need
16. Individual development	16. Provides a human resources development system to improve performance, promotability, flexibility, decision-making, anticipation, problem solving, delegation and follow-up skills resulting in establishing the right person/right job fit.		
17. Organization direction	17. Identifies and rank-orders opportunities according to their practical potentials.		
18. Flexible	18. Capable of being used by individuals, teams, and all organization entities, including profit centers, departments, and jobs.		
19. Integrates	19. Provides one basic professional management system, which integrates planning, management, communication, coordination, delegation, control, compensation, development, organization, job and career planning.		
20. Positive	20. Builds on strengths and emphasizes opportunity under changing conditions.		
21. Asset Management	21. Focuses on management of people, money, materials, time, and space.		
22. Balanced	22. Balances profits with growth through profitability management.		
23. Motivational	23. Contributes to establishing a positive climate with an objective basis for measuring and rewarding performance.		
24. Practical	24. Based on sound concepts that are easily applied to the person's job and to the organization's requirements.		
25. Creative	25. Stimulates creativity and provides a system for identifying and moving sound concepts into reality.		
26. Measurable	26. Establishes measurable standards, sound objectives, supporting projects, costs, and benefits.		

(cont.)

FIGURE 10–4. (continued)
(Place a checkmark for each item in column HAVE or NEED)

Standard or Criteria	Measure of Performance	Have	Need
27. Developmental	27. Contributes to the growth and development of professional, promotable managers at all levels with measured improvements of increased management effectiveness.		
28. Profit-oriented	28. Establishes profitability centers with cost/benefit thinking by managers for all jobs.		
29. Management of change	29. Establishes living plans throughout the organization.		
30. Increases management effectiveness	30. Profit, growth, and job satisfaction are measurably increased through application of professional management skills on the job.		

Add total number of checkmarks in each column: ___ ___

a. Percentage of HAVE to total   ___%

b. Percentage of NEED to total   ___%

c. Percentage effectiveness (100% − B%)   ___%

d. Post C percentage by placing an "X" in the box on the scale that best describes the present overall status of your system:

0%	25%	50%	75%	100%
Nonexistent to Poor	Inconsistent to Fair	Satisfactory but Needs Improving	Excellent— Doing the Job	

0%   10%   20%   30%   40%   60%   70%   80%   90%

THE PARADOX OF POWER

*One Approach
to Power*... "I want to be president of this company more than anything else in life!" This statement was made several years ago by an executive vice president in response to the question, "What is your career target?" Anyone present at the time could see from his tense face that he really meant it. He looked absolutely stunned when I asked him why he wanted the job. After a moment, he answered the question essentially as follows:

> I want the job because of the power that will be mine from being president of the company. I will be able to run it my way and get rid of the people that have been getting in the way and impeding the progress that we should be making.

This response is really not exaggerated, and frankly similar remarks have been made by several hard-driving, dedicated executives who have focused their efforts on getting the top jobs in their companies. More interesting is what happened to many of these executives and to their companies after they reached the president's office. While the lengths of time for achievement varied, as did the circumstances, generally speaking the results were the same: These men failed, and they hurt their companies very badly.

How could such well-intentioned and ambitious executives fail? It wasn't because they were stupid: Many of them were very intelligent, well-educated, and thoroughly dedicated. Many had outstanding credentials based on track records of personal accomplishment. However, they shared the following common characteristics and approaches:

1. They created a very negative climate in the company with their one-man dominance, backed up by their frequently used authority to hire and fire, combined with the carrot-and-stick approach to managing.

2. They had little respect for people in general. Instead, they felt that the majority of people couldn't think for themselves, that they had to be told what to do, and that they had to be tightly controlled to see that the job got done the way it should be done.

3. They frequently lacked trust and integrity, resulting in poor to nonexistent communications—except for their edicts from the top and, because of high turnover, the often asked question, "Who's new?"

4. These top execs surrounded themselves with weak subordinates who "yes-ed" them to death and who much preferred to agree with the boss, as opposed to making decisions or taking action.

5. These executives said by the way they conducted themselves in, "Do as I say—not as I do!" They felt they were above others in their company, since they made the laws for others to follow.

6. Their general managerial philosophy and politics seems to be based on the traditional mind set, which sees business as a jungle with its most basic law being win/lose and survival of the fittest. This general view was usually supported by an overly active, inaccurate grapevine, as well as by an attitude of "do it to others before they do it to you."

One president, who had just become an ex-president due to an extremely vicious power struggle, lamented that he couldn't understand why he had been ousted. This broken, confused man spent most of our luncheon listing his impressive history with outstanding credentials and extensive accomplishments. Then, in a final fit of frustration, he said, "If only business didn't have people in it, so much more could be accomplished."

Another executive vice president, when asked for his career target, also replied that he would like to be president of his company. When asked the second question, "Why do you want to be president?" he answered:

> Because I feel that I can meet the enormous responsibilities inherent in the job and that, in this position, I could best serve the company, its employees, stockholders, and various other publics.

It was my privilege to watch closely this executive and his company over a number of years. He and the company had these readily identifiable characteristics:

1. The president understood and believed in people as individuals, trusting them with as much responsibility as possible. As a direct result, the company's positive climate was derived from a mutual trust, faith, cooperation, respect, and confidence among the members of the management team and of the team as a unit in their company.
2. The president concentrated on developing his management team and surrounded himself with the strongest managers—each of whom could have been considered as a potential backup.
3. Honesty was the policy. The president said as much in a talk:
   > Integrity is vital to being able to communicate. If you don't believe what I say—you won't hear what I say and you will be constantly second-guessing me or wondering if I really mean what I say. Without communication, we cannot have an organization, and without organization, we have no company.

   As a direct result, everybody in the company "told it like it was." While persons might be wrong in a statement or suggestion, they nevertheless were always honest. Communications were exceptionally good in this company.

4. The organization balanced individual freedom with the discipline of organizational direction. All the employees knew their jobs. They were dedicated to accomplishing the jobs'accountabilities and to monitoring their own performance with the idea of continued self-improvement.

5. There was not a lot of turnover. The policy of promoting "primarily from within" was supported by the growing, competent, self-reliant managers who blossomed in that rapidly, yet soundly, growing company. As a result, the company attracted and kept good and improving people.

6. The "power" of the presidency was based primarily on the authority of earned prestige, which resulted from the president's good example and work in support of his managers. He requested—he did not demand. Yet, if a tough decision had to be made and if his participating management team could not make it, then the president met his responsibility by making it himself and received the enthusiastic, total support of his managers, even if they disagreed.

The Paradox of Power

The president in our first example understood only power, that is, the possession of control, authority, or influence over others. The president in the second example, however, grasped the responsibility that went with the power; he saw in the top office position the need to be reliable and trustworthy—that is, responsible. He saw the paradox of power. When power is viewed in the context of the responsibility it entails, it implies, paradoxically, service more than mastery.

And when the holders of power approach their jobs from this point of view, they attract a more spontaneous and natural kind of power than they need to accomplish their goals. On the other hand, regardless of how big and all-powerful their positions—as the tragic events in our own nation have shown—if those in top positions exercise power without responsibility, they will ultimately fail through a lack of support from those they must depend on for their power.

In one sense at least, perhaps there is no paradox. Perhaps we are describing the same entity with two different words—power or responsibility—both simply reflect a different way of looking at the same thing. A business, a government, or any organization consists ultimately only of people. The cohesive ingredients of an organization must, therefore, be mutual trust, respect, and confidence, which are derived from an understanding of and a belief in the fundamental reliability of people. In this light, you can see how foolish it is to attempt a separation of power, politics, people, and morality. All these distinctions reflect only the aspects of a group acting either in mutually responsible concert or in confusing conflict.

Granted, being honest or meeting the other tough demands of the presidency is not always easy. But history has shown that, to survive as a productive president, a person must fully understand the paradox of power and meet its inherent responsibilities.

KNOWING WHEN YOU REACH THE TOP

How do I reach the top? And when I've reached the top, what do I do next? These two questions are frequently asked by those who are ambitious and who are experiencing boredom and failure in their success. In business, "the top" traditionally means the most senior managerial position. In the case of a specialist, this job might be the Vice Presidency of a function. For the professional business manager, it would mean the Presidency with Chief Executive Officer responsibility.

But do those jobs constitute the top for everyone? After many years of experience with a number of companies and several thousand managers, I observe that there seems to be no such thing as *the* top. One individual's life-long goal can be another person's misery. Many people have risen to the level of their own frustration (observed frequently as their level of incompetence, as in the Peter Principle). Instead of reaching a dream, they experience a nightmare and often failure.

So how do *you* reach the top? Perhaps the first step is to identify which job you would most like to have in the future and work toward the job that is the next intermediate milestone toward your ultimate objective. Whatever your next target, it should be reasonable and attainable. Equally important, the next position you are seeking should have a good personal fit with you. The responsibilities of the next job should provide you with challenge and satisfaction, because, unless you have both, the job—regardless of the related title or prestige—will probably not be a worthwhile, productive, or happy experience for you.

To reach your "top," you first have to know yourself pretty well, including what you would really enjoy doing, as well as what you are competent to do well. You might consider preparing a written description of the type of situation you want, and then examine the jobs and the descriptions that exist, could exist, or should exist in your company or chosen field. Once you have identified your next "compatible" position, you identify the gap between your present capabilities and the job requirements. This gap then becomes your personal development plan. You have to repeat this process of knowing who you are, where you want to go, and what you need to do to achieve your goal until you reach your top.

So, how do you reach the top? You have to answer this question for yourself. Your answer depends on what you think the top is, on how you objectively relate your present self as compared to your future goal, and on how well you manage your personal development gap.

In many cases, getting to the top means having no where else to go—having nothing else to do. Success can then mean "topping out." If so in your case, you generally hear yourself asking the second question, "I've reached the top of my profession or my company—what do I do now?" These individuals are often worse off than those who never quite have their ambitions satisfied, but who are therefore alive, interested, dynamic, striving, and growing. Individuals who "have it made" are frequently unchallenged, bored, and sometimes afraid they will lose what they have worked so hard to achieve. Yet they really don't enjoy their success any longer.

What do you do after you reach the top and have nothing left to accomplish? One suggestion is to involve yourself in supporting someone else's process of reaching the top. Teach someone else to do your job as well as or better than you do. Consider developing such a replacement. This suggestion is not usually accepted with great enthusiasm, but it makes sense for several reasons:

1. The best way to learn a subject better is to teach it to someone else.

2. Structuring your knowledge and experience in such a manner that others want to and can learn it brings you great satisfaction and challenge. This is the way to multiply yourself and to become more productive. It is certainly better than remaining a one-man show that never grows beyond you and that is perpetually in danger of not living longer than you do.

3. The growth and development of the enterprise depend directly on the growth and development of the individuals who comprise it. So if "each one will teach one," you then have a very dynamic organization that attracts and keeps individuals who are constantly growing and increasing their productivity. The result is an obviously productive, profitable rapidly growing company.

A word about teaching: Along with delegating, teaching is one of the most important responsibilities and opportunities for managers. Managers who advance have usually mastered this important skill. They realize that teaching is not knowing all the answers; rather, it is more like knowing the right questions to ask at the right time. Growing managers realize that they have a responsibility to the people who work for them, more than a power over them. As these managers advance, they become more aware that moving up the ladder requires key skills, as pictured in Figure 12–1.

Will you work yourself out of a job? Yes, possibly—at least your present job. But as you do so, you will probably identify your next goal. Then you will once again involve yourself in the most satisfying process of all, as reflected by the continuing gain from your own life's activity.

Mastering a Creative Skill For Fun and Profit

Many people feel that creativity is a rare gift and that only a few people are blessed with it at birth. In actuality, one of the greatest resources that we all possess is our capability to be creative. Every person has the capacity for it. Furthermore, anyone can continuously increase his or her personal creativity through an understanding of creativity, together with certain concepts and tools that are available to all. Properly channeled, this unique capability can bring us both the supreme satisfaction of accomplishment and bountiful monetary reward. Frequently, the individuals and organizations that lead their chosen field have mastered their creative skill. As a result, they are

FIGURE 12–1. Skills required to reach the top and a guideline of time spent on developing and applying these skills

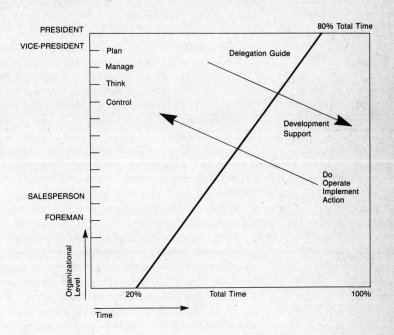

recognized as the ones who usually come up with the new, the different, or the better idea, product, or service that becomes the new standard.

Open a dictionary and read the various definitions of "creative." You will likely conclude that the term is fairly nebulous and that the ability for creativity is pretty much undefined. Yet the following definition of creativity may be helpful in more clearly understanding this "shadow of the substance":

> Creativity is a positive mental attitude with the synergistic skill of uniquely combining known elements, while at the same time challenging the unfamiliar.

This definition allows us to realize that the capability for creativity is within our minds and that, through applying our mind's process in a certain disciplined manner, we can develop a skill of creativity. Dr. Alex F. Osborn, who founded the Creative Education Foundation, said that:

> Creativity will never be a science. In fact, much of it will always remain a mystery . . . as much of a mystery as what makes our hearts tick. At the same time, I submit that *creativity is an ART—an applied art—a workable art—a teachable art—an art in which all of us can make ourselves more and more proficient, if we will.*

Extensive research by a number of people has identified certain characteristics that are almost always present in creative individuals (Figure 12–2). Many of these characteristics are listed in the Excellent Creative Thinking Program, as developed by Earl Nightingale and Dr. Whitt Schultz. We can compare our own personal profile with this profile of creativity. In doing so, we can identify our own personal creativity gap areas, which show us the areas we need to work on to increase our creative capabilities.

Few creative people have all of these characteristics, but each of these traits contributes to establishing a creative capability. Compare yourself against each one of these characteristics. Work on those you lack or on those you are weak in applying. Then you can increase your skill of creativity and become more creative as a result.

Increasing this skill takes effort on your part, but you will probably find doing so to be well worth the effort. Few satisfactions are greater than coming up with a truly creative idea and then making that idea a productive reality. This ability to create and to implement productive ideas has often been the basis for establishing a successful business and a great life.

Deciding to Be Creative

Many people do not make up their minds to be creative until they decide which point of view they wish to adopt. This continual procrastination in turn serves only to reduce creative capability due to lack of use. Examples of these diverse opinions follow:

> An important factor in the achievment of success is the area of original and creative thinking. Trust your mind to deliver fresh ideas. Trust it to sort material and deliver insights and solutions.
> —Norman Vincent Peale

FIGURE 12–2. Characteristics of creativity

1. These individuals have a thirst for acquiring knowledge and then an ability to process that knowledge into useful or new insights and decisions.

2. Truly creative persons would not just generate ideas, but they would also take action on them. They are *cre-active* individuals, insofar as their action frequently strengthens their idea, modifies it into a better idea, or generates new ideas—and then the process starts over. It is a closed-loop, continuous system.

3. Creative persons do not necessarily see things as they are, but rather how they could be. For example, Michelangelo was walking through a stone quarry when he stopped before a large block of marble and said that he saw an angel imprisoned in the rock. He later chipped away the pieces of the rock and created the angel, which became one of his many masterpieces.

4. Drive, direction, self-discipline, and constant self-development are additional characteristics of creative individuals. These characteristics, in turn, are supported by courage and a tenacity of purpose—they see the idea through to completion.

5. Basic integrity, with an uncompromising intellectual honesty, is another key strength.

6. Entrepreneurially oriented, they will take a needed risk.

7. Optimistic, they have a strong positive attitude.

8. They are superior in their judgment and in applying common sense.

9. Their enthusiasim reflects their zest and love for life.

10. These enterprising individuals challenge the unknown.

11. Highly persuasive, they have a superior skill to sell and to inspire action with sound reasoning.

11. With their outgoing nature, they normally have good people skills, as well as an ability to encourage people and ideas to grow in their presence.

13. They are dynamic, healthy, vital, energetic, with a sound balance of exercising the mind and the body.

14. Their conversation skill is superior.

15. They possess open, inquiring minds.

16. These good listeners are perceptive and empathetic.

17. They believe in themselves with a faith that they can do better, that any situation can be improved, and that a great unrealized potential can be tapped.

18. Creative persons are flexible. They balance a freedom of the mind with a discipline of supportive action.

19. A skill of anticipation, together with an ability to react to changing situations, characterizes their approach to things.

(cont.)

FIGURE 12–2. (continued)

20. Engaged in a constant pursuit of excellence, creative persons strive toward the perfect—the ideal—but their striving is realistic, practical, and measurably productive. They are impatient with their progress, but patient in their pursuit.

21. Versatility, inquisitiveness, individualism, and imagination are additional traits of creative individuals.

22. A good sense of humor is part of the creative make-up, since it is often required to alleviate disappointment and to prevent discouragement. It is a valuable outlet of tension and a welcome change to a serious pursuit.

23. These people frequently have the ability to see the best in others, while continually giving the best that is possible to give.

The human mind cannot create anything. It produces nothing until after having been fertilized by experience and meditation; its acquisitions are the germs of its production. —Buffon

I may safely predict that the education of the future will be inventive-minded. It will believe so profoundly in the high value of the inventive or creative spirit that it will set itself to develop that spirit by all means within its power.

—Harry A. Overstreet

It is better to create than to be learned; creating is the true essence of life. —Niebuhr

The full-grown modern human being who seeks but refuge finds instead boredom and mental dissolution, unless he can be, even in his withdrawal, creative. He can find the quality of happiness in the strain and travail only of achievement and growth. And he is conscious of touching the highest pinnacle of fulfillment which his life-urges demand when he is consumed in the service of an idea, in the conquest of the goal pursued. —R. Brillault

I criticize by creation, not by finding fault. —Cicero

Ideas are the roots of creation. —Ernest Dimnet

Quite a variety of view points! The important point, however, is not to be confused. Rather, pick one view, based on your own research and your own opinion. Being right is not as important as is picking one, along with its supporting approaches, then *use it*. In fact, there is no right answer. Pick the answer that fits you best, and then continually apply the concepts, as well as its supporting tools and techniques. You will become more creative, because any one of the disciplines contribute to creativity, while using no discipline will not. As an appropriate analogy, any one grain of sand (a creative discipline) acts as a catalyst to the oyster (your mind) and results in the forming of a pearl (an idea). Put another way, "The Lord gave us two ends to use. One to think with; one to sit with. Success depends on which we use. Heads we win; tails we lose."

The use of our minds is more important than the discipline we pursue.

AMERICA:
WHAT WE WERE,
WHAT WE ARE,
WHAT WE CAN BE

Like the citizens of any great nation, Americans don't like to think that their country's greatness and power may be diminishing. Certainly no one likes to consider the possibility that right now the United States could be joining the dominant civilizations who have risen and fallen before us.

Yet why should we be different from all the others before us? If you examine the analogy between our predecessors and us, you're obliged to admit strong parallel trends—first up and then down. In fact, the United States has gone through many of the steps associated with the life cycle of a civilization. Let's take a look at these steps, keeping in mind that this is only one person's view of a civilization's life cycle.

Life Cycle of a Civilization

1. BONDAGE

The first step of a new civilization is bondage. To be a slave is to start a dream of a different and better way of life.

2. SPIRITUAL FAITH

The second element of the life cycle, faith, becomes the foundation on which the dream is built. It is the touchstone, the philosophy, and the mission that continually nourish and sustain the dream even in the worst of times. As William James put it:

> Our belief at the beginning of a doubtful undertaking is the one thing that insures the successful outcome of our venture.

3. COURAGE

Courage provides the stimulus for taking the actions required to bring about the desired change. This change is built on the dream for something better and is supported by a common faith and philosophy.

4. LIBERTY

This "quality or state of being free" results from applied courage, and it establishes the new civilization as an independent functioning entity with its own power to do as it pleases. In this stage of development the people enjoy various social, political, or economic rights and privileges, including the individual's precious right of choice. The climate of the civilization at this point in its history balances individual freedom within a discipline of understood direction and action in support.

5. ABUNDANCE

As the civilization functions productively, it emerges into the era of abundance. Perhaps in this state, the civilization begins to plant the seeds of its own destruction.

6. SELFISHNESS

History has shown that the next phase in the development or evolution of a civilization's life cycle is selfishness. People tend to become "concerned excessively or exclusively with themselves"—which contributes to their going in ever diminishing circles. Progress is replaced by narrow and frequently unproductive self-serving activity. Individuals begin to concentrate on manipulating situations and others to their own personal advantage without regard for others or for what is right.

217

7. COMPLACENCY

The next stage, complacency, keynotes an evolving and now obviously declining civilization. In this case, the complacency is a kind of self-satisfaction accompanied by an unawareness of actual dangers or deficiencies. It is a major contributing factor to the demise of great and nearly great civilizations. In today's age of change, this suspended animation leads quickly to a loss of position and negative movement. Today you just can't stand still and expect to progress in a positive way!

8. APATHY

Complacency turns into apathy. This lack of interest or concern results in the negative philosophy, expressed as:

> My job is not to run the train
> Or even clang the bell,
> But watch the train jump the tracks
> And see who catches hell.

The people who comprise the civilization lack feeling or emotion. In a sense, they are spiritless and impassive, and so they contribute in large measure to the ninth step of the civilization's cycle.

9. DEPENDENCE

Evolving from apathy, dependence becomes the identifiable nature of the now rapidly declining civilization. No longer are the civilization and its people self-reliant. Their future is determined by someone—or by something—other than themselves. The people are basically responsive, allowing change to manage them, rather than managing change through the courage, faith, and common direction that were their original strengths. These strengths were somehow depleted along the way, perhaps by the very abundance that was the product of the original progress. The original dream, slowly and then more rapidly, has become a nightmare. Integrity is compromised, either for expediency or for political positioning, which is characterized by ever diminishing circles. Individuals become obsolete. And the civilization, with its organizations comprised of these obsolete individuals in a growing majority, gradually dies, returning to the original state before existence and thus completing the cycle.

10. BONDAGE!

The once proud civilization now becomes the slave of others. No longer is there a freedom of choice. Prerogatives are replaced by policies and procedures. The builders are inundated by the bureaucrats and the ever-diminishing circle disappears up its own apathy and dependency.

Apparently twenty-one of twenty-two civilizations have experienced this common life cycle—and *the average life of these civilizations has been two-hundred years!*

Can the wonderful dream that is the United States be dying? Is history repeating itself with our own great and beloved nation? Certainly the articles being written, more than ever before in our history, put the United States in a very poor light. We seem to be experiencing some sort of self-incrimination, to the point that some feel we can no longer depend on or trust our presidents, our government, or ourselves.

Resurgence Those who feel this way should also feel obliged to offer some answers: What, specifically, can we do to reverse the trend and to re-establish the strength of the nation, which has been built on the most challenging and rewarding dreams ever conceived?

Part of the answer is to acknowledge the life cycle stage we're in, because a new cycle can start at any time (Figure 13–1). The other part of the answer is to realize that the task is up to no one else but us.

We have the capacity—no question about it. But we must want it, and we must have the faith and courage to undertake it. In the final analysis, the capacity lies within each individual, not with "the city" or "the government." We cannot blame the establishment or some other scapegoat for our own shortcomings. We must recognize simply that each individual has the opportunity and responsibility to bring about the needed improvements. And that, conversely, all we need to stop progress cold is for everyone to wait for someone else to take action.

If, then, resurgence is up to the individual, what do we do? "The Four D's" are one answer to that question:

1. drive,
2. direction,
3. discipline, and
4. development.

Let's look at each a little more closely.

219

FIGURE 13–1. Conceptual resurgence

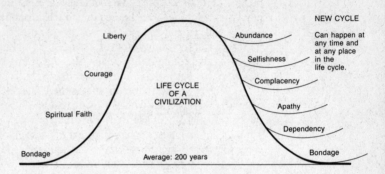

LIFE CYCLE
OF A
CIVILIZATION

Liberty

Courage

Spiritual Faith

Bondage

Average: 200 years

Abundance

Selfishness

Complacency

Apathy

Dependency

Bondage

NEW CYCLE

Can happen at
any time and
at any place
in the
life cycle.

DRIVE

The drive that individuals have frequently determines how far they travel during their lifetimes. Much attention is given to motivation these days, and a number of psychological tests are used to measure "drive" or the desire to get the job done, or to be successful. Some people even feel that drive is everything. Probably all of us have heard someone say, "He really has drive—he is bound to be successful."

DIRECTION

Whether a person is successful, however, frequently depends as much on the second "D" as it does on drive, because all the drive in

220

the world is of little importance unless it is harnessed to a sound, well-defined direction.

Direction aims drive toward meaningful accomplishments. It is truly sad to see a hard-driving individual, or a great and energetic nation, going off in all directions, so that progress is painfully slow, or perhaps nonexistent.

Few people take the time to apply their inherent capability to create their "grand design." They go through life working hard, but they do not have a defined mission. Because they lack direction, they plan the game of life without a par. Consequently, they neither win nor lose in their day-to-day management of their momentum.

These individuals—whether they comprise a company, an industry, or a nation—do not employ the planning process they have available to them, and consequently they are like a ship without a rudder or a course. All the drive in the world will not get them to where they could go, because the direction has not been established and their destination is undefined.

On a national scale, if individuals do not have direction, then collectively their country will lack direction, and progress will be minimal at best. Or, at worst, they might tend toward self-recrimination and even destruction.

DISCIPLINE

The importance of discipline has been emphasized over and over again throughout the book and in several contexts. Suffice it to say that it is the one trait that we need now.

DEVELOPMENT

Continual self-development provides constant growth. Every individual has a choice between two basic kinds of life: one that peters out in obsolescence or one that spirals outward in ever bigger circles. The latter alternative is the route of development and of growth. So, particularly in this great nation, each individual has the capability, the opportunity, and the responsibility to increase his or her own rate of resurgence through a personal commitment to The Four D's.

In turn, just as the success of an organization depends on the success of its individuals, so the outcome of the entire nation rests with the personal commitment of each of its citizens. Make no mistake about this point: We are blessed to live in a country where the choice is still ours. But we could easily damn the nation if we continue to opt for the easy choice. The choice that each of us makes for our future determines in large measure our country's future and, consequently, whether we will always have that choice.

Momentum Versus Renewal

A person, an organization, or a nation has essentially only one set of alternatives: to grow or die. Yet growth or death—the life cycle as a whole—depends much more on mind sets than on chronological age. So an individual, a firm, or a country can "think" old, stop growing, and die.

The more you grow, the more wary you must become of the mental posture that says, "It's okay to let go now." In other words, success frequently provides the foundation for failure. When goals are reached, the individual or the organization stops being challenged and starts to coast. Commitment starts to mutate into complacency. Tomorrow's dreams are replaced by yesterday's achievements. The drive, which was the dominating force, dissipates into a haze of comfort, supported with an income from established momentum instead of from accomplishment.

On a larger scale, history has clearly demonstrated that selfishness, complacency, apathy, and dependency follow a sustained period of abundance. The eventual death of the civilization comes when it is dissolved or absorbed by another civilization in the growth phase. The same fate awaits individuals and organizations.

In a world so fraught with change, however, it is sometimes hard to keep going and growing. Few things are certain, but we can rely on at least three constants:

1. The future will not be like the past, and so extrapolation forecasting is obsolete, yet still predominates.
2. The future will not be like what we think it will be; it is essentially unpredictable.
3. The rate of change will be faster in the future than it has been in the past.

In the teeth of these certainties, most organizations and individuals still use the obsolete practice of extrapolative forecasting, which views the past and the estabished momentum as the basis for estimating the future. This dangerous approach often causes movement in the wrong direction, but with a higher degree of assurance. The results achieved are disappointing and frequently disastrous.

Perhaps this sort of forecasting fails because it discounts the effect of individuals, who are in the last analysis responsible for their success or failure, as well as for that of their organizations and cultures. Individuals determine the future. More specifically, their mind sets determine the future.

If you can "predict" the future of an organization at all, you must rely on the mind sets of the individuals in charge of management. The first step in this forecasting approach, then, is to assess the leadership's mind set, according to the scale in Figure 13–2. Associated with each stage on that scale is a type of strategic organizational mission:

1. comfort ←→ maintenance,
2. commitment ←→ improvement,
3. conquest ←→ aggressiveness,
4. challenge ←→ expansion.

MAINTENANCE

In this first area of the scale, the status quo is comfortable and, therefore, the dominating influence. A strategic mission may not exist, or if it does, it is fuzzy. The measurement of performance is to survive—to maintain and defend the existing market share. Management of momentum, together with a "don't-rock-the-boat" management style, describe the existing character of this dying organism.

FIGURE 13–2. Mind set scale

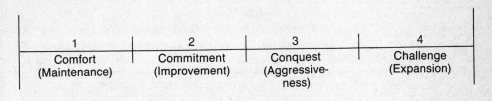

1	2	3	4
Comfort (Maintenance)	Commitment (Improvement)	Conquest (Aggressiveness)	Challenge (Expansion)

IMPROVEMENT

In this second phase, a commitment to improvement is made. The strategic mission is to define and analyze the existing situation, and then, based on this evaluation, to determine how the situation might best be improved. This plan for improvement is supported with the required systems to establish a stronger position in the markets served through a better product—service and human resource mix to establish the right person in the right job.

Characteristically, in this phase, the organization optimizes its results by balancing what is good with what it needs to achieve an improvement or gain from an existing strength and capability. Analysis, design, decision, and discipline are the key supporting skills required to implement improvement. Inertia is replaced by energy. Comfort is transformed into commitment, which provides the foundation for moving into the third phase of the mind set scale.

AGGRESSIVENESS

The strategic mission in this phase is conquest through expanding market share until a dominant position is achieved. The emphasis is on maximizing performance, which might be measured either in terms of increased profits in a profit-making organization or in terms of increased mission accomplishment in a nonprofit organization. Aggressive organisms are characterized by a strong drive, a clear direction, and a dominating discipline in support of approved plans. Commitment is converted into actions and accomplishments.

EXPANSION

In this fourth phase, the strategic mission is to provide a constant challenge, which is measured by how far the opportunities stay ahead of the growing resources of people, money, materials, time, and space. In support of this mission, the key still is a keen diagnostic ability, supported with a formal management system. This system consistently manages inconsistent situations in a way that produces constant gain. It does so by identifying and ranking opportunities in accordance with their practical potentials, and then by judiciously allocating the available resources in accordance with these prioritized opportunities. This management system establishes a balance of sound growth with maximum profits by achieving the best possible profitability through the management of the organization's potential. This gain may be measured by the increase in return on assets employed, together with the increase in assets employed. Aggressiveness and action become calculation and challenge in this fourth phase.

The profitability chart in Figure 9–6 displays the mind sets and corresponding strategic missions, along with the impact of each on the performance and future of the organization and the individual. Yet, obviously, charting such progress is a lot easier than making it a reality. So the practical question is, "How does an organization start moving from the comfort phase toward the challenge phase?" To answer this question, you have to understand the process of organizational and individual renewal. This process moves organizations from managing momentum to managing potential, combining the mind set sequences of a commitment to improvement, of conquest through aggressively better positioning the person and organization, and of accepting the challenge of constant expansion. This rebuilding process also demonstrates the crucial importance of the renewal process to the survival of an individual or an organization.

FIGURE 13–3. Profitability profile chart

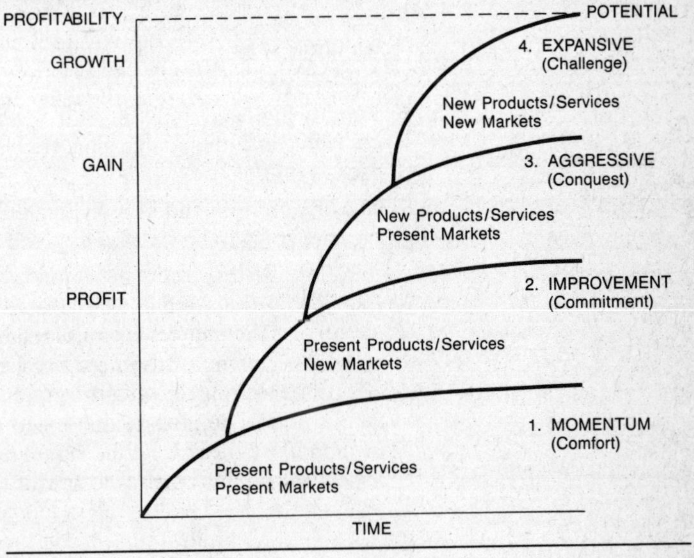

PROFITABILITY — — — — — — — — — — — — — — — — — — — → POTENTIAL

GROWTH

4. EXPANSIVE (Challenge)

New Products/Services New Markets

GAIN

3. AGGRESSIVE (Conquest)

New Products/Services Present Markets

PROFIT

2. IMPROVEMENT (Commitment)

Present Products/Services New Markets

1. MOMENTUM (Comfort)

Present Products/Services Present Markets

TIME

225

To begin renewal, an organization must exhibit the following characteristics and climate:

1. A growing dissatisfaction with the status quo is a starting point.

2. It needs an effective selection system that identifies and attracts talented people, since competent and ambitious people are the key to renewal. Such people are in short supply, so the organization that out-competes for talented people will establish the capability for renewal.

3. Also necessary is a positive climate that encourages open, effective communications and honest self-criticism. The truth must be welcome and respected, even if it hurts.

4. The internal structure and managerial style needs to be flexible, so that change may be anticipated and managed to advantage.

5. The organization and its individuals must not become prisoners of their own policies and procedures. As the policy and procedure manual gets fatter, the ideas grow fewer. Well established habits and routine tend to limit imagination and flexibility.

6. Mutual trust, respect, and confidence need to be emphasized as the modus operandi, along with a participative orientation toward decision making and toward the established programs.

7. Empire building, politics, and vested interests must be combated and made subordinate to the organization's philosophy and plan.

8. The organization and its individuals need to focus on what they are going to become, as opposed to emphasizing what they have been.

9. Individual freedom should be balanced with organizational discipline. The individuals must believe that what they do makes a difference. They need to care and know that their efforts are moving the organization and themselves toward their mutually defined destinies, and that each is working in support of the other. The future of the organization is dependent on this type of dedication.

10. The reward system should be objective and fair, based on achievement and results, rather than on position, activity, and length of service.

11. Reasonable mistakes need to be tolerated and put into the perspective that the road to success is paved with some failures along the way. Even a turtle can't make progress unless it sticks its neck out. The entrepreneurial spirit needs to be nurtured if the process of renewal is to be established and maintained.

12. A system for stimulating and managing creativity, as well as for operational improvement, should be consistently implemented, and the results should be carefully measured. This type of system provides the spark to insure that the renewal process is a continual, living process, as opposed to an occasional program that starts and then dies.

Between managing momentum and managing potential, the difference and results are enormous. The crucial choice you make between these two extremes directly determines the kind of future you achieve. In addition, it establishes which organization is to die and which is to live.

Last Word: a Beginning, Not An End   You have come to the end of this book, which, hopefully, has contributed to generating a commitment on your part always to plan and manage professionally yourself, your career, your job, your organization, and your future. Obviously, you need a great deal of self-discipline and a continual program of self-development; however, this is a small price to pay when compared to the enormous rewards that the pro earns.

Perhaps one of the greatest insights that professionals share is that the price paid to be a professional isn't a price after all. Striving toward a grand design and the pursuit of excellence itself are the most rewarding elements in life. As a result, the achievements, acquisitions, and rewards turn out to be a by-product of the learning and work the professional manager loves to do. It is not difficult to identify individuals who have reached this level of professional excellence. It is my earnest hope that you will be a member of this elite group who say, "Thank God It's Monday."

APPENDIX:
APPLY THE SEVEN-STEP PROCESS

Application of the seven-step process to establish the critical path you need to develop professional management in your life is illustrated in the following *brief example plan summary.*

Section One:
Definition

A. *Definition of Self*
I am a committed person dedicated to attaining purposeful professional management in my life. I realize the need for diagnosing my situation, analyzing my surroundings, setting purposeful objectives, establishing effective strategies, and taking action-oriented steps to execute the strategies. I have not been able to sustain this process in the past, but I am dedicated to seeing this process become a common response in all areas of my life.

The professional manager is one that engages in a pursuit or activity professionally and has developed the management skills required to identify the inherent potential in a situation, and then to be able to manage that situation is such a manner that the potential will be both enlarged and achieved as much as it is possible to do so.

B. *Purpose of this Plan (the most important results desired)*
1. To identify the skills of the professional manager.
2. To learn the methodology of the professional manager.
3. To make professional management a way of life.

C. *Resources and Skills that are most important to the success of this plan*
1. Ability to think and make analytical, long-range decisions.
2. Willingness to learn; ambition to grow and to be challenged.
3. Desire to "go the extra mile" to succeed.
4. Ability to lead and positively influence others.

D. *Accountabilities and Responsibilities (most important responsibilities in order of their importance)*
1. Identify the characteristics of professional management.
2. Spend time applying the disciplines and methodology of professional management.
3. Internalize the attitudes, disciplines, and methods of professional management.

Section Two: Analysis

A. *My Most Important Strengths*
1. Good mental capabilities; the untapped potential of my mind.
2. Ambition; willingness to learn and to try new things.
3. Ability to get along with and influence other people.

B. *My Most Important Weaknesses*
1. Lack of clear life/career direction in the form of a comprehensive, workable common sense plan.
2. Lack of discipline in fully utilizing the untapped resource of my mind.
3. Tendency to procrastinate; to not manage my time properly.

C. *My most Important Actions and their Results*
1. Apply the planning principles exhibited in the book, *Thank God It's Monday!*

Result: More direction, better planning, better results.
2. Apply the principles of creative thinking.
Result: Improved utilization of my mind; better ideas, alternatives, and results.
3. Apply the technique of Time Management illustrated in this book.
Result: Better utilization of personal time, greater productivity.

Section Three: Judgment

A. *Assumptions*
1. I will be able to express in written form the right plan to accomplish my purposes.
2. I will develop the needed self-discipline to achieve my plan.
3. The application of the principles of this book through a written plan will make me much more effective in my life/career.
4. The application of the principles of this book through a written plan will lead to the following potentials:
   a. more financial success.
   b. greater job satisfaction.
   c. greater effectiveness and efficiency.
   d. more balance in my whole life.
   e. greater learning ability and creativity.
   f. greater self-esteem.
   g. greater productivity.

Section Four: Decision

A. *Objectives (What by When)*
1. Develop a life/career plan in writing by April 15, 19XX, which will identify development gaps and list self-improvement programs.
2. Review the methodologies of professional management illustrated in this book over the next 90 days.
3. Learn how to apply the methodologies of professional management by this time next year.
4. Establish a time management schedule by February, 19XX.

**Section Five:
Action**

A. *Strategies—How I am going to accomplish the plan?*
   1. Write down a life/career plan.
   2. List the skills of a professional manager.
   3. Develop and identify the methods of acquiring the skills of a professional manager.
   4. Practice the disciplines of professional management.
   5. Join support organizations such as the American Management Association, the Professional Management Institute, and the Planning Executives Institute.
   6. Develop a program of time management.
   7. Review the techniques of professional management given in this book on a regular basis.
   8. Practice methods of creative thinking to develop the ability of the mind.
   9. Acquire and use additional material on becoming a professional manager.

**Section Six:
Results
(Justification)**

A. *Economic Gains*
   1. More financial remuneration on the job.
   2. More effective use of resources.
   3. More efficient use of resources.

B. *Professional Gains*
   1. More recognition based on higher performance.
   2. Greater probability of promotion.
   3. Greater learning skill and potential.
   4. More job satisfaction.
   5. Greater productivity.

C. *Personal Gain*
   1. More balance in personal life.
   2. Greater self-esteem.
   3. Better time management.
   4. More personal enjoyment and personal satisfaction.

**Section Seven:
Feedback
(Exception
Report)**

As my life/career plans change, I know I must adopt the following steps to keep my plan living. The exception report will:
1. Identify the changes that have taken place that will impact my plan.

2. Identify actions that can be taken to manage these changes to advantage.
3. Identify the specific impact of the change on the plan.
4. Identify the sections of the plan that will have to be changed and updated.

Congratulations! Now You May Begin

Once you have completed your written plan, you will have joined a very rare group of individuals who have established an understood direction from what they wish to achieve in the future.

Whether or not you accomplish your plan depends on you and how much self-discipline you use in support of your plan. Part of this self-discipline will be taking the required actions in accordance with the priorities and time schedule you establish as part of the plan.

In addition, you will need to develop self-discipline to manage changes to your plan, including those which you have not been able to anticipate. There will be times when you will need to update your plan. By following this procedure continually, you will establish a "living plan" and develop an increasing skill to manage consistently inconsistent situations in a way that will produce constant gain.

In other words, you have now started a never-ending process of exercising your mind with the Professional Manager's system and tools in support of this continual process. Your written plan, therefore, is the beginning—not the end—and while you will find your written plan very useful, it is the never-ending Professional Manager's process which is indispensable.

GLOSSARY

assets:	People, money, material, time, space; used interchangeably with resources.
assumption:	The expectation and the anticipation that a certain event will occur. A best quesstimate of what will happen by when. A reflection of judgment.
balance:	That important word that represents a commitment to "wholeness" (see "whole person").
brain:	That physical part of the human being that creates and employs the logic process.
brainstorming:	A group technique for stimulating ideas attempting to generate as many ideas or alternatives as possible.
cause and effect management:	A type of management that focuses on the 20% of the factors that impact at least 80% of the results, emphasizing problem prevention rather than problem solving.
climate:	The internal environment that exists within an individual or an organization, which may be referred to as a state of being, which, in turn, may be positive, negative, or neutral in nature and is subject to being changed.

233

common sense:	The conscious application of the mind's process in order to make better decisions faster, and, through using this systematic approach, being able to do more in less time with better results.
comprehensive plan:	Written statement of the present situation; the desired ends; the controls and the methods, formulated beforehand, of proceeding to bring the desired end to reality. This overall plan will encompass and summarize the strategic, marketing, profit, capital, and other tactical plans and includes Sections 1 through 11 of the Planagement System.
communication:	The process of transferring an image accurately from one mind to another mind. The responsibility for successful communication is with the communicator!
creactive:	That process existing in each individuual that blends and stimulates the creative capability to generate ideas, with the actions required to make the idea happen.
creativity:	That process which combines a positive mental attitude with the synergistic skill of uniquely combining known elements, while at the same time challenging the unfamiliar; achievement in finding new ways to do things.
delegation:	To entrust or assign responsibilities or authority to another.
development:	The continuous process of identifying the best that can be done and then doing the best that can be done on an ever enlarging basis.
diagnosis:	That important skill of investigation or analysis of the cause or nature of a condition, situation, or problem.
discipline:	Self-control, a systematic code or pattern of behavior.
education:	That process of asking a continual series of questions, the answers to which contribute to increased interest and/or confusion, which develops a new series of questions at a higher level in regard to more important considerations.
effectiveness:	The ability to identify the right actions and to do the right things.
efficiency:	The ability to accomplish goals with precision and to do things right.
enterprise:	A systematic, purposeful activity.
entrepreneur:	A risk taker, who builds an enterprise toward achieving its potential.
excellence:	The striving toward and accomplishment of the best that is possible.
exception report:	A mechanism for changing or updating a plan.
gap:	A deficiency; a difference between what is the actual situation and the desired or ideal situation.
goal:	Basically the same as an objective, but frequently of a shorter time span and supportive to objectives.
greatest unrealized potential:	That unused capacity of the human mind, estimated at between 80 percent and 95 percent of the total capacity available.

234

growth:	Increasing total assets and the rate of return on those assets, sufficient enough to attract the assets (men, money, material, time, and space) needed to accomplish the plan.
guideline objectives:	The continuing general aims, desired results, that management is planning to accomplish.
human hang-ups:	Those negative human elements that get in the way of using more of the capacity of the human mind and impeding the capability to take sound concepts to reality, primarily due to the human being not wanting to, or knowing how to, think, use orderly procedures, do paperwork, or employ the self-discipline required to identify and manage potential and change.
innovation:	The process of initiating creative change.
integrity:	The truth, the whole truth, and nothing but the truth.
job profile:	A position or job description with measurable standards of acceptable performance.
key operating ratios:	Those basic ratios that, if maintained, will insure that the desired results from the plan will be achieved.
key milestone:	Those key supportive activities that must be completed by a specific date in order to accomplish the objective on time.
logic process:	The functioning of the brain; is the same as the decision-making process, problem-solving process, planning process, management process, innovative process, all of which are comprised of the seven sequenced steps of defining the situation, analyzing the situation, evolving alternative actions, making a decision in regard to a future that cannot be predicted with accuracy, taking the actions required to make the decision a reality, identifying the gain from the activity, and establishing a living closed-loop process through managing exceptions and changes on a continuous, never-ending basis.
management:	The art and science of getting things accomplished through other people, regardless of reporting relationships.
management principles:	A statement of the moral and ethical business creed and practices, standard of conduct, that the company and its people, which comprise the company, will follow.
market dominance:	A significantly larger share of the market, as compared to the nearest competitor.
marketing:	That continuous process that provides an individual or organization with the capability correctly to identify, anticipate, and communicate the needs of the market, while continually organizing and utilizing the resources required in such a manner as to meet the market's needs as well or better than anyone else while achieving optimum profits and growth. (Oriented from the outside to the inside and is longer range in nature.)
matrix:	A format for presenting the interrelationship of elements, based on something within which something else originates or develops.

maximum:	The greatest quantity or value attainable or attained.
MBO:	Management by Objectives; a management system based on systematic goal-setting.
mind:	That element within an individual that feels, perceives, thinks, wills, and reasons through a blending and balancing of logic with emotion.
mission:	A statement of philosophy and direction with emphasis on the major results to be achieved. The mission or purpose is considered as the "leading edge" and provides the guidance for developing supporting plans.
motivation:	That internal process which develops sound direction and motives, while establishing the commitment for taking the required action to make the directions and motives a functioning reality (Motive-Action).
objective:	A statement that clearly communicates what will happen by when.
optimist:	Sees the opportunity in every difficulty, problem, or situation.
optimum:	The best possible balance and level of interrelated elements.
pessimist:	Sees the difficulty and problem in every opportunity or situation.
plan:	The written answers to the questions in the Planagement Model and presented in Sections 1 through 11 of the Planagement System.
Planagement®:	The registered trademark and service mark of Planagement, Inc.; defined as that process which integrates the art and the science of taking a concept to reality through use of a practiced method.
planagement model:	A series of questions and thought stimulators generated by the questions, "What is the minimum amount of information you require to make a sound decision and in what order do you consider it?" These questions are arranged in a logical sequence and recorded within the eleven-section framework of the Planagement System and designed to develop a sound written plan based on the written answers to the questions and thought stimulators.
planagement method:	The generation of answers to at least the questions contained in the appropriate Planagement Model of key questions and thought stimulators arranged in a logical sequence and documented in Sections 1 through 11 of the Planagement System.
Planagement® process:	The seven sequenced, continual steps resulting from the conscious application of the mind, including, (1) Logic/Facts/Beliefs (Science); (2) Analysis/Alternatives (Science and Art); (3) Judgments/Assumptions /Potentials (Art); (4) Decision/Objectives (Direction); (5) Plan of Action (Discipline); (6) Why/Justification (Gain from the Activity, Development); (7) Control/Exception/Update/Deviations/Changes (Living Plan, Closed Loop System).
Planager®:	One who continually employs the Planagement System. A profile of this licensed individual will include the following:

236

1. Be a professional.
2. Have common sense, a keen analytical skill, a disciplined mind, and an ability to communicate well.
3. Possess an economic sense that will constantly emphasize a continuing gain from an activity through an understanding and belief in the profit system, the entrepreneur, and private enterprise.
4. Have a respected reputation and background, with sound and diversified experience, and a solid "track record."
5. Be eager to learn and have demonstrated a superior capacity to do so.
6. Be a builder . . . never an exploiter.
7. Believe in and respect the individual and have faith in something greater than self.
8. Be a giver and possess the skills of a good teacher.
9. Have sound judgment in regard to people and situations, with superior interpersonal skills, empathy, and an ability to listen well.
10. Be strongly motivated, while possessing innovative, creative capabilities, combined with a practical method of application and a positive attitude.
11. Constantly emphasize dependability and self-improvement, so that he will be able continually to enlarge the contribution he makes to self, the organization, and to others.
12. Have a good sense of humor.

planning: The process of defining and analyzing the present and projected situation, and of specifying a desired future and the steps required to make the desired end a reality.

planning/management center: The individual—his/her mind, his/her situation including the job, and his/her future including a career plan.

plan summary: A brief statement of *all sections* of the plan (Sections 1 through 11 of the Planagement System and Manual), which provides the minimum information needed for effective communication, decision making, and control. The plan's summary (Section 0) provides guidelines in order to develop other supporting plans. Also, it is the plan's summary that is reported on by exception.

policy: A principal course of action that establishes and regulates the parameters within which the company will operate. Delineates acceptable areas and types of business activities. In addition, policies guide and provide a framework for operations, supporting plans, and decision making.

potential: The maximum that exists or could exist that can be developed or become actual.

practical potential:	Potential, less the modifying factors of cost benefit; probability of success expressed as a percentage and synergistic fit with capability and available resources. Practical potentials are basic to identifying sound growth.
Pareto's law:	Based on the frequently occurring circumstances that 20% of the items within a situation control and have great influence over the other 80%. Pareto's Law provides the foundation for the key account approach and may be applied to products, markets, key operating ratios, and other controling factors.
procedures:	Usually a precise—how to do it—statement that defines the operating steps to be taken.
professional:	A totally honest person engaged in the pursuit of excellence and committed to a conduct of continually seeing the best in others, while giving the best he/she has.
professional manager:	One that engages in a pursuit or activity professionally and has developed the managerial skills required to identify the inherent potential in a situation and, then, to be able to manage that situation in such a manner that the potential will be both enlarged and achieved as much as it is possible to do so.
profit:	The amount that the benefit exceeds the cost. In a profit-oriented organization, profit would be measured as the income derived from revenues less expenses.
profitability:	A continuing gain from the activity, which is achieved by establishing an optimum balance of profit and growth.
program:	A systematic series of specific projects, steps, or actions designed to implement strategies and contribute to the accomplishment of objectives. Programs are normally broader in scope than projects and incorporate several related projects in support.
projects:	Plans of action that sequence, schedule, and assign the activity required to make the objective happen.
psychology:	The science of the mind and behavior.
purpose:	A brief description of the organization's mission that justifies the organizations' existence and use of resources and states the organization's intentions, as well as the major results that are desired from the organization's activity.
quality:	Degree of excellence of individual and/or organizational performance, as measured by established standards and potentials.
sales:	That process which maximizes the demand for the existing products, processes, services, and other capabilities and provides these to the served customers in the greatest possible volume at the highest possible price (oriented from the inside toward the outside and shorter range in nature).

238

self-concept:	How you perceive yourself —that is, self-respect and self-image. What a person feels and believes about what he/she does, is, and will become.
skills inventory:	A profile of a manager; strengths, weaknesses, skills, experience, ambition, and the like.
strategic sequencing:	A process of effectiveness that identifies, prioritizes, and integrates the individual's and organization's opportunities in order of their practical potentials, resulting in the development of a sound strategic plan.
strategy:	The science and art and method for organizing basic actions designed to deploy, with critical timing, the organization's resources into the most advantageous position; provides guidance for developing and implementing the programs and projects required successfully to accomplish the plan.
success:	When persons are able to spend time as they want to, rather than as they have to.
synergism:	The process that causes the whole to be greater than the sum of its parts.
synergistics:	A management process which insures that the whole will be increasingly greater than the sum of its parts.
systematics:	A process of efficiency that identifies, designs, prioritizes, interlinks, implements, and improves the required systems in support of plans for action, resulting in the development of operating plans that are required to implement the strategic plan in the most cost-effective way.
systems approach:	Systematically considering and relating all variables that determine an optimum end result.
tactics:	The business methods used in the short run to measure, allocate, and control all resources in an effort to maximize the gain from the activity and achieve an optimum position in relation to potential.
theory b:	The professional manager's philosophy and style, which establishes a sound balance that fits the requirements of the situation and individuals involved.
theory x:	Autocratic management philosophy and style.
theory y:	Participative and supportive management philosophy and style.
three-level forecast:	A best, worst, and average estimate of future events; a technique for forecasting.
whole person:	The established priority and balance of the mental, spiritual, social, and physical interrelated elements that comprise an individual.

BIBLIOGRAPHY

Allen, Louis, A., *Management Profession*. McGraw-Hill Book Company, 1964.

Batten, Joe D., *Tough-Minded Management*. AMACOM, 1963.

Benge, Eugene J., *Elements of Modern Management*. AMACOM, 1976.

Dale, Ernest, *Management: Theory and Practice*. McGraw-Hill Book Company, 1973.

Drucker, Peter F., *Management: Tasks, Responsibilities, Practices*. Harper & Row, 1974.

Ewing, David W., *The Human Side of Planning*. The Macmillan Company, 1969.

Gellerman, Saul W., *Motivation and Productivity*. AMACOM, 1963.

Golightly, Henry O., *Managing with Style*. AMACOM, 1977.

Kepner, Charles H., and Tregoe, B. B., *The Rational Manager*. McGraw-Hill Book Company, 1965.

Kootz, Harold and O'Donnell, Cyril, *Essentials of Management*. McGraw-Hill Book Company, 1974.

McGregor, Douglas, *The Human Side of Enterprise*. McGraw-Hill Book Company, 1960.

McGregor, Douglas, *The Professional Manager*. McGraw-Hill Book Company, 1967.

Odiroine, George S., *Management by Objectives,* Pittman Publishing Corp., 1965.

Randolph, Robert M., *Planagement—Moving Concept Into Reality*. AMACOM, 1975.

Reeves, Elton T., *Practicing Effective Management*. AMACOM, 1975.

Sampson, R. C., *Managing the Managers*. McGraw-Hill Book Company, 1965.

Sloma, Richard S., *No-Nonsense Management*. The Macmillan Company, 1977.

Steiner, George A., *Top Management Planning*. The Macmillan Company, 1969.

INDEX

Abundance as part of civilization's life cycle, 217
Account management approach to selling, 81
Accountabilities, personal, 48
Action thoughts, 22–27
Active listening, learning, 11
Actualizing approach to life, 128
Administrative sense, lack of, as cause of business failure, 169
Administrator's vs. builder's philosophy, 130, 131
Administrator's philosophy, 130, 131
Agenda, results-oriented, 177, 178
Amateurs and professionals, differences between, 126–128, 129
America, past present and future, 216–227
  life cycle of civilization, 216–219
    abundance, 217
    apathy, 218
    bondage, 216, 219
    complacency, 218
    courage, 217
    dependence, 218–219
    liberty, 217
    selfishness, 217–218
    spiritual faith, 217

America, past present and future (cont.):
  momentum vs. renewal, 222–227
    characteristics necessary for, 226–227
    extrapolative forecasting, danger of, 222–223
    mind set scale, 223–225
    profitability profile chart, 225
  resurgence, 219–222
    conceptual resurgence, 220
    "four D's," 220
Apathy as perennial problem, 43
  as part of civilization's life cycle, 218
Assistant, profitable delegation to, 85, 87

Background differences as roadblock to thinking, 8
Backup, inadequate, as cause for business failure, 168–169
Behavioral sciences, importance of, 64–65
Bondage as first and last step of new civilization, 216
Boredom as possible cause of business failure, 171
Brainstorming, 19, 20
Brillault, R., 214
Buonarroti, Michelangelo, 61
Burnout of entrepreneur, 170

Business, autonomous and successful,
    how to build, 159–186
  failure, ten reasons for, 167–171
    administration, lack of, 169
    backup, inadequate, 168–169
    boredom, 171
    capital, lack of, 168
    delegation, lack of, 169
    discipline, lack of, 171
    innovation, lack of, 170
    interpersonal skills, inadequate,
        170–171
    management, poor, 167–168
    marketing orientation, lack of, 170
    time management, poor, 170
  within going concern, 159–160, 172–186
    meetings, productive, 175–179 (see
        "Meetings, productive")
    participative management, 172–175
        (see "Participative management")
    synergistics, 179–186 (see also
        "Synergistics")
  profile/position description of ideal
      entrepreneur, 161–164
  steps, 160–167
    commitment, 160
    flow diagram, 166
    manager, becoming professional,
        160–164
    phases, managing, 164, 166
    philosophy, balanced, 167
    resource base, establishing, 165
    venture, five functions of, 165, 166

Capital, inadequate, as cause of business
    failure, 168
Career planning, 29–41
  career and job, differences between,
      29–30
  choices, three, 40–41
  future, planning toward, 30–35
    day-by-day management, 31–34
    illustrative plan, 32–33
  philosophical considerations, 36–38
    about human nature, 36–37
    management philosophy, 37–38
    responsibilities, importance of
        accepting, 38–40
  planning process, step-by-step, 35–36
Cause and effect, management by,
    101–120
  approach, implementing, 112–117
    organizational needs, five, 113–115
    survey, 115, 116
  building blocks for, 100–101
  discipline, 106–112
    checklist, 106–108
    habit, 110–112
    logic process of resurgence, 111
    types, 109–110

Cause and effect, management by (cont.):
  80/20 rule and diagnostic skill, 117–120
    Key Results Areas, 118, 119–120
  reactive management, 100–101
  skills, 101–103
    diagnosis, 103–106 (see also
        "Diagnosis")
    "fuzzy" skills, 102–103
    "thermostat" managers vs.
        "thermometer" managers, 101
Chairperson, selecting competent, for
    productive meetings, 177
Change:
  managing through written plan,
      104–106
  passive reaction to as roadblock to
      thinking, 8
  reaction to as measure of performance,
      57
"Charisma" as nonverbal communication
    form, 17
Cicero, 214
Client relationship essential to a "good"
    job, 46–47
Closed-loop learning thinking process,
    12–13
Commitment to building your own
    business, 160
Committees, proper management of,
    175–179 (see "Meetings,
    productive")
Communication, direct, with client
    systems in "good" job, 48
Communication as potential roadblock to
    thinking, 8
Communication skills, strong, essential
    for leadership, 17
Communications and knowledge gap,
    bridging, 97–99
  guidelines for, 98–99
  reasons for gap, 97–98
Compensation, linking to performance,
    55–60
  change, reaction to, 57
  premises, basic, 56–58
  system, establishing, 58–60
Complacency as part of civilization's life
    cycle, 218
Coordination/Communication Report, 48
Courage required of leader, 17
Courage as part of civilization's life cycle,
    217
Creative, 12–13
Creative Education Foundation, 212
Creativity, 18–22, 210–215 (see "'Top,'
    reaching")
  brainstorming, 19, 20
  characteristics, 212, 213–214
  decision for, 212–215
  definition, 211

Creativity (cont.):
  skills, 211
  tensions and opposites, 21–22
  thinking techniques, 19–21
Crisis management, 100–101
Critical path necessary to develop
      professional management, seven-
      step, 228–232

Day-by-day time management plan, 31–34
Delegation, 83–89
  definition, 83
  and development, 85–89
    downward delegation, 85–86
    formula, 86–89
  extension of, 85
  lack of as cause for business failure,
      169
  making, 85
  system for, 84
  what to delegate, 84
Demanding of followers essential quality
      of leader, 17–18
Dependence as part of civilization's life
      cycle, 218–219
Determination essential for leader, 17
Development and delegation, 85–89 (see
      "Delegation")
Diagnosis, 103–106
  conceptual view of managing change,
      105
  early warning system, 104–106
  as function of management, 106
  how it works, 104
  teachable, 104
  what it is, 103
Diagnostic skill, learning, 11
Dimnet, Ernest, 214
Direction, 221
  to utilize time best, 77–78
Discipline, 106–112
  balancing with freedom to motivate
      employees, 63
  checklist, 106–108
  essential for leader, 18
  habit, 110–112
  lack of as cause of business failure, 171
  logic process of resurgence, 111
  role of in national resurgence, 221
  types, 109–110
Drive, 220–221
  for self-improvement, 11
Drucker, Peter, 118

Early warning system for good
      management, 104–106
Education, motivation through, 69–72
  educated person, characteristics of, 70–71

Education, motivation through (cont.):
  resistance of managers to teaching, 69–70
  teaching, manager's responsibility for,
      69–74
    feedback of results, 73
    lack of ability for, 74
    practice, teaching by, 72–73
    at student's level, 73
    techniques, using varied, 73–74
Education in selling trade, continuing,
      81–82
Educational system, failure of to teach
      thinking process, 15
Efficiency of American business offices,
      188
"Eight Ingredients of a Good Job,"
      46–49
80/20 rule, 117–120
Emotion and logic, problem of balance
      between, 9
Empire building defeating to profitability,
      194
Entrepreneur activities, successful,
      159–186 (see "Business,
      autonomous and successful...")
  profile/position description of ideal
      entrepreneur, 161–164
Entrepreneurial organization structure,
      144
Example setting, consistent, essential for
      leader, 17
Excellence, pursuit of, 27–28
Excellent Creative Thinking Program, 212
Experiential differences as roadblock to
      thinking, 8
Expertise, emphasis on in "good" job, 47
External motivation non-existent, 62, 66
Extrapolative forecasting, danger of,
      222–223

Failure of entrepreneurial businesses, ten
      reasons for, 167–171 (see
      "Business, autonomous and
      successful...")
Faith as part of civilization's life cycle,
      217
Feedback, getting to measure motivation,
      65–66
  profile of motivation, 66
Feedback of results, direct, essential in a
      "good" job, 46
Feedback system for effective teaching, 73
Feelings and logic, problem of balance
      between, 9
Ford, Henry, 11
Forecasting, 147–148
  "living-rolling," 150
Formalization, 195
Fosdick, Harry Emerson, 110

Freedom, balancing with discipline to
    increase motivation, 63
Future, career planning for, 30–35 (see
    "Career planning")
Future, formula for facing, 150–157
    example, 153–157
    growth expectations, defining, 151
    opportunities, identifying, 151
    plan, developing, 153
    potentials, charting, 153
    present and future, comparing, 153
    serendipitous approach, 150
    systems approach, 152

Guesstimating, 147–148
Guide for Bank Planning, 89
Guideline plans, writing, to facilitate
    management team building, 174

Habits, establishment of as roadblock to
    thinking, 8
Herzberg, Dr. Frederick, 45–46
Hierarchy of needs through organizations
    and individuals, 68
    organizational, 180
Human being, four parts of, 2–3
Human nature, thoughts about in career
    planning, 36–37
Human resource development, creating
    system for, 63–64
The Human Side of Enterprise, 124
Humanistic management style, 62–63
Humphrey, J. Carl, 70
Huxley, Thomas Henry, 72

Inefficiency, cost of, 7
Innovation, lack of as cause of business
    failure, 170
Integrity, personal, essential for leader, 18
Integrity as absolute for effective
    communication, 98
Interpersonal skills, inadequate, as cause
    of business failure, 170–171

James, William, 217
Job, proper, setting up, 45–49
    client relationship, 46–47
    communication with client systems, 48
    Coordination/Communication Report,
        48
    "Eight Ingredients of a Good Job,"
        46–49
    expertise, area of, 47
    feedback of results, direct, 46
    learning function, 47
    over-communciation, problem of, 48
    personal accountabilities, 48
    resources, control over, 47–48
    "right" people in "right" job, 49–52

Job, proper, setting up (cont.):
    flow diagram, 50
    position descriptions, developing, 51
    rank-ordering, 52
    selection kits, 51–52
    scheduling one's work, 47
Job and career, differences between,
    29–30
Job descriptions, developing, 51
Job profile, documented, as part of
    Management Development
    Program, 53–55

Key account approach to selling, 80–81
Key Results Areas, Drucker's, 118,
    119–120
KISS principle, 193

Language, differing definitions of as
    roadblock to thinking, 8
Leadership, learning, 1–28
    action thoughts, 22–27
    creativity, 18–22
        brainstorming, 19, 20
        tensions and opposites, 21–22
        thinking techniques, 19–21
    excellence, pursuit of, 27–28
    human being, four-part composition of,
        2–3
    learning/thinking process, 1–2
    maximizing performance and work
        satisfaction, 4–6
    option-loaded decisions, 22–27
    performance, optimum, keys to, 14–18
        "charisma," 17
        communication skills, 17
        courage, determination and
            persistence, 17
        demanding of followers, 17–18
        discipline, 18
        educational system, failure of, 15
        example-setting, 17
        integrity, personal, 18
        learning to lead, 16–18
        management ability, superior, 18
        needs and goals, sensitivity to, 17
        philosophy, 17
        positive, emphasizing, 14–16
        problem-solving orientation, 15–16
        self-image, positive, 17
    Planagement System, 4–6
        learning skill, developing, 11–13 (see
            also "Learning skills...")
    roadblocks to thinking, 8–10
        logic process of mind, 9–10
        management process, professional, 10
        overcoming, 9–10
    Thinking Gap, 6–7
        inefficiency, cost of, 7
        potential for improvement, 7

Learning discipline, 109–110
Learning function essential to "good"
    job, 47
Learning skills, developing, 11–13
    active listening, 11
    closed-loop learning thinking process,
        12–13
    diagnostic skill, 11
    multisensory learning, 11–12
    questioning, art of, 11
    repetition, 12
    selectivity, 12
    thinking and acting parts of brain,
        developing balance between, 12–13
    visualization skill, 12
Liberty as part of civilization's life cycle,
    217
"Living-rolling forecast," 150
Logic and emotion, problem of
    unstructured balance between, 9
Logic process of mind, 9

McGregor, Douglas, 63, 124
Management, poor, most common cause
    of business failure, 167–168
Management ability, superior, essential
    for leader, 18
Management Development Program,
    practical approach to, 53–55
    ideal manager, practical, 53
    job profile, documented, 53–55
    skills inventory, 55
    steps, 54
Management philosophy, sound, essential
    in career planinng, 37–38
Management process, professional, 10
    learning and growing, decision for, 11
    learning skills, developing, 11–13 (see
        also "Learning skills...")
    learning targets, developing, 13
Management team, building, 172–175 (see
    "Participative management")
Managers, selling as responsibility of, 79
Managing yourself, 1–28 (see
    "Leadership, learning")
Market researcher, salesperson as, 80
Marketing orientation, lack of as cause of
    business failure, 170
Maslow, Dr. Abraham, 64–65
Meetings, productive, 175–179
    agenda, 177, 178
    chairperson, selecting, 177
    documenting, 177–179
    members of team, selecting, 176–177
    team charter, establishing, 176
    team meetings, 176
Mental discipline, 109
Michelangelo, 61
Mind set scale, 223–225
MIS, 194

Motivation, 61–74
    behavioral sciences, importance of,
        64–65
    definitions, 62
    through education, 69–72
        educated person, characteristics of,
            70–71
        resistance of managers to teaching,
            69–70
    external motivation non-existent, 62, 66
    formula for increasing productivity,
        62–65
        feedback, 65–66
        freedom and discipline balance, 63
        human needs, 64–65
        human resource development, 63–64
        organizational direction, 63
        participative management, 62–63
        profile of motivation, 66
    hierarchy of needs of individuals and
        organizations, 68
    as internal process, 62
    self-actualization, 67–68
    teaching, steps for, 72–74
        feedback of results, 73
        lack of ability for, 74
        practice, teaching by, 72–73
        at student's level, 73
        techniques, using varied, 73–74
    understanding of individual human
        beings, 67
Multisensory approach to teaching, 73–74
Multisensory learning, 11–12

Needs, human, hierarchy of, 64–65
Needs of customer, diagnosing, 80
Needs and goals of group, sensitivity to
    essential for leader, 17
Niebuhr, 214
Nightingale, Earl, 212

Opportunities as point of emphasis of
    professional managers, 101
Organization charts as cause of over-
    communication, 48
Organizational direction essential for
    motivation of employees, 63
Organizational discipline, 110
Organizational pyramid, traditional, 142
    entrepreneurial, 144
    inverse pyramid concept, 143
Osborn, Dr. Alex F., 212
Overextension as cause of business failure,
    169
Overstreet, Harry A., 214

Paperwork as discipline for mind, 8
Paretos law, 91
Participative management, 172–175
    company guideline, writing, 174

Participative management (cont.):
  consolidation and integration, 175
  individuals, selecting, 174
  supporting plans, individual, 175
Peale, Norman Vincent, 212
People as the organization, 42–60
  apathy, problem of, 43
  compensation, linking to performance,
      55–60
    change, reaction to, 57
    premises, basic, 56–58
    system, establishing, 58–60
  management development, practical
      approach to, 53–55
    ideal manager, practical, 53
    job profile, documented, 53–55
    skills inventory, 55
    steps, 54
  "recycling" resources, 43, 44
  steps, 43–49
    Planagement Selection System, 49–52
      (see also "Planagement
      Selection...")
    right job, setting up, 45–49 (see also
      "Job, proper...")
Performance, maximizing, 14–18 (see
      "Leadership, learning")
Performance reviews, 55–60 (see
      "Compensation...")
Persistence essential for leader, 17
Peter Principle, 208
Philosophy, defined, essential for
      leadership, 17
Philosophy of professional manager,
      128–130 (see "Professional
      manager's approach")
Planagement: Moving Concept into
      Reality, 164
Planagement Selection System, 49–52
  flow diagram, 50
  position descriptions, developing, 51
  rank-ordering, 52
  selection kits, 51–52
Planagement System, 4–6
  career planning, six steps in, 35–36
  climate for increasing productivity
      formula for, 62–65
  diagnostic process, 103–106
  "Eight Ingredients of a Good Job,"
      46–49
  job planning system, 45–49
  learning and growing, decision for, 11
  learning skills, developing, 11–13 (see
      also "Learning skills...")
  learning targets, developing, 13
Planning, 89–92
  criteria for, fifteen, 90–92
  Paretos law, 91
PMI Mind Set Profile Scale, 133–141
Position in life, planning, 29–41 (see

Position in life, planning (cont.):
  "Career planning")
Positive working climate, creating,
      143–145
Potential, turning into results, 146–158
  definition, 146
  future, formula for managing, 150–157
    example, 153–157
    growth expectations, defining, 151
    opportunities, identifying, 151
    plan, developing, 153
    potentials, charting, 153
    present and future, comparing, 153
    serendipitous approach, 150
    systems approach, 152
    three-level forecast, 147–150
      "living-rolling," 150
Potential for improvement in thinking, 7
Power, paradox of, 203–207
Practice, teaching by, 72–73
Problem-solving orientation inhibiting to
      growth, 15–16
Procrastination as roadblock to thinking,
      8, 35
Professional discipline, 109
Professional management to increase
      profitability, 195–202 (see
      "Profitability")
Professional Management Institute, 164
Professional manager's approach, 121–145
  philosophy, 128–130
    administrator's vs. builder's, 130, 131
    self-esteem, 128
  positive climate, creating, 143–145
  profile, 125
    characteristics, ten, 126–128, 129
  Theory X and Theory Y, 124–125
  top-down organizational theory,
      inverting, 142–143
    inverse pyramid concept, 143
    organizational pyramid, traditional,
      142
  traditional vs. professional
      management, 121–123, 130–142
    characteristics of managers, fifty,
      133–140
    PMI Mind Set Profile Scale, 133–141
Profitability, 187–202
  as key to human progress, 187
  managerial productivity, 188–189
    asset-management approach, 190–192
    definition, 189
    growth orientation, 189
    management by exception, 191–192
    position description, 189–190
    supporting job plan, 190
  productivity at root, 188
  professional management, 194–202
    action plan, developing, 196, 200–202
    and business needs, five, 195–196,

Profitability (cont.):
   198
     cost-effectiveness, measuring, 196
     gaps, identifying, 196
     questionnaire, 197
     specifications for management
      system, 196, 199
     understanding, deepening, 195
     short-term and long-term, difference
      between, 187–188
     think planning, 192–194
      empire building, danger of, 194
      KISS principle, 193
      MIS, 194
      project management, 194
Profitability profile chart, 225
Project management as key to efficiency,
   194
"The Pursuit of Excellence," 182

Questioning as stimulator of thought, 8–9
  art of, learning, 11

Rationality and feelings, problem of
  balance between, 9
Reactive management, 100–101
"Recycling" resources, 43, 44
Repetition as learning skill, 12
Resilience essential for leader, 17
Resources, control over in "good" job,
  47–48
Responsibilities, importance of accepting
  in career planning, 38–39, 40
Responsibility accompanying power,
  203–207
Results, producing through action
  thoughts, 22–27
Roadblocks to thinking, 8–10
  logic process of mind, 9–10
  management process, professional, 10
  overcoming, 9–10

Sales plan, developing, 81
Scheduling one's work important to
  "good" job, 47
Schultz, Dr. Whitt, 212
Secretary, profitable delegation to, 85, 87
Selection kits, 51–52
Selectivity as learning skill, 12
Self-development, role of in national
  resurgence, 221–222
Self-discipline to use time wisely, 76–77,
  109
Self-esteem essential for sound
  philosophy, 128
Self-image, positive, essential for
  leadership, 17
Selfishness as part of civilization's life
  cycle, 217–218

Self-management, 1–28 (see "Leadership,
  learning")
Selling more in less time, 79–83 (see
  "Time, wise use of")
Skills inventory as part of management
  development plan, 55
Social discipline, 109
Stewart, George Craig, 101
Strategic sequencing, 95–97 (see
  "Strategy")
Strategy, 93–97
  definition, 93
  example, automotive, 94–95
  example, business, 94
  example, military, 93–94
  process for developing, 95, 96
  sequencing, 95–97
  Systematics, 95–97
Synergistics, 179–186
  hierarchy of needs, organizational, 180
  how it works, 182–186
   organizational chart, favorable, 184
  in large conglomerate, 182
  in small business, 180–181
Systematics, 95–97

Teaching, manager's responsibility for,
  69–74 (see "Motivation")
  feedback of results, 73
  lack of ability for, 74
  practice, teaching by, 72–73
  at student's level, 73
  techniques, using varied, 73–74
Teaching as essential responsibility of
  managers, 210
Team terminology instead of committee,
  176
Tensions and opposites, use of to
  stimulate creativity, 21–22
Theory X and Theory Y of management
  styles, 63, 124–125
"Thermostat" managers vs.
  "thermometer" managers, 101
Thinking as basic skill for increasing
  productivity, 193
Thinking Gap, 6–7
Time, wise use of, 75–99
  communications and knowledge gap,
   bridging, 97–99
   guidelines for, 98–99
   reasons for gap, 97–98
  delegation, 83–89
   definition, 83
   and development, 85–89 (see also
    "Delegation")
   downward delegation grid, 85–86
   extension of, 85
   formula, 86–89
   making, 85

Time, wise use of (cont.):
  system for, 84
  what to delegate, 84
 planning, 89–92
  criteria for, fifteen, 90–92
  Paretos law, 91
 selling more in less time, 79–83
  customer needs, diagnosing, 80
  key accounts, concentration on,
   80–81
  knowing and comparing product,
   79–80
  learning more, 81–82
  managers, selling responsibility of, 79
  professional, importance of, 79
  sales plan, developing, 81
 starting, 76–78
  direction, 77–78
  self-discipline, 76–77
 strategy, 93–97
  definition, 93
  example, automotive, 94–95
  example, business, 94
  example, military, 93–94
  process for developing, 95, 96
  sequencing, 95–97
  Systematics, 95–97
Time management, poor, as cause of
  business failure, 170
"Too-many-hats" syndrome of
  entrepreneur, 169

"Top," reaching, 208–215
 creative skill, mastering, 210–215
  characteristics, 212, 213–214
  decision for, 212–215
  definition, 211
  skills, specific, 211
 Peter Principle, 208
 teaching as essential responsibility of
  managers, 210
  skills required, 211
 what it is for you, 208–210
Townsend, Robert, 125
Traditional management, failures of,
  121–123 (see "Professional
  manager's approach")
20/80 rule, 117–120

Up the Organization, 125

Venture, business, five functions of, 165,
  166
Visualization skill, 12

Warning system, early, for good
  management, 104–106
Wolf, Rev. John, 75
Working climate, creating positive,
  143–145
Written plan, using to manage change,
  104–106

249